THE

Glamour Magazine

PARTY BOOK

THE

Glamour Magazine

PARTY BOOK

BY ELEANOR ELLIOTT

DOUBLEDAY & COMPANY, INC., GARDEN CITY, NEW YORK

1965

LIBRARY OF CONGRESS CATALOG CARD NUMBER 65–10616

Acknowledgments

Principal thanks are due to Kathleen Aston Casey, Editor of *Glamour*, for entrusting this book to me, and for her invaluable suggestions, careful editing, and encouragement.

Glamour and I are grateful to the following young hostesses who answered questions on party customs in their communities and contributed many ideas:

Mrs. Marvin Barrett, New York, N.Y.
Mrs. Harriman Borland, Lake Forest, Ill.
Mrs. Michael F. Brewer, Berkeley, Calif.
Mrs. Joseph W. Cochran III, Hillsborough, Calif.
Mrs. Richard Colt, Houston, Tex.
Mrs. William Creighton, San Francisco, Calif.
Mrs. Thomas G. Hardie II, Baltimore, Md.
Mrs. John Harding, Omaha, Neb.
Mrs. Rodney M. Layton, Wilmington, Del.
Mrs. Worthington Mayo-Smith, Mt. Kisco, N.Y.
Mrs. Stephen C. Morris, Cleveland, O.
Mrs. Bernard Rogers, Chicago, Ill.
Mrs. Charles H. Russell, San Francisco, Calif.
Mrs. Henry See, Minneapolis, Minn.
Mrs. John Shapleigh, St. Louis, Mo.
Mrs. Olin G. Shivers, Jr., Atlanta, Ga.
Mrs. Farwell Smith, Chicago, Ill.
Mrs. H. Lloyd Taylor, Wilmington, Del.
Mrs. Russell E. Train, Washington, D.C.
Mrs. George F. Vietor, Jr., Houston, Tex.

Mrs. John D. Weidlein, Pasadena, Calif.
Mrs. Roy Weinberger, New York, N.Y.
Mrs. Edward B. Winn, Dallas, Tex.
Mrs. David M. Winton, Minneapolis, Minn.
Mrs. C. Bagley Wright, Seattle, Wash.

Thanks are also due to Mr. Kenneth Dean of Sherry Wine and Spirits Co., Inc., in New York for his expert assistance with the sections on cocktail parties, wines, and liqueurs.

In a broader way, credit goes to my mother, Mrs. James A. Thomas, and to Mrs. John Foster Dulles, for whom I worked as social secretary in Washington. From them I learned most of what I know about the specifics of entertaining, and their talent and enthusiasm for giving good parties have always been inspiring.

Finally, to my favorite host, John Elliott, Jr., go fervent thanks for cheerfully putting up with short-order meals during the writing, and for managing to seem interested in his wife's endless talk about the essentially feminine subject matter.

E.E.

Contents

ACKNOWLEDGMENTS   v

FOREWORD   ix

Part I

TODAY'S PARTIES

1. The Party Spirit   3

2. Who's Invited and How   9

3. Launching a Cocktail Party   30

4. Dinner Parties Big and Small — Table Settings, Simplified Service   42

5. Buffet Suppers Two Ways   56

6. A Do-It-Yourself Dance   64

7. Parties Out of Doors   78

8. When It's a Family Affair   90

9. Tea and Coffee Parties   98

10. When a Lion Comes to Dinner — The Formal Party   109

Part II

THE INDISPENSABLE INGREDIENTS

11. *The Manners of the Host and Hostess*   125

12. *Being a Good Guest*   141

13. *Dressing for Parties*   152

14. *The House That Lends Itself to Entertaining*   163

15. *Your Party "Staff" – Part-Time Helpers and What to Expect of Them*   176

16. *Party Food and Drink*   186

17. *Easy Menus and Recipes*   197

18. *Party Economies*   242

Part III

THE PARTY OF A LIFETIME: THE WEDDING

19. *The Wedding Preliminaries*   251

20. *Planning the Wedding Reception, the Ceremony, Wedding Parties, Wedding Clothes*   269

INDEX—GENERAL   293

INDEX TO MENUS AND RECIPES   299

Foreword

This is a book about giving parties, with plans and suggestions for certain forms of entertaining. Its object is also to show how you can work creatively with the basic ingredients of any party, so that it may be a full-blown pleasure, not flat and dull.

Why such a book? Aren't there standard etiquette books and hundreds of cookbooks, with old reliable and way-out recipes? Doesn't everybody read articles on all kinds of parties, from brunches to wedding breakfasts, and how well-known hostesses attained their popularity? Can't you pick up ideas from your friends?

Of course you can, and you do. But the editors of *Glamour* thought there was a need for a helpful and up-to-date book for today's party givers who have less time, less help, and higher food bills than those of yesterday, and whose enthusiasm for quality in entertaining might be flagging under these pressures.

They heard rumors about coffee cups being passed minus saucers, and about tarnished silver and shredding place mats betraying a defeatist attitude on the part of hostesses. One young hostess said that the things she read about perking things up made good escape literature but they didn't apply to her; where would she find time for flair and still get urgent things done?

Glamour maintains that women, married or single, however snowed under, can still have parties as nice as they used to be, "befor" . . . before the war, before the new tax rates, before the third baby came, before help became scarce.

You can still entertain with flair, and enjoy doing it, no matter what else life asks of you. That's what this book is about. It doesn't give any one prescription for entertaining, nor is it a standard work on a single aspect of social life, such as etiquette, menus and recipes, clothes, or dinner parties. There are no absolute rules about parties, especially in so diverse a country as ours; the one requirement is the human and heartfelt attitude toward people that makes parties pleasant and rewarding.

We do hope we have included a little inspiration, plus some generally accepted rules and a lot of ideas, that will refresh your own supply of talents, reinforce your inclinations about manners, party planning, and what to do in emergencies. We hope, too, that this book will present alluring reasons for raising your party-giving sights within your own environment. You will find tips, points of view, and instructions that should help you maintain a high entertainment standard, however modest or elaborate your facilities may be. Among the myriad ideas, many will already be second nature to you. Others may give you a new slant or be adaptable to the kind of entertaining you most enjoy. At party time you should be able to present yourself and your home as attractive, a little special, and with an atmosphere that will make present and future friends look forward to a repeat performance. A performance, incidentally, that you will welcome the chance to put on over and over again.

Part One

TODAY'S PARTIES

CHAPTER **I**

The Party Spirit

As everyone knows, parties don't just happen. They are work, before, during, and after. There have always been parties and always will be—because everybody likes them, even needs them. Like vitamins, a new hat, a vacation, parties change things for the better. They can even influence history—your own personal history, or events in the world.

That is, *good* parties can do all this. But what makes them good parties? One word, we think, says it: spirit. The difference between a good party and a flop is spirit and only spirit. Everything else about a party may be perfect, but without the right spirit it won't be what you'd hoped for, and all your work will have been wasted.

What is party spirit? The spirit of friendship. No matter what the reason for a particular party may be, the underlying one is to encourage friendship between people. If man were merely gregarious, people would just collect in bus stations, ball parks, and offices. He wants more than that: he wants to please and be pleased.

When a party starts with friendly spirit it can take off in any direction—hilarity, or serious discussion, or just relaxing small talk. Some parties are not successful because the spirit of friendship is given second place. Often huge cocktail parties are not quite successful, perhaps because their main purpose was to kill off obligations, and the spirit gets lost in the shuffle. It doesn't need to. A mutual feeling or interest can create it, even among perfect strangers, or parties given by politicians, or testimonial dinners in grand ballrooms, or weddings. Guests who share sympathetic feelings for an idea or a person share the pleasure of one another's company as well.

Party spirit is generated by people, of course, first by you, the hostess. Then, if you are married, there is your willing collaborator, the host, and then the guests. You don't invite sworn enemies, obviously, or people who have nothing in common, such as a pillar of the community and the local barefoot existentialist. But you don't have lawyers' night this month, bankers' night the next, and artistic "Thursdays" in April, either. You ask people you like who you think might like each other and have a mutual interest or two, so that the meeting can be fun and perhaps start new friendships. People who make a party cannot do it in a vacuum. A mood must be set. It isn't necessary to hire a band or befriend Danny Kaye. The right atmosphere comes mainly from (1) a sense of something better than usual, or "best-ness"; (2) novelty; and (3) good manners.

Best-ness

Hosts and guests bring the right spirit to a party by wanting to be at their best and by going more than halfway toward others who are trying to befriend and entertain them, even in less than ideal circumstances. When you go to a party with a splitting headache and say nothing about it, you are trying to be at your best.

Pride comes in here; the right kind of pride is natural and desirable. It is human to want to serve the best menu you can and to present the best appearance. It also happens to be polite. Exaggeration for "show" is another thing entirely. People can always tell whether you can afford expensive food and whether you have always spoken with a broad *a*. Showing off is just the opposite of bestness; of doing what comes naturally the very best you can.

Novelty

A good party seems gay partly because it is not an everyday event. If it were, you would die of boredom like those poor nobles in the courts of the Bourbon kings, who seemed to be living at a perpetual party, wearing party clothes and party manners from morning till night. It palled fast at Versailles, and it would pall today. For most people, heaven knows, the problem of too many parties doesn't exist, so there is novelty enough in planning for fun and in the thought of seeing one's friends.

Novelty in the detail of a party is trickier to come by. Sometimes playing a new game is perfectly appropriate and adds to everyone's pleasure. Sometimes it really is an asset if one of the men decides to do imitations. The trick is to know that time, since novelty for novelty's sake seldom works and must not be forced. Someone once thought an all-red dinner would be fun for George Washington's birthday (cherries and all that). The women were told to wear red dresses, the men were given red carnations. Tomato soup, baked ham, beets, red jellied salad, cherry pie, and red wine made up the menu. It all tasted fine, but the guests, overcome by redness, soon deflated like old red balloons. A novel idea, paradoxically it was a colorless party.

Novelty can be achieved in light touches of something special, beyond what your guests might ordinarily expect. Invite them to meet someone new in town. Decorate the party differently. Or vary your usual party pattern. City dwellers are likely to enjoy eating in a back garden; barbecue fans might prefer a sit-down dinner for a change. If your bank account looks good, the novel touch could be extravagance—raspberries out of season, lobsters flown from Maine, or vintage champagne.

Certainly dress has much to do with novelty. Costume parties have built-in novelty, inducing a sort of instant camaraderie. "Black tie" on an invitation makes it seem an occasion, and when the hostess says, "Wear shorts," you look forward to an easygoing party that has its own special—and friendly—appeal.

For introducing party spirit, novelty is the middle point between two extremes: the usual and the bizarre. Later on there will be ideas about menus, decoration, dress, and amusements, to underline this point. For now, just remember it's the *artful* use of these ideas that counts.

Manners

A big subject. What are manners? A philosopher once said, "Manners are morals in little things." Naturally they are; morals have to do with the way people treat each other—sometimes in profound matters like love, honor, truth, and sometimes in relatively minor matters like behavior among friends. Another explanation of manners is psychological: manners come from the basic instinct of self-preservation. Self-preservation seems a long way from finger bowls, but it is only another way of saying, "Do unto others . . ." You create friendliness by acting toward people the way you wish they would act toward you. If "putting yourself out" for others seems a lot to pay for pleasure, remember that the other side of the coin is "getting out of yourself," one of the dividends of parties.

Manners, as *etiquette*, constantly change through history and vary greatly among nationalities. No one would think of rushing around to leave calling cards on a hostess the day after a party, though this custom was a must in the etiquette books before World War II. You would be astounded to be greeted by kneeling servants but this is still the custom in some houses in Thailand and Japan. But manners, as *morals*, never change basically; there has never been a time, nor will there ever be, when consideration for others is out of fashion.

Although the word "etiquette" sounds stuffy and somehow antiquated, its rules usually have practical, not artificial, reasons. In Roman times it was "etiquette" to bring your own napkin to a dinner, because hosts didn't provide them. In the Elizabethan period it was proper to eat with your fingers because many houses didn't offer forks. There is nothing stuffy about that sort of etiquette; it is just plain practical. But there are always a few carry-overs from former times that don't seem to make sense at a given moment. As Harold Nicolson, the English authority on behavior, has said, "The society manners of one generation become the provincialisms of the next." Sometimes we cannot even trace the reasons for them. A puzzling example is the matter of butter plates never being laid on a formal dinner table. We tried to discover why. Old etiquette books, usually good sources of reasons for social usage, shed no light. Butter plates are absolutely forbidden; at a formal dinner bread must always be put on the tablecloth! Was it a space problem with all those wineglasses and nut dishes, was butter too prosaic, or did waitresses enjoy crumbing the table? No one had an answer. We finally called on a ninety-year-old dowager, who revealed that Emily Post had consulted *her* in the twenties. Slightly shocked at the question, she replied, "It's just custom, my dear, custom. Butter plates are not correct, never, never at a formal dinner!" Maybe by the time there are moon manners and undersea etiquette, butter plates will be unimportant. They're not really worth worrying about now.

Most customs we cling to—such as a man pulling out a lady's chair—continue to be good manners because extra attentions inevitably help to create the right spirit. In Chapter 11 they are discussed in greater detail.

Now on to the hostess, who is largely responsible for creating the right atmosphere. Under your roof people may or may not have fun, may or may not become friends. If you feel reluctant, somehow not in the mood for a party, your feelings can react on everybody else. But if you look forward to the pleasure you hope to give and get, it will show from the start, and you are on your way to being the best hostess in town.

Rules for a Good Hostess

Rule 1 for being a good hostess: Wanting to give a good party. Of course you must have your house in order and the best possible to eat and drink. When the party begins, devote yourself to your guests. You have to do some thinking in advance, to work out a system that runs well for you, that suits you, your house, equipment, and cooking skill. You have to accept the particular limitations of your system, realizing it will never truly be ideal. Plan your party sensibly and creatively within your own limits. If you want to give a good party this sort of planning is fun.

Some people hesitate to give parties because they feel their houses are never quite right or that they won't entertain well enough. That's foolish. A good hostess knows her guests will only remember whether or not they had a good time. So she spruces things up the very best she can and gives the kind of party she wants to give and can give well. If you balk at more than eight for dinner, don't worry about it. So do many famous hostesses. If you cook only three dishes well, stick to those until you've mastered new ones. Better unsurpassed lamb stew than passable duckling à l'orange. If Sunday lunch is the only possible time for you to have friends in, just give Sunday lunches, even though you often dine with others.

Facilities don't enter the picture either. A good hostess could give a good party anywhere from a sports arena to a one-room apartment on well-dusted packing cases. So Rule 2 for being a good hostess is: Give your kind of party and don't be intimidated by your setting.

Rule 3, whether you do the party alone, or have all the help imaginable, is this: Accept no substitutes—for yourself. What you do for the party can't be bought or borrowed for the occasion, like extra dinner plates. Caterers and party bureaus *arrange* parties: only a hostess can *give* one.

In the chapters that follow we hope to take the place of your private banquet manager or arrangements committee, from invitations right on through to emptying the last ashtray. We shall outline several types of parties and do what one hostess called the "constructive worrying" for you. That is this book's plot and you are its heroine. You will be doing what only you can do, giving the party, and like all forms of giving, it is the spirit in which you do it that counts.

CHAPTER 2

Who's Invited and How

You can plan a good party in half an hour. All it takes is thought and a pad and pencil.

Indoors or out, there are really only two types of parties: those at which you provide a meal and those at which you don't. Decide which it's to be, how many people to have, then jot down the date and the hour. The hour should match the time most people give parties in your community or, if you're being different, make sure it's a time when people will be able to come. If you plan to ask a few mothers who work, don't have the party on a Sunday, when they want to stay home with the children. If half the men in your group think of Saturday as golf day, save Saturday lunches for the winter months, or skip them entirely if many friends head for the ski slopes at the first good snow report.

Write down everything else from now on. Your pad, not your memory, can be guardian of what's been done and what still needs to be done.

When to Send Invitations

One invitation should go out well ahead of the others—to the maid, or bartender if you need one. Line your helper up immediately. Then on to the guest list.

There are no unbreakable rules about this, but you should try to get them all out within a day or two, to reduce the chance of a friend hearing about the party before he receives his invitation. Give people enough advance notice—ten days or two weeks—so that they are likely to be free, but *don't ask them more than three weeks ahead.* If they shouldn't want to come, it would be hard for them to refuse. And most people can't predict their plans more than three weeks in advance.

The guest list is just names, but it is where party artistry is most important. You are trying for a mixture of people who will sail through the evening together. It takes thought and imagination.

Small Party Lists

The list for a small party is the hardest to plot because, the fewer the people, the more they cluster together and the less chance there is for regrouping in different combinations. Say you decide on having ten or twelve people. Parties of this size usually break up into only two or three groups, and conversation may be general part of the time. For this, since you need lines of communication that are already open, the first names written on the list should form a nucleus—two couples, or four single friends, who know you well. Or who know each other well enough to have an evening's worth of things to chat about. When everyone knows only you, the beginning of the party is spent in "placing" people: "The Smiths have just come from Chicago," or "Tell us about your new job, Helen." It can be pretty slow going. But "nucleus guests" will have things to say to each other right from the start, and a conversation in which others can join soon gets under way.

Always have a nucleus, but never repeat an old list. If a friend can say beforehand, "They always have me with the Browns, Wilsons, and Newtons," you haven't thought enough about the list, and your parties probably suffer from sameness.

After jotting down your nucleus names, think some more. It is nice if the other guests have something in common even if they may not suspect it when they arrive. Though they don't know each other, Henry Stillwell and George Robinson both love to fish. Bill O'Neill would probably enjoy meeting Anne Bigelow because both are wild about photography—and neither is engaged. Sue and Jim Cummings, who have just started a little art gallery, would have things in common with Paul Osborn, who works at the museum.

Most women's brains are like small central intelligence agencies: they remember things about people, what they do, where they come from, how they spend free time. If you think for a few minutes, your "intelligence file" will build the list for you. There are usually hidden resources, too. Henry is the best storyteller you know, Paul plays the piano, and George is a party dream man, who talks easily to anyone about anything and makes friends fast.

So much for the men. Women are just as important to parties but generally adjust to them quicker. They are usually good listeners, but also love to talk and are freer with opinions than most men. This may not do for serious things in life but it is great for parties. Finally, women love to be with men and are loath to waste time in male company talking of their jobs or household problems—unless specifically asked. And what man in a party mood does that?

Some women, sad to admit, cannot shift into party speed; they cluster together, cataloguing life's boring routines, while the rest of the party goes ahead without them. Save these women for lunches. Or, if you ask them to a mixed party, decide to be social director (in fact, that's what you are) and firmly push them into mixed company. A party at which men collect on one side of the room and women on the other is out as far as we are concerned.

For a small party list, here are a few types, regardless of sex, to think twice about:

One-subject people, who are so involved with their particular jobs that they can talk of nothing else. The category also includes the egotist. His one subject is himself.

Lecturers may know about many things, but once a subject comes up they are apt to start a filibuster. This lulls other guests into a stupor or makes them restless as they wait to get a word in edgewise. The true conversationalist knows how to pick his audience.

Sensitive plants are those humorless people whose feelings bruise so easily that a chance remark, no matter how innocuous, causes them anguish or anger that they can't disguise. This puts a strain on everyone else. Good, heated argument can refresh a party, but sensitive plants are so subjective that whatever is said cuts them down or makes them close up and wither.

Big Party Lists

The list for a big party demands much less depth perception. There are fewer hazards about people getting along with each other, more possible combinations to start with. A big group breaks off more easily into smaller ones, and most people can find one in which they feel at home.

A big party is probably best for one-subject people, lecturers, and sensitive plants. After being bored for a time, their companions will walk across the room for something, "forget" to come back, and be replaced by others. The rule of thumb for any big party is to ask yourself, "Would I like to have such-and-such a couple?" If the answer is yes, it means that you like them and think they'll have a pleasant time. That is reason enough to put them on the list.

More Pointers for Making a Good List

Never ask anyone you really dislike. Perhaps this sounds too obvious to mention, but sometimes you become obligated to people you would rather not see. It is not that you are unkind: to have a sense of discrimination is human, and *necessary* at list-writing time. Don't think, "Oh dear, I suppose I could ask X without ruining the party." Be firm. Don't ask X. If you don't like him it is better to be obligated—for life—than to continue the relationship and risk putting a damper on what could be a wonderful party. If you dislike someone your friends are not apt to swoon over him either.

Sometimes you have to invite such a person. He may be allergic to you, too, but invitations go back and forth because he is unavoidably in your world—he may be an irritating relative or a cranky person married to a good friend whom you never want to stop seeing. Remember that when you add him to a list you take a calculated risk of losing some of the party spirit. As a safety measure, check the list carefully and try to include others who will help him have a good time. You never want people in your house to have a bad time, and taking pains over their pleasure is smart: you won't have to cope with them if they get along nicely with others.

In making your list, give thought to a mixture of age groups. We want to come out *for* this in our party platform. Sprinkling a few people from different age groups into a list could add to everyone's fun, and older people, always flattered to be asked to younger people's parties, will probably be at their best.

Perhaps you are cautious about inviting older people because you are afraid of becoming involved with them as you are naturally involved with parents or in-laws. Family invitations often do come week after week, but there is no reason to think that other older people will hound you.

Don't hesitate to invite older people for fear that your party won't come up to their standards. They probably have an idea of how you entertain, and if they don't like it they won't accept. And don't avoid asking older people for fear they will cramp your style or inhibit your contemporaries. Your elders have heard jokes, gossip, and violent political argument a lot longer than you. Not a rare species, they are (sobering thought!) what you will be in twenty or thirty years.

On the other hand, it is best not to ask older people to a party—a sit-on-the-grass supper, for example—when you can't make them comfortable. Don't have them with a group that takes until midnight to warm up and likes to "really get going" around two in the morning. And don't have them at all if they are older prototypes of the one-subject person, the lecturer, or the sensitive plant described a few pages back. Good party prospects are those older friends who have a real interest in the present and future, which you personify.

Having families around is pleasant, and at a party a brother or sister can help you with shy guests or strangers. But the complexion of a party can be marred if your friends think they are coming to see you and find themselves faced with the whole family.

Your parents probably think you're extraordinary. The only trouble is, they are inclined to talk about it. When they rhapsodize about you, no one can disagree even in fun, and a one-way conversation ensues—that is, no conversation at all. Another hazard about inviting parents is that they know you awfully well. They may cramp your style. Consider parents or any relatives as you would anyone else: ask them only if you think they will contribute to the party and will have fun doing so.

Speaking of families, a word about the very young. Christenings are the only adult parties at which babies belong. At the start of a party you might carry in your baby to be admired, but the most you can ask of a guest is a minute's concentration on him. Even a TV commercial doesn't ask for more than this. Bring the baby on—he's a fantastic new product—then take him off and resume the evening's program.

The same applies to young children. For fifteen minutes or so guests will enjoy seeing them, and they will enjoy being at the party. They can also help by passing things that will not ruin the rug if spilled. Having children around is a good way to teach them party behavior. If they do not behave, even after one minute, out they must go. There is no shakier start to a party than a hostess alternately smiling at guests and scolding children.

Older children might be invited to the start of your party but should not be asked to spend the whole evening. However sociable the child may be, the guest's interest in the new baseball coach or the high school band is limited.

Pets, like babies, have no place at parties, unless you have the rare one that lies drowsing under the piano and never claims attention in company. Remember, too, that some people are frightened of dogs, allergic to cats, or repelled by rodents, a class that embraces hamsters, guinea pigs, and white mice.

This advice about babies, children, and pets applies only to parties, not to family gatherings or the night when a couple of close friends come for dinner. But try never to let your pet annoy anyone.

A final word about the list. After you have built one that looks good, put down some substitute names that go well with the others. Unless you are a Queen or First Lady you cannot expect a hundred per cent acceptance. Having thought of good alternates in advance, you won't be panicked into asking just anybody when you receive a regret. In case of last-minute dropouts from a seated dinner, you can always send a cry for help to one of the standbys, especially if he is a close friend. Don't hesitate to do this. He will come if he possibly can, no matter how near party time you call. Next time, you might put him at the top of the list so he won't feel that he is a perpetual second thought.

Who Gives Invitations?

You, the woman, must always give invitations and reply to them. You are mistress of your house and the work of the party will be done by you. People want to know that *you* want them, so *you* ask them.

A husband may initiate a party by asking you to give one, or he may invite friends to come on a certain date. But a wife should follow up with "official" invitations. It's more efficient. Women are better about keeping family engagements in mind and a woman-to-woman handling of invitations avoids mix-ups. This applies to single hostesses too. When inviting a couple, always get in touch with the wife.

To Write or to Telephone Invitations?

There are no binding rules about whether to write or telephone invitations. Whichever is more convenient is proper. Some people think it is simplest to telephone, others prefer to write. Both have advantages.

If you telephone, you don't have desk work or the bother of checking addresses. You may find out right away whether people can come. You can give more information about the party: not only what to wear and whom the party is for, if anyone, but an extra word or two that may set the mood: "Dick's promised to play the piano" or "I thought we'd turn on the hi-fi after dinner and dance."

If you write, you know people have the essential facts—date, time, place—straight, and the invitation acts as a reminder. A written invitation also makes a party seem more of an occasion. And it is reassuring, as the hour grows late and a guest hasn't yet appeared, to have sent and received written words about the party.

For any party other than a formal dinner (which is discussed in another chapter), we say take your choice about writing or telephoning. But if you are having a cocktail party or buffet supper of twenty or more, writing is faster than trying to telephone everyone. In either case, keep your list at hand and check each person off as you hear from him. A plus, whether you write or telephone, is an address book with addresses and numbers kept up to date.

Written Invitations

If you decide to write, there are two choices. The first is in the form of a note, on your good paper. The correct writing paper is a single or double sheet of white, off-white, pale blue, or gray (no pink or lavender, please), with or without a border, with or without your monogram or address. Paper marked "Mrs. James S. Hughes" or "Miss Priscilla Ogilvy" is for business letters, not invitations. The stiff white vellum card, like an outsize visiting card, with the address engraved across the top is also popular and in good taste for an invitation in the form of a note. You need say no more than this:

Dear Mary,

Will you come for a cocktail on Thursday, April twenty-seventh, between six and eight? If you would like to bring an escort let me know and I'll send him an invitation.

I do hope you can come.

Love,
Louise

April eleventh

OR

Dear Adele,

Will you and John have dinner with us here on Thursday, April twenty-seventh, at seven o'clock?

I do hope you are free that evening.

Sincerely,
Dorothy

April eleventh

No need to ask for a reply: saying "hope you are free" implies that you want to hear. If the invitation is to a new acquaintance and your paper does not have your address on it, add it, and the telephone number if you wish, below the date.

Writing notes, though a very personal and polite way to invite, is time-consuming and seems a bit heavy-handed for most parties today. Visiting cards, which no one "leaves" any more, are better. The writing goes quickly and the engraved or printed name and address are clearly readable. "Mr. and Mrs.," or "Mr." or "Miss" for unmarried people, is always used, and if the address is given it is completely spelled out: no abbreviations for Street, Boulevard, Avenue. Conversely, for what you write by hand, any sort of understandable abbreviation is considered all right.

Visiting card invitation to a cocktail party:

Thursday, Jan. 7th
6 to 8 o'clock

Mr. and Mrs. John Hamilton, junior

R.s.v.p.   105 Valley Road

Or, if the name is engraved at the top:

105 Valley Road

Mr. and Mrs. John Hamilton, junior

Friday, May 5th
6 to 8

R.s.v.p.

It is not necessary to say "cocktails" but you may if you want to above the date. If it is a party in honor of someone, write "For . . ." or "To meet Mr. and Mrs. James Fitzgibbon" as in the samples that follow. To say "In honor of" is too formal for this sort of invitation, but putting "For . . ." or "To meet" is nice for the Fitzgibbons—who doesn't like to have a party given for him?—and nice for the guests who can be sure of the name beforehand. If it is to be a small party, or a party for people who are not strangers to your group, you could say "Jim and Lucy Fitzgibbon," but if you are asking a crowd, some of whom will not have met them before, stick to "Mr. and Mrs."

To meet Mr. and Mrs. James Fitzgibbon

Mr. and Mrs. John Hamilton, junior

Thursday, Nov. 3rd
6 to 8
R.s.v.p.   105 Valley Road

Fold-overs or informals. These are white cards folded at the top with the name engraved on the outside. Less formal than the unfolded card, they are perfectly correct for most occasions, and convenient for writing short notes. When using them in place of visiting cards, give the same information about the party, but write it on the inside, leaving the outside blank except for the engraved name. *Note:* Cards shown are not actual size. Postal regulations now require that envelopes be no smaller than 3 by 4¼ inches.

Although we prefer the plain white visiting card or the informal fold-over for cocktail invitations, because they are good-looking, quick, and clear, you may also use the colorful invitations that you can buy in stationery stores. Resist those illustrated with pink elephants or people dancing in martini glasses. And the "We're having small bash" type never seem really funny. It's better to choose something plain, with enough room for writing in the information you want to give.

Using "R.s.v.p." For cocktail invitations, there are two schools of thought about using "R.s.v.p." Some people always add it, because they want to know in advance how many may be coming. Others, planning to provide extra glasses and sandwiches anyway, prefer to leave off "R.s.v.p." To them, a cocktail party is not a momentous occasion, and the card is just a way of saying, "We are going to be at home on Thursday afternoon and would love to see you." If you use "R.s.v.p." you can make it easier for people to reply by adding your telephone number underneath.

With or without "R.s.v.p." there is no accurate way to predict the number of cocktail guests you will have: some will come who haven't replied, and others who have accepted won't. A point in favor of "R.s.v.p." is that you can give the guests of honor a list of those who have accepted which will help them remember names at the party, and after.

Usually half to two thirds of those invited come to a cocktail party, unless it is a very special occasion—a birthday, or a semi-business event to which people feel they should come. In these cases you can expect about three quarters. In bad weather the total is anyone's guess. You may be eating leftover appetizers for days afterward.

Telephoned Invitations

If you decide to telephone cocktail invitations, make sure you work pertinent details into the call, as italicized here: "I'm having a few people for cocktails to meet Judy Scott. She's an old classmate of mine who's just come to town. . . . On *Tuesday, the fifth,* from *six to eight, here.* . . . Good! It will be fun to see you. . . . Yes, *Tuesday, the fifth, six to eight.*" With luck, your friend has the information on her calendar by then.

Invitations to Dinner Parties

The choices for an invitation to dinner are the same as those to a cocktail party. You send a note or a card or telephone. Just be sure to give essential details.

Here are examples for a dinner invitation on a visiting card. The "R.s.v.p." is always used.

(1) To dinner:

Dinner, Tuesday, September 10th
7:30 o'clock

Mr. and Mrs. Hugh Cameron, junior

R.s.v.p.   105 Valley Road

---

(2) To a buffet supper:

Buffet Supper, Sunday March 4th
9 o'clock

Mr. and Mrs. Hugh Cameron, junior

R.s.v.p.   105 Valley Road

---

(3) To a dinner in honor of someone:

In honor of Mr. and Mrs. Matthew Frost

Mr. and Mrs. Hugh Cameron, junior

Wednesday, April 11th
8 o'clock — black tie

R.s.v.p.   105 Valley Road

Or, less formal:

For Peggy and Dave Howard

Mr. and Mrs. Hugh Cameron, junior

Friday, June 17th
7 o'clock

R.s.v.p.   105 Valley Road

(4) To a dinner held elsewhere than at your house:

Dinner at the Green Meadow Club

Mr. and Mrs. Hugh Cameron, junior

Tuesday, August 9th
7:30 o'clock

R.s.v.p.

Black tie

105 Valley Road

Note that you put the "R.s.v.p." above the address to which you wish the reply to be sent. If your cards do not have the address engraved, the bottom of the card could read:

> R.s.v.p.
> 105 Valley Road   Black tie

Or when the invitation is not "Black tie" just run the address across the bottom, like this:

> R.s.v.p.   105 Valley Road

As in the invitations to cocktail parties, use any abbreviations that seem clear, and place the information about the party wherever it looks neatest and easiest to read.

If men are to wear dinner jackets, "Black tie" is the correct wording, not "Tuxedo" or "Formal dress." Never say "Informal" either. A party *is* informal unless otherwise stated, and anyone in doubt about what to wear will call and ask.

Reminders

If you telephone a dinner invitation you naturally include all the information you would give on a written one. For a big seated party you might decide to follow up a telephone acceptance with a written reminder. Although this seems a touch official, it's a pre-party tranquilizer for you, especially if a few girls on the list are careless about writing things down. The reminder is written like the invitation on the visiting card, with "To remind" written across the top or substituted for "R.s.v.p."

Invitations to Special Events

When the invitation is to a birthday, anniversary, or christening party, say so, but look over the list carefully. Such parties should include only close friends, because an invitation to one raises the subject of presents. Close friends will want to bring presents (even though you protest), but it would be almost like charging admission if acquaintances felt they must. Weed out people you do not know well—they don't belong at this sort of party anyway—and then mention the cause for celebration when telephoning or writing. An invitation on a visiting card might have one of these across the top:

> *Birthday:* To celebrate Bill's birthday
> *Anniversary:* 1958–1968
> *Christening:* Tea after Mark's christening

If you are giving a birthday or anniversary party for someone outside your immediate family, you need not be so circumspect. Say whom the party is for, and why. Guests make up their own minds about bringing presents.

Accepting and Regretting

A hostess has the right to expect prompt replies, which include enough facts to show that the invitees understand the details. In the examples below, these facts are underlined.

Acceptance to a written note:

Dear Isabel:

Thank you so much for your invitation to dinner, on Tuesday, the twenty-third, at seven-thirty. It was good of you to think of me and I'll be there with great pleasure.

> Love,
> Marion

Regret to a written note:

Dear Isabel:

We are so sorry that we cannot come to dinner on the twenty-third. Peter has to go to Pittsburgh and is taking me along. Thank you for thinking of us. We shall miss being with you, and hope to see you soon.

> Affectionately,
> Lucy

Written replies to a cocktail party invitation are the same; mention the date, and if you cannot come give some polite excuse. If you accept, it isn't vital to mention the time since a meal will not be served.

Acceptance or regret to an invitation on a visiting card:

The traditional rule about replying to any sort of invitation is to use the same degree of formality as the sender does. A note calls for a note, a third-person invitation is answered in the third person, and a return call is the correct response to a telephoned invitation. Today this rule has been relaxed for replies to visiting card invitations. You might write a regular note in the first person ("Dear Susan, I would love to come . . .") or in the third person ("Mr. and Mrs. Duncan Dillon regret . . ."). It is all right to telephone or to reply by writing a line across the top of your own card:

"Delighted to accept for dinner on the 23rd at 7:30," or, "So sorry we cannot come on the 23rd. We will be in Atlanta. Hope to see you soon."

No need to sign these, but if, in replying to a close friend, you begin with "Dear Caroline" and end with "Love, Mary," cross out the engraved name.

In the etiquette books there are endless elaborations on accepting and regretting special parties, but for general purposes, here are the main points: invitations demand prompt replies, with pertinent facts included, and regrets demand some sort of polite excuse. Finer points are merely common sense: if you cannot accept the Smiths' invitation because you already have a date with the Browns, say so, unless you feel the Smiths will be hurt by not having been asked to the Browns'. If you cannot accept because you are having a party of your own that night, weigh your excuse against the reaction it might have: owing the Smiths, you won't want to say you are having a party without them, so "Terribly sorry, we are booked up for that evening" is enough. If you don't owe the Smiths, tell the truth, adding, "We hope to see you soon and thanks for thinking of us." No one expects to be invited to every party you give.

Invitation Menaces

One menace is the undecided person. You invite him, and a few days before the party there is still no word as to whether he is coming. Sometimes there is a good reason: he just doesn't know yet or has tried to reach you unsuccessfully or has left a message with someone else—your six-year-old, your cleaning lady, or your roommate, who has failed to relay it. Give the invitee the benefit of the doubt for a few days. But after that, since you still want to know whether to expect him, there is only one thing to do. Call him and keep calling until you get an answer. People don't mean to be irritating about delayed replies (even though they are!) and will usually say "No," out of politeness to you, if they are unable to give a definite "Yes."

Some people can always be counted on for indecision. It is best for your irritation quotient, even if you are sending others written invitations, to telephone them. Say politely, but meaning it, that you hope to know as soon as possible because you "may have to borrow extra chairs" or because "John thinks he'd like to invite someone from the office if we have space at the table." Give some reason that has to do with your problem of planning, not their problem of decision. And never say, "We must know if *you* can come," which implies "I can't face the party without you." That exerts unfair pressure. Even the chronically undecided have a right to refuse.

Speaking of unfair pressures, another menace is the clutcher. The telephone rings. A voice says, "I'd like to have you for dinner. Is there any evening in the next three weeks you could come?" You reply, guardedly, "What evening did you have in mind?" The caller says, "The sixteenth?" You reply, "I'm so sorry. I'm afraid we're busy on the sixteenth." With a bloodsucker's tenacity she comes back, "What about the eighteenth?" We doubt if you are ever guilty of this breach of manners, but if someone tries it on you, our advice is to pick a night and accept. You could go through the calendar, inventing excuses for the eighteenth, the twentieth, and the twenty-third, but you might as well settle on the eighteenth, if free, because a clutcher is not going to relax her hold unless openly insulted. And you don't want to do that.

Having been pressed into an acceptance, you have two courses: keep the date (as you do your dentist appointment) or call up later and make an excuse. Since those who go to parties dragging their heels don't make desirable guests anyway, a white lie is a kindness. Keep it as short as possible—it will be easier to remember, and you won't be in danger of stumbling over your words or "protesting too much."

Clutchers are usually people whom you don't know well or don't like. If good friends, who know you almost always want to see them, suggest a choice of dates, they will understand perfectly if you say you can't pick a night at the moment but hope for a rain check later.

Another menace is the late arrival. There are always a few of these. Some people just have no sense of time. Others (usually women, we admit) like to make an entrance, which *requires* being late. To achieve the desired effect, they must come into a crowded room. The simplest solution is to ask the late arrival for half an hour earlier than anyone else. Or you can say firmly, "Dinner's at seven, and I really mean seven because the Lloyds are flying in from the Coast that day and won't be up to a late evening." Or "Bill has to leave for Washington early next morning." Other solutions: plan a dinner that won't be ruined no matter how long it sits. Or whisk everyone to dinner as soon as the Janie-come-lately arrives. You might also decide to begin without her. Except in Washington, where eight means eight and everyone knows it, people hesitate to do this, since a party shouldn't begin with a stampede for the food or a veiled reprimand even to the most addicted late-comer.

In your circle there is probably an unwritten rule about lateness, with a margin of forty or so minutes before you and your sauces begin to boil over and the other guests stare glassy-eyed at empty hors d'oeuvre trays. Just observe that rule and try to forestall the late arrivals when you give the invitations. (In Chapter 12, "Being a Good Guest," we discuss the overlong cocktail hour in more detail.)

In praise of frankness. When accepting or regretting, if there is some qualification about your answer, be frank. If you must regret but wish you didn't have to, say so and explain why. Your sincerity will show and you'll be asked again. If you accept but know you will be late, say so, and if you know you will have to leave early, tell your hostess beforehand—it's better than seeming to be a wet blanket by skipping out with no warning in midevening.

When you invite, if you are planning something special for the evening, say so. Tell guests that you expect them to play a game, go out dancing afterward, or watch a slide show, giving them the chance to refuse if they don't like the idea. It's embarrassing for a guest to find that he is expected to play cards when he doesn't know a grand slam from a royal flush.

When one half of a couple you expect calls and says the other half can't be there but he or she would like to come alone, be frank. If it upsets your plans, say, "It would be better, to tell the truth, if you didn't come alone; we already have too many extra men (or women). We'll hope to see you another time soon." The same applies if someone asks to bring along uninvited guests. Say no if you feel that way. There are times when extra people are simply too much trouble or will crowd the party. Everyone understands this.

Recalling Invitations

Frankness is a factor here too. Once in a great while you arrange a party and later wish you hadn't. You may suddenly be busy or tired and the thought of guests is overpowering. Sometimes seeing it through will seem worth it. At others, it might be better to call it off. Imagining yourself as Mrs. Indomitable is all very well, but dragging yourself through an evening makes the party hard for everyone. People would much rather be asked again later when you feel in the right mood.

Asking People Back

Everybody wants to repay hospitality, and inviting people because it is your turn has been the motive behind many a great party. But perhaps too much emphasis is put on taking turns, to the detriment of the parties. You may be guilt-ridden about "those nice Clarks who had us to supper six months ago," or hesitant about asking special favorites three times in a row, especially when they haven't asked you back.

You should ignore these feelings and *believe* that you will get around to the Clarks sometime, when they are likely to fit in and have fun. Don't worry about inviting your favorites over and over again, unless you feel that you are overworking them or that others may think they are your indispensable props. If you feel this way, your favorites probably will feel overworked, too, and won't come.

Of course, no one goes on inviting people who keep turning her down, or asking people who never show interest in repaying her. But stop worrying about who owes whom among your real friends. When you are unable to return invitations—because the budget won't stand it or your husband's besieged with work—friends will understand and know without being told that they will hear from you when the right time comes.

Remember, too, that asking back is not an eye-for-an-eye matter, a dinner to be repaid with a dinner, concert tickets with concert tickets. If evening entertaining is impossible for a long period, you can repay couples by inviting the women to something in the daytime. Repay single women this way too. And since all you are trying to show is a desire to continue the friendship, you need give no invitations at all for a time. Instead pay back with a telephone call, flowers, or anything that shows you are thinking about friends as *friends*, not social obligations.

If you are a busy career girl and don't get around to doing any of these things you still have a way to repay: when you are invited again repay with *yourself*, by being the most thoughtful, appreciative, and outgoing person at the party.

Two situations do need special attention. When someone asks you to dinner for the first time, do something in return as soon as possible. They have made the first move and should feel that you agree it was a good idea, if it was. However, if you discover that you really have nothing in common, don't return the invitation and don't accept another one. There's no percentage for either side in encouraging a friendship you're not interested in.

The other situation is this. When you meet someone at a friend's party and want to invite him or her right away because you hit it off so well, invite the hostess who brought you together, the first time. Every hostess enjoys having her friends enjoy each other; but if you don't invite her with them the first time, she might feel you were side-stepping her or using her party as territory in which to stalk for new game.

CHAPTER 3

Launching a
Cocktail Party

There are two kinds of cocktail parties—those at which guests stand up and those at which they sit down. The big ones are harder to launch, but after you master the preparations for one of these a small party is child's play.

A big party is probably best given by a married hostess or by roommates, not so much because of the preparation as because of the difficulty of being a good hostess alone to so many people. Married or single, the hostess who works full time should give a big party only on a weekend, because it is a big investment in time as well as money.

After drawing up a good guest list, write down each step of the work and make a time schedule. Let's say it is now a week before the party. You sent out invitations a week ago and you expect fifty people for cocktails between six and eight o'clock. The countdown that follows should bring you to the hour—6 P.M. on the day—with everything done and you in your best party spirit.

Well before the day of the party you should engage any help you need. Since fifty people—or even twenty-five—are too many for a host to keep supplied with drinks, we advise hiring a bartender. This is a must if you are unmarried. You shouldn't ask a friend to act as host for so many, and letting fifty people mix their own drinks will cause terrible confusion.

A hostess for whom expense is no problem might have more help: two men, one to make drinks, the other to pass them, and one or two waitresses, to open the door, help with coats, serve appetizers, and clear glasses and ashtrays. All these are expendable, except the bartender. You can leave the door on the latch and empty ashtrays yourself. Guests can hang up their own coats, pick up their own drinks, and help themselves to appetizers.

You should also arrange, several days in advance, to have enough of the following in the house by party time.

Ice

If you have a freezer, this is easy. Just keep making ice cubes and store them in plastic bags in the freezer. Let the bartender worry about unsticking them. If you have no freezer you will have to buy ice; it adds only a few dollars to total expenses. Three hundred and fifty ice cubes should be plenty for fifty people. Remember that the iceman comes late on the afternoon of the party and you don't want to worry about him *then*, so be sure he has the date, time, and address accurately.

Glasses

To rent or to buy? This depends on how often you give big cocktail parties. You may want to rent them from a caterer, but even if you give a party only once a year, we think it is still easier (and cheaper in the long run) to buy. Good-looking plain glasses from any dime store cost ten or fifteen cents each. For fifty people, you should have thirty tall glasses, thirty old-fashioned and twenty martini glasses, which comes to twelve dollars at the most—a smart investment as opposed to renting every time you give a big party.

Eighty glasses sounds like a lot extra, but you can't predict who will drink what. Most people take on-the-rocks drinks or tall drinks (whisky with soda or water, gin and tonic), and a few will ask for actual cocktails. In summer almost everyone will ask for a tall drink, so allow for that. Don't, however, pad out the supply with "good" glasses that might get broken and cost a lot to replace.

If storing glasses is a problem, ask your liquor dealer for a couple of cardboard liquor cases and stack the glasses two or three at a time in the partitions with pieces of paper between them. Lay paper over the top and put the cartons in the cellar or a cupboard where they won't get knocked about.

Serving Equipment

The more helpers the less serving equipment needed. One tray per waitress will do since each can refill it as often as necessary. With a minimum of help, or none at all, the more trays the better. Put appetizers on them beforehand, and when one is nearly empty exchange it for another already arranged. Or leave several full trays around where guests can help themselves.

If you are short of trays, go to the five-and-ten for plain round wooden or plastic ones. Or use your largest, flattest dinner plates. Glass or china plates are especially good for stuffed eggs and other food that must be kept in the refrigerator until served. Never put stuffed eggs on silver trays; they work their tarnish magic right through doilies.

Doilies

A pottery platter of raw vegetables needs no doily, but this is about the only exception. Use the white paper lace mats from any grocer, housewares shop, or five-and-ten. Colored or plastic doilies don't look right.

Bowls

Four or five bowls filled with nuts and olives and spaced around the room are a good idea no matter how much help you have. They are on hand in case of delay in serving other food, and within reach of people sitting in corners who often get missed by the waitress threading her way through the standees.

Ashtrays

At a big party ashtrays are apt to be used for olive pits, crumpled paper napkins, and toothpicks as well as ashes. Small ones just won't do, so put them away. Get plain heavy glass ones at the five-and-ten; they are virtually unbreakable and perfectly nice-looking.

Liquor

You could offer as many cocktail choices as a restaurant and have a couple of bartenders who can make up anything from an Alexander to a Zombie. This is not only unnecessary, it looks ostentatious. Better to have an ample supply of the basic drinks, based on what you know of your friends' preferences. Although one or two choices are sufficient, it is more expansive, and no more expensive, to offer a wider range.

For fifty people, you might have this on hand:

4 fifths of scotch
4 fifths of bourbon
4 fifths of gin
2 fifths of vodka
2 fifths of rye
2 bottles of dry sherry
2 bottles of Dubonnet
1 bottle of dry vermouth
18 pints of soda water
18 pints of ginger ale
18 pints of tonic water
12 bottles of a cola drink

That sounds like an orgy. It will cost something, too, and is much more than enough. But liquor keeps, and a cardinal rule for cocktail parties is to have more than enough ready and waiting.

Today some brands of liquor come in quarts, which cost more but are relatively cheaper than fifths and can represent a saving over a period of time. Consult your dealer and let him suggest the best brands for the best price. (More about this in Chapter 16, "Party Food and Drink.")

Our liquor man tells us that rye and rum are becoming popular in some areas of the country, and that in others vodka is moving up on gin, so adjust the amounts of each liquor to the "local conditions." It isn't strictly necessary to have sherry, Dubonnet, *and* extra vermouth, for vermouth on the rocks. Generally a person who likes one will be satisfied with either of the others, even though they taste different.

The list above provides for only one kind of cocktail, the martini, because both epicures and "good drinkers" seem to agree that a martini is *the* cocktail. Increase choices if your bartender is up to juggling orders for manhattans, sours, and rum drinks as well. At any rate, decide beforehand what you will offer, have the ingredients ready, and tell the bartender to turn down requests for anything else. Cocktail guests, like motorists, require efficient and speedy service, and the bartender will have no time to rummage around for special fixings while the party is in full swing.

For those who do not drink alcohol, you might have, in addition to ginger ale, tonic, and cola, a pitcher of seasoned tomato juice in the refrigerator. Consider having a pot of coffee on the stove to offer late-stayers.

The Bar

Your bartender must have enough room to work in, all equipment within reach, and be stationed where he is accessible. You can use anything for a bar—the dining table, two card tables pushed together, or even a desk—so long as it is high enough to work at without stooping and is covered with a floor-length cloth. Arrange the glasses at one end and a few bottles of liquor and soft drinks (removed from their paper carriers) at the other. Then people can see what they may ask for. Remaining bottles can be put under the bar table until needed, and the ice bucket, if it is big—and it should be—can go on a small table to one side, or on the floor behind the table.

Place the bar so that the bartender faces the guests and so that they do not have to run an obstacle course around furniture to reach him. The dining room, except in a house where it is not on the same floor as the living room, is a good spot for the bar, especially at a crowded party. People in search of a second drink will move there and start a group near the source of supply. But if you use the dining room or dining alcove as a bar location, do not also have all the food there. It will create a crush and concentrate the party in one area.

Equipment for the Bar

Linen or cotton cloth with waterproof pad underneath to protect table
Cocktail shaker or martini pitcher
Water pitcher
Bottle opener
Ice pick or bar knife
Tray for passing—at the start the bartender will have time to do this
Cocktail-size paper napkins
Two linen bar or dish towels
Ingredients for special drinks (lemon peel, orange and lemon slices, limes, bitters, sugar, cherries, olives, onions, etc.)

All of the above can be checked off days ahead of the party. You will have had time to do the shopping, order liquor, ice, and so on, between daily chores.

Food

Food comes closer to that six o'clock deadline, and calls for an accurate time schedule. Divide it into three categories: advance food, same-day food, and emergency food.

Many things you might serve can be ordered days in advance. Nuts, popcorn, olives, and crackers can sit in the kitchen ready to be put in bowls just before party time. Most cheese spreads, pâté, dips, and anything to be heated during the party can be prepared ahead and kept in the refrigerator. Sandwiches made the day before won't suffer at all if covered with damp towels or transparent wrap and piled in the refrigerator. Raw vegetables can be cut and floated in ice water the day before. Eggs can be hard-boiled and fresh shrimp can safely be cooked and refrigerated twenty-four hours ahead.

Same-day food includes true perishables, such as stuffed eggs or open-faced canapés, which could crust over or dry up. Since anything spread on toast or crackers that might get soggy is also a last-minute proposition, allow an hour or more on the afternoon of the party for preparing these. Nothing is more delicious than hot appetizers, but skip them unless you have enough help to assign someone to keep checking the oven.

Plan only one or two same-day things. Save elaborate last-minute concoctions for smaller parties, or assign these to a waitress who comes early for that purpose. Leave nothing for yourself to do in the food department—beyond setting trays around—later than the early afternoon of the party.

Emergency food is important. You can't be sure how hungry guests will be, how long they will stay, or for that matter how many will show up. At most cocktail parties nothing is eaten in the beginning, everybody takes something in mid-party, and a few seem to get really hungry near the end of the party, so it is virtually impossible to predict how much will be eaten. The solution is to have something on hand that is easy to fix but will keep for later if not used. Nuts, olives, corn chips are useful, but more glamorous emergency food—jars of pâté and cheese spreads with a couple of boxes of toast rounds, or sliced icebox rye—can be opened and served in seconds. Don't forget Italian antipasto. Canned rolled anchovies and artichoke hearts keep indefinitely, and sliced bologna and salami can be used in sandwiches or for cold supper days after the party.

The key words for the food at a big party are: simple, substantial, and attractive. Appetizers are basic refreshments for those who drink only a little or nothing at all, and ballast for those who drink a lot, so forget about little canapés with more eye appeal than substance.

Here are some suggestions. For fifty people, four choices would be plenty, along with a few bowls of nuts and olives, and emergency rations in the background. Recipes for the starred concoctions are given in Chapter 17.

*Pâté maison made from two pounds of liverwurst
Swiss cheese sandwiches ⎫ made from two loaves
Water cress sandwiches ⎬ of bread with slices
                        ⎭ cut in fours
*Tartar steak on icebox rye made from two pounds of top round
  and two loaves of thin-sliced bread
Stuffed eggs made from three dozen eggs
Sardine spread on white bread made from two boxes of sardines,
  one loaf of bread cut into rounds
Shrimp—three pounds of fresh shrimp with cocktail sauce
*Crab meat canapés—two cans of crab meat, one loaf of bread cut
  into small rounds
*Cheese Taj Mahal—one pound of club cheese spread, two boxes of
  toast rounds
Raw vegetable platter with dunking sauce
*Breadless salami, bologna, and cheese-slice "sandwiches"—one pound
  of each, filled with cream cheese

After you have written down the menu, make a master grocery
list of every ingredient you need.

Cleaning

You can swish a dustcloth up to the last minute, but this is not
the moment for vacuuming and polishing. Polish tables and any
silver you plan to use well ahead of time. Polished silver can be
wrapped in treated tissue paper days in advance and come out shining. A good investment, this paper can be used many times and
silver put away between parties is much easier to clean. Polishing
silver a day ahead and covering it with clean, dry towels is also perfectly safe. Or you might assign the silver to a helper on the day
of the party, but only if she comes early. Her final pre-party hour,
like yours, will be fully occupied without this chore.

Glasses may be washed three or four days in advance, stacked, and
covered with dish towels. Those stored on shelves may need
thorough washing; stored in boxes, they may need only to be wiped
off and carefully inspected for smudges.

Everything must look clean and be clean—no strain if you schedule ahead. You might want to budget some of your cocktail party cash for extra cleaning help the day before, in answer to the often-heard question: "How am I to get the house looking right and still look right myself when the first guest arrives?"

Now we begin to close in on the party launching. Here are a few more things to do no later than the day before, if you haven't yet attended to them:

If you plan to have flowers, order them now. The florist will tell you what he has that's fresh and economical. Ask him to deliver first thing on the morning of the party, so that you will have time to arrange them.

Make a house check. See that you have enough

> cigarettes
> ashtrays
> candles
> fresh soap
> guest towels
> bathroom tissue
> matches
> cocktail napkins
> paper coasters

Do any light bulbs need replacing? Have you others in readiness? You may have decided to rent a coat rack, but if not, is the hall closet neat? Most coat closets are family catchalls, so if you plan to use yours, straighten it up now. Move your own things elsewhere temporarily. If you expect fifty people, a big hall closet could probably hold all the men's coats (don't forget extra hangers). Women's coats can be laid in the bedroom.

Look over the bathroom or powder room to see that it is properly equipped and that everything works.

You can also set up the bar the day before. Tall glasses and old-fashioned glasses can be stacked in twos and threes, or left on trays in the kitchen to be carried in as needed. If your cigarette boxes have lids, fill them now. Put matches, coasters, napkins around.

If ice is not being sent in, start making batches of cubes and putting them in the freezer in plastic bags or containers.

Go to the hairdresser. You won't want to be fretting under the dryer on party day.

The evening before the party is the best time to do the heavy work: lay the fire, move furniture, haul out the ladder to replace ceiling light bulbs.

As the shadows lengthen, have a good dinner and forget about the party until you wake next morning. You are really organized and will have time to spare for everything to be done next day.

After breakfast and any necessary housework are out of the way, ask yourself whether you are worried about the ice, bartender, or any other details. If the answer is yes, call and check.

Now do the flowers and any same-day food. Guided by your list, defrost or chill foods that need these attentions. Peel hard-boiled eggs, cut out rounds of bread. This may take a couple of hours, so it should be about noon now. As you check your list, for almost the last time, you will be surprised how little is left to do. You may even have time to see to the mail or do some telephoning. Have lunch. Press your dress.

At last you can begin the final touches. Set out bowls and trays with the non-perishable foods, nuts, crackers, etc. The potato chips and crackers for dips can be arranged, with the dip to be added later. Put out cigarettes, matches, cocktail napkins, if you haven't already.

There is an air of suspense in the house now. Everything is ready —except you. This is the time, about four o'clock, to retire from the scene to bathe, rest or read, and dress. Allow an hour even if you normally dress as fast as a fireman. Inevitably, there will be interruptions and you will need time to straighten up your room and bathroom.

Now it's about five-fifteen. Forty-five minutes to go. Get out what's waiting in the icebox and arrange platters. The bartender and other helpers, if you're having them, will need instructions when they arrive. If they are new to your house, take them on a tour, pointing out where people are to leave coats, where the washroom is. Divide the labor among them, deciding who will be responsible for clean ashtrays, fresh food platters. If you hire a "team," it is important to organize it. You may want to pay helpers now, to avoid having to think of it later.

Ask the bartender to check his bar. Get out anything that's missing. If he asks for something you don't have, don't be upset. All the truly essential things are there.

During the last half hour, turn on the lights, air the living room, close doors that need to be closed—guests don't like to wander into places they are not supposed to be. If you have pets in the house put them out of the way. There will be other distractions: the telephone, delivery men. A married hostess will be busy with her husband's inevitable questions. "Where's my new tie? What's Bill Montgomery's wife's name? Did we ask the O'Donnells? Did you tell the bartender to make the martinis six to one?"

Serene as Buddha, you answer his questions, find his tie, and assure him that all is fine, while you clean up the bathroom again.

Then you go to the living room, close the windows, and wait.

A few minutes later the doorbell rings. Here you go.

The Small Cocktail Party

After a big cocktail party this will seem like nothing. Organization is still the watchword. Spick-and-span house and equipment are, if possible, more important, because blemishes will be more noticeable. You won't need extra glasses, "bought" ice, or a week to get ready. Furniture can be left in place, and you can use whatever serves as a bar when you are home alone. Although you don't need help for a party of twelve or so, someone to open the door, pass food, and straighten up afterward can be very pleasant.

A small cocktail party is the best time for fancy appetizers and for special drinks, the makings of which can be assembled in advance. There is time enough, and room enough, to do these things well. One or two kinds of appetizers are all you need, and you won't mind being in the kitchen until the last minute preparing them when only a few people are coming. Also, with a small number of guests, you might make appetizers—spread pâté and cheeses—in the living room, and pass them without having to fade out of the conversation.

Here is a check list for a cocktail party of twelve or fourteen people.

  2 fifths of scotch
  2 fifths of bourbon
  2 fifths of gin
  Dry vermouth—a half bottle is plenty
  1 fifth of vodka
  1 bottle of sherry or Dubonnet
  6 pints of soda water
  6 pints of tonic
  6 pints of ginger ale or cola
  2 dozen sandwiches or crackers with a spread
  2 dozen of something else—hot canapés, sausages, cheese puffs, or shrimp
  2 bowls of nuts, chips, or vegetables
  1 big ice bucket filled in advance with four extra ice trays ready in the refrigerator

You won't need all this liquor, but have it there in case many guests ask for the same thing. The food supply is more than adequate, too, but delicious sandwiches and hot things usually go quickly, and the food in bowls is insurance against constant nibblers. You won't need more than an hour or so in the afternoon (or, if you have a job, in the early morning) to set up the bar, etc., as long as the house is in order.

Small cocktail parties can be delightful. Relatively little work, they leave you free really to talk, not just drop in and out of conversations. But they still take doing, and sometimes you may feel that as long as you have to be ready for action, you might as well ask a crowd. A big party is also more economical than several small ones.

One last point. If you decide on a big party, make sure it is big. If you want a small one, keep it small. A big party won't seem successful if you empty the living room of furniture and then only half fill it with people. And remember, don't let a small party get bigger without adjusting supplies.

CHAPTER 4

Dinner Parties Big and Small — Table Settings, Simplified Service

THE SMALL SEATED DINNER

All seated dinners seem special, but except for rare occasions, most people agree that the ideal size is no less than six nor more than twelve. At small dinners people can get together, become friends, the work can be done well with little or no help, and most of us have space and equipment to handle six to twelve comfortably, without borrowing extras and rearranging furniture.

Let's say the dinner we will now describe is for ten people and that your dining room or dining area will comfortably take that number. Let's say that your table stretches to seat ten and that you have ten of everything you'll need for serving. Let's have a three-course dinner, and, for now, let's assume you will have hired one helper. (Later we will show how the same dinner can easily be put on singlehanded.)

Setting the Table

Tablecloth or place mats? It's up to you, of course. What do you have? What do you like? If you have full tablecloths and don't mind the laundry expense they are always nice. Place mats are popular and correct for all except a formal table setting.

If You Use a Tablecloth

The virtues of a tablecloth are that it is traditional and festive, the table looks all of a piece, and you can put more on it without its looking crowded.

Tablecloths look and feel better with a mat under them. The mat also prevents damage to the table top. If you don't have a standard table pad, use an old blanket. A quilted mattress pad also works well—it feels right, and no one can tell what it is without peeking.

The pad should hang over the edge of the table three or four inches. A too big one can be secured to the underside of the table with tape or thumbtacks, or temporarily hemmed with basting stitches or safety pins.

Laying a cloth for a big table by yourself is almost impossible because with a pad beneath it you have to lift it completely away from the table to even it. Get someone to lend a hand.

The folds of a cloth that has been laid away for a long time may look too pronounced. Since ironing a big cloth is no job for an amateur, a solution is to heat the iron, unplug it, run it over the already laid cloth. You won't get a completely smooth cloth, but a few regular folds won't be noticed, and if you lay it early heavy creases tend to smooth out.

What Kind of Cloth?

White linen with a damask pattern is conventional and attractive. Lace or a combination of linen and lace is fine too. Some lace cloths are ecru to start with, or because they have aged that color. With these, it's better to use ecru napkins rather than white.

There's nothing against cloths of other pale colors. We recall a table laid with the palest pink damask, which set off the hostess' cobalt-blue and rose candlesticks. Another table in a dark green room looked lovely laid with damask pale as lime juice. White or ecru cloths with borders or insets of another color can be beautiful, too, as long as they don't jar with other colors in the room.

For special parties try something less conventional. On a Christmas or Thanksgiving table you might lay red or green felt, or a white cloth overlaid with wide bright velvet ribbons. If you have a round table, you might cut a circle or star of felt to set off the centerpiece, or run ribbons across the table like wheel spokes.

On her Christmas table one hostess we know lays a snow-cover of white nylon plush, sets a grove of small fake Christmas trees in the center. For Thanksgiving, a country hostess uses an antique patchwork quilt in reds, browns, and white. Another uses an old curtain of green documentary chintz printed with game birds.

We have also admired Spanish cotton rugs, Indian bedspreads, and Balinese batiks on tables. Consider the color scheme, including the patterns and colors of china, then let your imagination wander.

If You Use Place Mats

Place mats have these advantages: they are not usually expensive, are easy to wash, easy to store, and there is so much choice in the shops that you can always find something that goes well with the rest of your equipment.

The traditional place mat is oblong or round. Stick to these. Odd shapes, like fans, or baroque shells, or those outsize doilies that hang over the side of the table like tongues, make your table look busy instead of organized. Probably for this reason round mats, the exact size of dinner plates, or smaller, are becoming more and more popular. Since you see them only between courses, they add to a clear, understated look. They are an especially good choice if the table has a beautiful finish or an inlaid veneer; it is a decoration in itself and shouldn't be covered more than necessary. Oblong mats, which have the advantage of giving an absorbent base for glasses, are fine on a table big enough for them to be laid fairly far apart.

Place mats may be lace, linen, cotton, leatherette, plastic, or even wood—felt-backed and mounted with reproductions of old prints. Good shops sell plain round plate-size fake lace or linen mats, for about two dollars apiece. When buying plastic or leatherette, pass up tricky surfaces and patterns in favor of something that resembles woven material with traditional designs of fruit or flowers. While most non-material mats are all right for informal parties, the plastic ones with splashy scenes of Paris or Japanese fishermen belong, if anywhere, at an outdoor lunch.

Plates, Flatware, and Napkins

Place plates—or service plates, as they are also called—may seem a bother, yet they make a table look attractive and are part of traditional table setting. We think you should use them when the first course is to be passed *after* the guests enter the dining room. The napkin then goes in the center of each plate.

However, at a dinner for ten, with one maid, it is easier to have the first course already on the table when guests come in, and place plates, as such, are unnecessary but correct. If the first course is hot soup in a soup plate, the plate under it *is* the place plate. If it is a cold first course—pâté, eggs in jelly, or stuffed tomatoes—one plate is enough. Oysters or clams on the half shell, served in a soup plate, should have another plate underneath. A stemmed glass for shrimp cocktail or a shell or ramekin for hot sea food also requires one. If the first course is (hot or cold) soup in a consommé cup, etiquette says you should have a place plate under the cup and saucer. This seems unnecessarily complicated. We would omit the place plates and just use the saucers that go with the consommé cups.

When the first course is put on the table in advance, the napkin goes on the left, next to the forks.

Forks, knives, and spoons. Silver should be lined up evenly, with each piece about an inch from the edge of the table. Forks go on the left, with tines upward. Knives go on the right with cutting edges facing inward. Soup spoons go to the right of knives. This is elementary, but what often confuses hostesses is the placement of extra knives and forks. It is simple: the implements to be used first are laid farthest away from the plate. If the first course is soup, the spoon goes at the far right. Farthest away from the plate go the knife and fork for a first course, nearest the plate go the larger knife and fork for the main course. Or, should dinner begin with a main course, to be followed by salad, the order is reversed: big knife and fork on the outside, salad knife and fork nearest the plate. Grapefruit or melon spoons go on the outside right, like soup spoons; oyster forks go wherever they would best balance the pieces of silver on either side of the plate.

Traditionally, dessert forks and spoons are not laid on the table but served on the dessert plate on either side of the finger bowl. There is no doubt that this is a nice detail: it keeps a table from being cluttered with silver at the start, and finger bowls help you leave the table feeling fresh. But keeping well-paced, easy service in mind, you won't be a social outcast if you skip finger bowls. If you do, the dessert silver goes above the plate parallel to the side of the table, with the fork handle to the left and the spoon handle to the right. Dessert plates are laid on empty.

With or without finger bowls, it is easier to set up the dessert service on a sideboard. After the main course is cleared, the waitress or hostess doesn't have to return to the kitchen for each dessert plate.

Glasses. Water glasses go to the right and a little above the plate, almost directly over the knives. If you serve wine or beer, these glasses go to the right of the water glass.

Some people omit water when serving wine. It's a temptation. Getting out glasses, providing ice water, is tiresome, especially when it is often left untouched. But since some guests may not drink wine, better take the trouble and have water too.

All glasses on the table should be goblets—that is, have stems— except when you serve beer, iced tea, or iced coffee.

The centerpiece can be anything—or nothing. If your table is small, omit it.

If an important flower arrangement would crowd your table (or your budget), poke around the house for something else. Do you have any silver hidden away? An old-fashioned breadbasket or an ice bucket that's too small to be practical can be polished up, filled with simple greens, and used as a centerpiece. A silver or pewter tankard filled with a few blossoms or greens is good-looking. Among a husband's collection of Things Never to Be Thrown Away you may find an old sports trophy or beer mug with possibilities.

What do you have in glass or porcelain? A low vase or a bowl with a single flower floating in it could be lovely. Perhaps some figurines elsewhere in the house would make a pretty centerpiece.

Or just buy an assortment of fresh fruit (to be eaten later) and pile it on an ordinary plate.

It is amazing what a garden can offer when you search it with a centerpiece in mind. Perhaps you have dogwood or fruit tree blossoms. Spirea (bridal wreath) is beautiful, and laurel or rhododendron, blooming or not, arranges easily. So does pine, hemlock, or spruce. Having no garden of your own, you may have a friend who wouldn't object to a little careful "pruning" of hers. Or you might buy wheat sheaves or dried flowers.

If you live surrounded by city cement you can't search gardens, but you can buy long-lasting greens to use on the table and put somewhere else afterward. Sprays of eucalyptus or lacy ferns? Two pots of ivy put in a bowl and trailed from the center of the table? Do not be tempted by fake flowers or fruit. They can be enchanting elsewhere, but as a centerpiece they look stiff, dead.

Candles, traditional on dinner tables, are a must as far as we are concerned. Any amount of candlelight is festive, and a dining table lit entirely in this way is not only romantic but more becoming to women than a weekly facial. If your dining room or area does not lend itself to total candlelight, candles on the table are enough. At a table seating ten, you need four candles. If all you have is two silver or china candlesticks, use glass ones instead. You can buy these anywhere for a few dollars. The simpler they are the better. If you have two pairs of candlesticks that do not match, use them— one pair at the head of the table, the other pair at the foot. Just be sure that the tops of the candles are of even height.

Always try to have tall new candles at parties. Use burned-down ones at other times. Have white or ivory candles only, except perhaps for holiday dinners when the whole table is set in bright colors.

On a small table you might group a few low candlesticks in place of a typical centerpiece. A crowded table often looks better with candles placed single file down the center. Otherwise, pair them about halfway between the centerpiece and the ends of the table.

Salts, peppers, and ashtrays. Once these are on, the table is set. Salts and peppers should be placed in an organized pattern. For ten people, four pairs are plenty. With one pair at each end and one pair at the center of each side, they are within "please pass" reach of everyone. If you have several pepper mills, use them instead of shakers. If you have but one, put it at the head or foot of the table to be passed around.

Ashtrays can be placed according to what you know of your friends' smoking habits. One ashtray for every two should be enough, but one per person is better. Laid on irregularly, small glass ones are the least noticeable. It is not necessary to have urns or boxes for cigarettes. Just lay two or three cigarettes in each ashtray and put a small matchbox or ten-strike matchbook beside it.

In these diet-conscious days, compotes filled with nuts or candy seem superfluous, but it's up to you. If you want them, and have room, put a compote at either end of the table. It is more important, with only one maid (or none), to make room for the wine, which will be self-served. For ten people you will need two bottles on the table to start (with two more in readiness).

While there is nothing wrong with having bottles of wine on the table, it is prettier, perhaps, to decant it into carafes. Neither a bottle nor a carafe goes directly on the table or cloth. A *sous-carafe*, a sort of outsize coaster with a high rim, is the old-fashioned answer, but any small silver, china, or glass dish does just as well.

What have we left out? Bread and butter plates. While there's no rule against using them, the *serving* of this dinner is easier without them. When you do use them, they go to the left of the plate above the forks. If you should serve salad *with* the main course, the salad plate goes on the left, too, when you set the table.

Table-Setting Check List

Basic Equipment:
   Place mats or tablecloth and napkins
   Plates for all courses
   Forks, knives, and spoons
   Water goblets
   Candles
   Ashtrays, cigarettes, and matches
   Salts and peppers
   Coffee service in readiness

Optional:
   Wineglasses, and coasters for wine carafes or bottles
   Centerpiece

Compotes for nuts or candy
Butter plates
Finger bowls and doilies

On the sideboard:
Runner or mats
Serving forks and spoons
Trivets for hot dishes

Serving a Small Seated Dinner

Since the point of a seated dinner is to have organized service and comfortable guests, there must be a minimum of getting up and down. You and the maid should agree on a division of duties ahead of time. There should be a sideboard or extra table in the room for serving, because you do not want to go to and from the kitchen.

Set the sideboard with a runner, mats, or trivets for the hot dishes. Add all the serving silver you will need: fork and spoon for the main course, vegetables, salad (if you are having it), plus whatever you need to serve dessert, including ladles for sauce or whipped cream.

Now here are suggested stage directions for you and your waitress in proper sequence.

When it is time for dinner the maid pours the soup and puts it on the table. Or she brings the first course, already on plates, to the table.

Maid announces dinner.

You seat the guests as they come in. Dinner begins.

Maid passes crackers. Or a bowl of crackers is on table and you ask guests to hand it around. Mayonnaise or any accompaniment to the first course is also passed around by guests.

During first course the maid takes a tray to living room, collects cocktail glasses and ashtrays, and plumps pillows.

She returns to kitchen and brings main course to sideboard.

You or the host (if the entree needs to be carved) serve the main course to guests while the maid is clearing the first course. If she is quick she may be able to pass plates to the last few people.

You return to the table. Maid passes buttered rolls. The wine is poured by hosts or guests at each end of the table.

When guests are almost through eating, the maid passes main course around for second helping. With a casserole too heavy to pass, you or the maid ask if anyone cares for a second helping. You ask aloud; she goes around the table, asking quietly and not bothering with those who still have plenty on their plates.

When the main course is finished (or, if there's a salad course, when *it* is) the maid clears the table of salts and peppers (all together on a small tray), then comes back and crumbs it. This is done with a folded white napkin and a small plate onto which are swept crumbs, spilled salt, and so on. Although brushes and crumbers are things of the past, crumbing still enhances the looks of the table, if you have someone to do it. Then the maid lays dessert plates and passes dessert. If it is a two-trip one such as pie à la mode, or a flaming one, you may think it better to serve it from the sideboard yourself, and have her pass the filled plates around.

During dessert, the maid fills the coffeepot and takes the coffee tray to the living room. It's best to serve it there so that the maid can get started on the dishes early.

When you leave the table the maid retires to do the dishes. You serve coffee.

Later, the maid comes out to refill coffeepot, or you can disappear for a minute to do this.

Finally, the maid clears coffee cups away.

This system works well. It is smooth and quick, and you have to get up only once or, at the most, twice during the meal. An experienced or well-rehearsed waitress can easily do her part. Obviously the menu chosen is important. One maid cannot be expected to cook, whip cream, or watch a sauce during the serving of dinner. At best, she can heat rolls and keep the main course on the stove until the last minute. This sort of service works well with roasts that do not lose their heat quickly, and with casseroles and entrees that don't have to be put on platters before being brought to the sideboard. Desserts can be as elaborate as you can make them without needing last-minute touches: fresh fruits, mousses, pastries, puddings, or even hot crepes or cherries jubilee because the pancakes or cherries can be prepared ahead and moved from stove to sideboard when the time comes.

Ten people is the most you should try to serve this way. Twelve or more is too much for one maid, and no matter how many times you get up to help, which is disruptive to the party, there will still be delays and an athletic atmosphere to the serving.

When You Have No Maid

Without a maid there is much more to do, but a few details can be skipped and the dinner still run smoothly with a little assistance from the host or, if you are unmarried, the "guest host" you enlist. Here are the revised stage directions:

Before the party, put a couple of trays in the living room. As you go out to serve the first course, load one tray with the remains of appetizers and full ashtrays.

When the first course is on the table and you announce dinner, the host carries the other tray, filled with cocktail glasses, to the kitchen.

The first course is managed exactly the same as when you have a maid, except that crackers are on the table to be passed around by guests. You and the host divide the work of clearing and bringing the second course to the serving table. Perhaps you put food on the plates and he passes them to the guests. Or you do all that and he brings in the bread and condiments, if any, and puts them on the table. When you both sit down, wine is poured. Or you might ask one of the other men to do this while you are serving.

Second helpings can be served by you *or* the host. It is not necessary for both to get up.

When the main course is finished, the host clears it while you bring in dessert and dessert plates. (Forget about crumbing the table.) A dessert in a bowl can be passed hand to hand around the table, as can a tray of pastries or *pots de crème*. If it is something to be cut, like pie or cake, it is easier for the guests if you cut and serve it from the sideboard, plate by plate.

When the time comes to leave the table, ask guests to go on without you. (If the men are having coffee separately from the women, tell the women where they should go. The host guides the men.) You retreat to the kitchen to get the coffee.

To make a maidless dinner of three courses easier to serve, you might have a first course in the living room. For this anything that can be eaten with a fork is fine—sardines on toast, crab meat served hot in ramekins or cold on lettuce. Oysters baked in a variety of ways are an excellent choice, or just serve them raw on a big tray lined with cracked ice. Have cut lemons or a sauce mignonette, or go all out and put a tiny bit of caviar on each oyster. Do not have soup as a living-room first course; it's too difficult to serve and to drink, and is no partner for cocktails.

A living-room first course could simply be more than usually elaborate and filling appetizers, such as fresh shrimp or smoked salmon on pumpernickel. Also good are hard-boiled eggs with the yolks curried or mixed with ham paste or chopped herbs. When melon is in season, prosciutto wrapped around melon balls is a filling delicacy. Or you might have two or three cheeses with assorted crackers, or well-seasoned steak tartare on rye bread.

This is a good time for hot appetizers because, having no help, you have to make one or two trips to the stove to check on the dinner anyway. Sausages, or cheese pastries, tiny meat balls in a piquant sauce, or the old standby, bacon wrapped around olives, water chestnuts, or chicken livers, make delicious living-room courses as long as you have enough.

Another way to make a maidless dinner less strenuous is to simplify after-dinner details. To recap: on going in to dinner you took cocktail things and ashtrays to the kitchen. Since you won't have had time to plump pillows, forget it. But you might have a pile of clean ashtrays somewhere in the living room, and after dinner put them around in place of the ones you took out.

Prearranged coffee service is a help too. Have cups, saucers, spoons, sugar (and an artificial sweetener, perhaps) on a tray in the living room or hall. After dinner you merely bring in the filled coffeepot. If men and women separate for coffee, fill women's cups first and then take the tray (now lighter by half) to the men. Or have another tray and a separate pot ready for them.

THE SEATED DINNER FOR
TWELVE TO EIGHTEEN

Let's expand the small seated dinner to include twelve to eighteen people. The basic pattern has these variations:

You will need two people to help. The cooking is done as before, by you, with first course and dessert ready in advance.

You might divide the work this way. One helper opens the door and passes appetizers. The other watches the food in the kitchen, and at intervals brings in hot appetizers, if any. You stand in for these jobs when needed.

The host makes the first cocktails. If you have hired a butler, he can make the cocktails or serve refills when the party is complete. An experienced waitress, too, might refill on-the-rocks drinks, but the men in the party will probably not trust her with martinis or other cocktails.

The table is set exactly as before.

With two people to help, you might serve dessert in etiquette-approved style—that is, dessert fork and spoon are brought in with the dessert plates when the main course has been cleared.

Serving the Dinner

The first course is put on the table before guests are seated. How you serve the main course depends on what it is. If it's something to be carved, you might serve it and accompanying vegetables from the sideboard. If it's a casserole and you are not sure the helpers will bring it in hot or ladle it out attractively, have it brought to the sideboard to be served by you and passed by them.

A main course easy to transfer to platters in the kitchen, such as quartered chicken, whole birds, mutton chops, or veal birds, might be served in the conventional way: by having two services each of meat and vegetables. If you eat at one big table, one helper serves half the group, starting with the woman at the host's right and going around to the left. The other helper serves the other half simultaneously. With two smaller dinner tables, each helper serves one.

Double service has many advantages; food stays hot, each person gets the complete course faster, and for more than twelve guests, your regular serving platters and bowls will probably not hold enough for everyone. Double-service bowls and platters need not match; just use whatever extras you have. (Big serving equipment such as you might use for buffet suppers is too bulky and heavy to be passed around easily.)

Decide ahead whether to have rolls and sauces passed by helpers or from guest to guest around the table.

Wine is probably better served from decanters on the table, just as at the smaller dinner. For twelve people at one table two decanters are enough. For a bigger group at one table, have three or four decanters spaced evenly around; at two tables, have two decanters on each. For any number of guests, have extra bottles of wine open and waiting.

Since you will have to double the recipes for most desserts, consider two dessert services as well—two puddings, shortcakes, or pies. Ice cream, or a mixed fruit dish, accompanied by cake or cookies, could be passed in a big bowl by one maid, the other following with the cake platter. Or two bowls could be passed simultaneously, then two cake plates.

After Dinner

A maid brings in the coffee tray. You pour, she passes. If you serve liqueurs, a maid might pass a tray with the bottles and glasses, or you or the host could pour and she could pass.

In other days, a tray of ice water and soda was offered during the evening. It seems unnecessary when there are coffee and liqueurs to clear and tall drinks in the offing. Anyone who wants plain water can have it when tall drinks are offered.

The maids clear away coffee and liqueurs, bring clean ashtrays, and refill the ice bucket. One of them might also help serve long drinks. But since one virtue in having this much help is that it relieves you of K.P., perhaps it is better to let the maids get to it at this point. Certainly by eleven or so you should expect no more service in the living room.

Would a hired cook help at this dinner? Yes and no. A dinner for twelve is hardly more work for you than a dinner for ten. Eighteen is something else again, since you will have to wield huge pots and pans, spend extra time paring vegetables and duplicating recipes. If you can do most of the cooking well ahead, and if helpers come early enough to set the table, a cook is not really needed.

The decision also rests on the kind of cook available. Many who hire out can cook only plain food, their real virtue being that they are in the kitchen watching it, as you cannot be after the party begins. In some communities the free-lance cook does so many parties that there is risk of monotony in the menus. Unless she has a chef's versatility, we would vote for not hiring a cook. You, if at all interested in cooking, are probably better. Your services are free, too, and extra dollars might be better spent for serving and cleaning help. Of course, this doesn't apply if you are like one hostess we know who says that cooking well enough for parties is, and always will be, a "mixtery" to her.

A WORD ABOUT LUNCH PARTIES

Since they differ so slightly from dinners, we have not devoted a special chapter to them. From guest list to demitasse, they are arranged in exactly the same way, with only two differences in table setting: candles do not appear on a lunch table, and brightly colored mats or cloths are appropriate. Food differs little, though for an all-girl lunch you might have lighter food than when men will be present. In Chapter 17 there are dinner first courses that make good main courses for lunch. In the chapter that follows this one, read "buffet lunch" for "buffet supper" when planning a daytime party.

CHAPTER 5

Buffet Suppers Two Ways

The buffet supper has come a long way since it started as a sort of indoor picnic on cook's night out, when food was left on hot plates in the dining room and people ate when they felt like it. Now, guests are invited for a definite hour, and everyone eats at the same time. The menu is often more elaborate than at a dinner, and people often wear evening dress.

The buffet supper is popular because it is an easy way to entertain a maximum of friends with a minimum of space and help. There are two ways of putting one on: the traditional buffet supper, a perpetual motion party where guests serve themselves and eat all over the house; and the "seated" buffet supper, at which guests serve themselves to one course, at least, but eat at set tables.

THE PERPETUAL MOTION PARTY

Let us say twenty are coming and let us have a "staff" of one to help set out dinner, clear plates, and clean up. (You can do this party singlehanded of course, by reserving time the next day for dishwashing and straightening up.)

The Food

Two courses are ample: one or two filling hot dishes, with salad and a cheese tray, perhaps, plus dessert. Have lots of everything.

Since people will be eating on laps or at folding one-to-a-person tables, have food that can be eaten with a fork alone. For some unfathomable reason, cold turkey and ham, which are difficult to cut without a knife, are universally favorite buffet supper dishes. Skip them in favor of casseroles and stews, hashes and goulashes. Let no one downgrade these dishes because they have the reputation of being easy and economical. They are often neither. Many gourmets think the best food in the world is cooked in the standard French *cocotte*, which is just a casserole with a more romantic name. Hundreds of casserole dishes can be gourmet food, not just cooking, if you know your wines and herbs. (See Chapter 17 for a few of our favorites.)

Setting the Buffet Table

The dining table is the natural place to lay out supper. Organize it so that first things come first. Nearest to where guests will approach the table put basic equipment: dinner plates, silver, and napkins. You may have room for a row of silver, then a row of napkins; if not, wrap the forks in the napkins. Guests can then hold plate, fork, and napkin in one hand, leaving the other free for helping themselves to food and for carrying their drinks.

Next come the hot dishes, placed in proper sequence: the main dish followed by the vegetable and hot rolls. If you are having a dish that goes *over* rice or noodles, put that second—no one can get rice *under* a curry. After the rolls, put the condiments, if any, then the salad, cheese and crackers, and lastly, glasses for beer or wine, or cups for coffee, with the appropriate drink alongside. If you are having beer or wine *and* coffee, you might have everything out except the coffeepot, which can be brought in with the dessert.

Equipment for keeping food hot is invaluable, and more ingenious inventions appear on the market every year. But you don't need electrical gadgets. Wires connecting hot trays are something of a hazard anyway when supper is laid in the center of the room. The metal stands of many sizes that have "church" candles underneath are inexpensive and satisfactory, as long as the food was piping hot when it left the stove. Dutch ovens with tight-fitting covers hold heat a long time, too.

Use the biggest serving spoons and forks you have so that guests do not have to dip in several times to get enough. A salad bowl the size of a punch bowl is none too big. Not because you necessarily fill it full, but because guests will find it simpler to help themselves from something sturdy and deep.

Serving the Supper

When all the food has been set out, supper is announced. The maid gathers cocktail glasses. You go to the dining table to direct traffic and help the guests' self-service. Since the hot dish can probably be handled with a spoon alone, a good place for you to help is with the salad and cheese, or with wine or beer. Perhaps you will have filled all the glasses ahead of time. If so, you might hand them out as guests go to sit down. When you have a maid, another way of serving drinks is to have her go around with a tray of full glasses after people are seated. If there is a shortage of side tables, guests will have to put their drinks on the floor. Stemmed glasses are easier to reach than tumblers.

After everyone is served, replace covers on the hot dishes. Have a napkin near each so that people returning for seconds can remove hot covers painlessly.

When the main course is finished guests take their plates back to the table or sideboard and pick up dessert, which has been set in the place left vacant by dinner plates and napkins. This position for dessert is best; it will be nearest the coffee and it allows you to leave the main course and salad out for those who may be slow about taking second helpings.

Another way to clear the main course is to have the maid load plates on a tray as they are put down, and carry out as many as she can *without stacking them*. This keeps the room looking neat and prevents guests from interrupting their talk until they get up for dessert.

Men guests at a buffet supper often carry out women's empty plates along with their own, and return with dessert. But no woman should expect this of them; a buffet supper is a do-it-yourself thing.

When dessert is ready everyone returns to the buffet table. Or kindhearted men bring dessert to the women. (With dessert *and* coffee, they will have to make two trips.) Or guests can get their own dessert and the maid can bring in filled coffee cups on a tray, several at a time. No matter how dessert is served, be sure that it is easy to eat with a fork or spoon. Pies, cakes, pastries, and puddings are good choices. To protect your rug, when you have fruit, do not add all the juice. With ice cream, have a thick sauce, not a runny one.

As each guest finishes, dessert plates are cleared by you, the maid, or the guests themselves. It is nice to keep refilling coffee cups for a while, but they too should be removed after half an hour or so.

A run-down on serving such a buffet supper without a maid would be pointless. You merely do everything she would do, with a few assists from the company. When supper is on the table you might ask each guest to bring his cocktail glass with him and put it on the sideboard. Knowing there is no help, most guests will be happy to help, putting used plates and cups wherever you say, including the kitchen sink. *You* will have to empty ashtrays and perhaps make a final roundup in the living room of coffee cups and wineglasses. But, as we said, it's a perpetual motion party.

THE "SEATED" BUFFET SUPPER

Perhaps this brings together the best of both party worlds: the informal atmosphere of a buffet supper and the organized setup of a dinner party, an ideal way to give a "black-tie" dinner for a lot of people in small surroundings. Guests can eat comfortably. The hostess can control the seating. But she does not have to have a complicated meal or experienced help, and she is not forced to live up to the great expectations guests may have on receiving invitations to a big dinner party. Yet the seated buffet supper could be the prelude to a ball. It could also be a day-dress party or, if served outdoors, guests could come from their tennis or golf games.

Setting Up for a Seated Buffet Supper

Let's call this a party for eighteen. You need a sideboard, a table or tables, and a chair for each guest. If you have no regular sideboard, bring in a table from somewhere else, or push two card tables together and cover them with a cloth. You won't need as much serving room as you did for the perpetual motion party because the small tables will already be laid with silver, napkins, and glasses.

We say tables, plural, on the supposition that few people have a table or a room big enough to seat eighteen people together. If you do, fine. If not, you have to do a little mathematics. How many does your regular table seat? Six? Ten? You can't put eight there, satisfactorily, because that would leave you five and five at the small tables, or six and four. With an equal number of men and women at the party, tables of five are out. Tables of six and four each are all right. It's just that if the tables can be the same size there is less suggestion that one is better than another.

If you find that having one table for only four people works best for space reasons, this is where you should sit. There is honor in being seated with the hostess, even if she is out in left field.

The mathematics will probably work out best with a "main" table of ten and two tables of four, or with three tables of six each. If you use your dining-room table to serve from, three tables of six is the most natural arrangement. All the tables do not have to be in the dining room or dining area. Just avoid having one table so far away that those who sit at it feel cast loose from the rest of the party.

Use card tables for each group of four people, or hire round tables that seat six. Many department stores have folding round tops that are grooved to fit on standard-size card tables. Some hostesses who often give seated buffets have solid ones made of plywood.

No one we know has eighteen dining chairs. Perhaps you can pad out with straight chairs borrowed from the hall, living room, or your next-door neighbor. Failing that, you will have to rent extras from a caterer. Don't give a thought to chairs not matching. Agreed, a unified look is desirable, but you can achieve it by keeping your regular chairs at your regular table and placing extra chairs together according to type.

In setting the tables, keep trying for a look of unity. You may have to use non-matching silver, plates, and glasses, but identical tablecloths will give you the look you're after—a cabaret effect, not only unified but gay.

Since this is an informal party, there is no rule about tablecloths. One hostess we know uses heavy red cotton at her seated suppers. Another uses upholstery material: blue tone-on-tone cotton damask. Or you might make a point of the cabaret look and buy cheap checkered cloths in red or blue with white.

The sheet department of your local store may offer inspiration. Flowered or striped percale, hemmed or cut with pinking shears to fit each table, might turn your dining room into a bower. One hostess we know basted pink sheets so that they touched the floor around each table. Yellow, blue, or green ones could be equally pretty.

Speaking of sheets, do you have any old linen ones yellowing in a trunk? Better to launder and cut them up for a party than save them indefinitely for a very important house guest. Other materials may come to light. One hostess discovered yards of unused curtain gauze. She cut colored felt to fit the tables and overlaid it with the gauze sewn into floor-sweeping circles, which gave her rather functional dining room a diaphanous, cloud-nine atmosphere.

A few more suggestions? Pale denims, perhaps floor-touching with white fringes, are charming. Chintz, washable velveteen—anything goes, depending on the season, as long as you stick to an all-of-a-piece look and don't strain your color sense by trying to be too original or by introducing colors that jar with the rest of the room.

Set all the tables as usual with the necessary number of forks, knives, salts and peppers, cigarettes and ashtrays. Two candles on the small tables and four on the big one contribute to the festivities.

Serving the Seated Buffet Supper

This is a compromise. Guests can do all the work, or they can help themselves to the main course only. It depends on how much help you have. Suppose this is your big event of the year and you are going afterward to a dance. You might then decide to have two maids and a three-course meal. Having pity for the women in full skirts, you would not want them to get up and down for each course. The first course would be on the table when guests came to the dining room. The maids would clear it while guests got up to get the main course. Maids would serve wine, pass rolls, and offer second helpings. They would clear again, and pass dessert in the conventional way, laying dessert plates with appropriate silver and passing platters of dessert.

The differences between this form of service and the seated dinner party described earlier are only three: you have to serve only yourself, not fill guests' plates, which gives you more time to be with your guests. Another advantage is that, with one course self-served, the maids have time to pass rolls, sauces, and so on. And tables will be less cluttered without sauce bowls, breadbaskets, and wine decanters.

A *seated supper with no help* can work just as well. Bring out the food, as usual, and let guests serve and clear on their own. You would have wine or beer on each table and would probably cut the courses to two. Perhaps the men would serve dessert to the women, to cut down on traffic. Or you could have individual bowls of dessert for each table, and ask one person at each to bring the dessert plates while you bring the dessert.

We picked twenty and eighteen as the number of guests for these buffet suppers arbitrarily. Of course there is no limit to the number of people you might invite, as long as you have enough equipment and the guests have enough room and are not called upon to work more than absolutely necessary. How much work is too much? It is the amount of work you would have to do at someone else's party that would prevent you from being a relaxed, entertaining, and self-forgetful guest.

Check List for Buffet Suppers

Cocktail equipment:
    Glasses
    Ice
    Liquor
    Cocktail shaker or pitcher
    Soda, ginger ale, tonic, water
    Bottle opener

Lemons, limes, olives, etc.
Napkins, coasters
Appetizers

Supper equipment:
Plates for all courses
Napkins
Tablecloth or cloths, mats or runners
Eating and serving silver
Trivets, hot plates, or candle warmers
Salts and peppers and other condiments
Glasses for water, wine, or beer
Ashtrays
Coffeepot and cups, sugar bowl and cream pitcher
Extra tables and chairs for the seated buffet

Don't forget:
Candles
Cigarettes
Matches
Extra ashtrays
Ice for after-supper drinks

Consider having:
Flowers or other table decoration

CHAPTER 6

A Do-It-Yourself Dance

No party is more likely to have spirit than a dance. It always seems special, and people start building up a party mood from the moment they get invitations. They arrive at the dance already elated and go on from there. The music and the exercise make people feel good—pleased with themselves, young and tireless.

Any reader who has the desire (and the bank balance) to give a dance at a country club or hotel might skip this chapter; the banquet department will take over. What we picture here is a small dance that any hostess, married or unmarried, who has three or more rooms might give at home, with the help, perhaps, of one maid. If you love the idea of giving a dance but have ruled it out because of expense, try this.

How Many People to Invite?

The number is controlled by the size of your house or apartment. Considering how crowded night club dance floors get, and how few people object, you can safely ask more people to a dance than to any other party. Say your usual limit for a buffet supper is eighteen; ask thirty-six. Or if a dozen is tops, ask twenty-four. It is not necessary for everyone to have a place to sit every minute. And if you have a summer dance in the country many couples will go outside from time to time. In cold weather, town or country, they can spread all over the house.

Which Room Is Best for Dancing?

Usually the dining room or dining area is best, because it is simplest to clear. A sun porch or playroom would do, as long as it is on the same floor as the living room. It breaks the mood of the party when people must go to a different floor to dance.

The front hall could also be the dance room. It is usually easy to strip and, if used for dancing, leaves the living room for sitting and talking, and the dining room for refreshments. Since every home is different, once again we have to invent a blueprint. Let's say you have a good-sized living room, a small dining room, and a small front hall. Our plan would be: dining room for dancing, hall for refreshments, and living room left as is.

Invitations

Once you have decided on your blueprint and how many people you can fit in, begin the list. Where the list for a small dinner might have one nucleus—close friends, some of whom know each other—this party might have people from other groups who, though they may not know your closest friends, know each other. Don't ask people who are complete strangers to everyone else. They are sure to have a drab time. It is also unwise, if you want a well-paced party, to ask older people, unless they happen to be the town's most enthusiastic dancers.

Let's say you want thirty-six to come. Invite ten more. Even if all ten came you could handle it, but they probably won't. What is more likely to happen is that, from the original group of acceptances, some people will drop out at the last minute and you won't have the party you wanted. Dances at home should *not* be as jammed as night clubs, but they should not look spotty either. As you do for other parties, make a list of alternates to ask when the first regrets come in.

The simplest, clearest invitation is one on your visiting card. Either of these wordings is correct:

Small dance
Saturday, Dec. 27th
10 o'clock

Mr. and Mrs. James Barton Read

R.s.v.p.   57 Windsor Street

Or:

Saturday, Dec 27th
10 o'clock

Miss Sarah Pitt Read

                                    R.s.v.p.
Dancing   57 Windsor Street

If you do not have "Mr. and Mrs." cards, write a note or buy a colorful invitation from the stationery store, the kind that says, "Date . . . Time . . . Place . . ." with spaces to fill in. At the top of this invitation write "Small dance," or at the bottom write

"Dancing." Sign it "Jim and Louise Read," or "Sally Stewart," if you are unmarried, not your formal title. You could also use the stiff white partially engraved card. The invitation would then read:

Mr. and Mrs. James Barton Read

request the pleasure of your company

at a small dance

on Saturday, January tenth

at ten   o'clock

R.s.v.p.   57 Windsor Street

Since this invitation is the most formal that you could correctly send, unless you had invitations engraved (which you wouldn't for this party), it is our last choice. You are not giving a coming-out party, and the gay evening you have in mind loses something at the start if the invitation looks too formal.

Incidentally, unless it is a ball, every dance is called a "small dance" on the invitation, even if three hundred are invited. The hour to start is up to you, but ten o'clock, the standard, gives people time for a leisurely dinner before they come.

You could telephone invitations. But just as the engraved card seems too formal, a telephone call seems too casual for this party.

The invitations should be mailed about three weeks before the date. Check off acceptances and regrets as soon as they come in, and if you have several regrets at the start, get right at the invitations to alternates.

Since many men are not crazy about dancing, and since some will leave the floor as soon as the music changes from a fox trot, it won't hurt to ask extra bachelors. They will keep the women on their feet and make it a better party.

Dinners before the Dance

Sometimes when word gets around that you are giving a dance one or two friends will offer to give dinners beforehand. This really makes an evening for everyone involved. The first one who calls gets first chance at your list. You read it to her and she takes down the names of those she wants to invite. It could be two couples or ten. Later, if another offer of a dinner comes from someone else, name only those who have not been chosen by the first hostess. You do not want two friends competing over the most popular people. One friend may offer to give dinner to everyone not already spoken for. What a friend you have in her! If this offer doesn't come, no matter. What does matter is that one lone couple should not arrive at the dance and discover that everyone else has been to a dinner. You *should* try to get them invited somewhere.

No doubt the first woman who decides to give a dinner will invite you. You may long to go, but think about how it will affect your pre-party mechanics. Perhaps the question will be resolved later on when we take a close look at the time schedule and arrangements.

Arrangements for the Dance

These fall into three categories: music, refreshments, and decorations.

Music

The music can be the most or the least expensive item in the budget, depending upon whether you hire a band or use your record player.

One instrument—piano or accordion—may be enough for dancing, depending on the player's virtuosity. A three-piece band is ideal. Of the three pieces, one should be drums or a string bass, because good dance music demands a distinct beat, usually not possible with melodic instruments alone. You have to have room enough for a band, and then there's the expense. A single musician or a good high school combo may sign up for relatively little, or perhaps you'll find pros who will come for union scale wages, but don't engage "cheap" second-raters. Recorded music played by experts is better.

If you decide on the record player, you will need several long-playing fox trot records, a record with Latin American numbers, and possibly a waltz record, if many waltz lovers are coming. You might also have a record with variety dance music, or music for some dance that's the fad at the moment. If you do not have good dance records on hand, let the man in the music shop advise you, and then listen to each one all the way through before buying. There are dozens of records to choose from, but you are looking especially for perpetual beat, not records with a few rhythm numbers interspersed with slow ballads and blues songs. The pace of the music makes the pace of the party.

After you have picked your custom-made dance orchestra, take it home and have a rehearsal in the room you've chosen for dancing. Decide about volume, the best order for the records, and the best place to put the record player, or amplifiers, if you have them.

Refreshments

At a do-it-yourself dance, the simpler the refreshments the better, even with a helper, because his or her time will be taken up empty-ing ashtrays, removing empty glasses, and keeping food and drink in supply. The guests will serve themselves—another reason for simplicity.

We picked the entrance hall as the place for refreshments. Set up a table there and cover it with a protective pad and a nice cloth. What goes on the table? First, the makings of drinks. Don't go in for too much variety. Have whisky and soda, gin and tonic, plus a few soft drinks or beer. It is best not to serve punch. Some people don't like it, and others will be satisfied with routine after-dinner drinks.

For thirty-six guests here is what you will need:

Equipment

Fifty tall glasses to allow for guests who inevitably put down one glass, forget it, and come back for a new one

A big ice bucket

A big water pitcher

Two or three bottle openers—so that guests do not have to wait to use a single one

Ingredients

4 fifths of scotch

4 fifths of bourbon

3 fifths of gin

2 fifths of vodka

24 pints of soda water

18 pints of tonic

18 pints of ginger ale

18 cans of beer

12 pints of cola

300–350 ice cubes

In summer you might increase the amount of gin and tonic.

For a special occasion such as this, champagne or some other sparkling wine may appeal to you. But it will make things a bit more complicated. Champagne cannot be opened in advance, and since it must be served chilled, you will have to put it in a big ice-filled washtub or metal-lined picnic hamper. You will also need special glasses, as champagne is not very satisfying drunk from a tumbler. And you'll have to plan for fresh bottles to be opened as needed.

However, champagne is appropriate for a dance and lends an extra note of gaiety. If you decide to have it, add these to your check list: Six or eight bottles of champagne—or half that amount of magnums. A bucket to bury the bottles in, filled with two hundred cubes of ice. A couple of napkins to wrap around the damp bottles while pouring. Eighteen glasses should be enough; probably less than half the group will take champagne when hard liquor is also being offered. Allow space to set out long-stemmed glasses; since you are going to the trouble of champagne it is nice to serve it in the traditional way. A good department store usually has champagne glasses for a dollar or so apiece. You may find even cheaper ones at the five-and-ten.

When it comes to the food, you might have either substantial cocktail party things or a one-dish supper brought out after midnight. It depends on space and which seems easiest. Since the dining room is now the ballroom, that's out for food. If the hall is big enough you might have a second table there for food, or set up one in the living room. Or simply have trays of sandwiches, plus bowls of popcorn and nuts on the living-room tables.

Should you decide on a hot supper dish, there are the extra details of plates, flat silver, and a hot tray. But if you have the space the supper itself need not be very complicated. Have chicken à la king or sea food newburg, with toast or rolls. Or a big casserole of paella, jambalaya, or Swedish meat balls in a spicy sauce, or some sort of pasta dish—ravioli or lasagne is easier to eat than spaghetti. You could have cold turkey or ham as well, but besides being difficult to eat with a fork alone, either one seems too much of a production when guests will have eaten dinner. Whether you decide on cocktail party food or supper food, all that's needed is something tempting to the appetite, which can be served easily at about midnight. Have a good supply of napkins, and reserve space somewhere for a big pot of coffee and two dozen cups that can be brought out late in the evening. A pitcher of milk might be welcome, too.

Decorations

A dance is the perfect party for decorations, and they can be fun to do if you allow time. Of course, you don't need any at all, beyond a few flowers in the living room. But a room that has been stripped for dancing may look a little unexciting without some attention.

Again, economy and the relatively small number of people coming suggest simplicity. Not for you huge flower sprays and banks of blossoms from the florist, or intricate special lighting. As you would for a children's party, go to the five-and-ten or the local party shop and make as small an investment as possible, with an eye to color.

Balloons are an obvious choice. You might buy fifty or so and cover the whole ceiling with them. Get plain round ones—no sausage or animal shapes. Since this is *not* a children's party, don't have misshapen cats and bunnies staring down at your guests. Pick colors that match your curtains or complement the color of the walls. Or take the opposite tack; buy as many assorted colors as you can, for a jelly-bean color scheme. Get small elastic bands to seal the ends, or just tie a single knot in the end of each balloon—a bit rough on the fingers, but just as airtight. Balloons will stay on the ceiling if rubbed on some woolen fabric—your skirt or sweater—to create electricity. Then gently toss them to the ceiling. They stick! This works better than anchoring them with tape, because they always move slightly with the air and can come loose. Also, tape may leave marks.

Other pretty balloon possibilities: Tie them in clusters across the tops and down the sides of the curtains, or around lighting fixtures (not touching bare bulbs—they may pop with the heat). One hostess got outsize balloons at a party shop, had them filled with helium, then taped ribbons over each from which were tied straw baskets filled with flowers. The balloons were hung by wire from the ceiling and swayed prettily above the dancing.

If your room has a central lighting fixture, crepe paper ribbons can be run from it out to the walls. Allow plenty of paper ribbon to loop down between the center and sides of the room and you get the look of a circus tent. At one do-it-yourself Christmas party the hostess decorated the dance room at no expense whatsoever; she taped a frieze of Christmas cards to the ceiling molding and hung Christmas baubles from lighting fixtures.

If your dance is held near any holiday, decorating is much easier since the stores are full of things on the holiday theme. At other times your imagination will be stretched further. See what can be done with paper flowers, party hats. Orientals are wizards with paper decorations, and you may find something original and pretty at a Japanese store, if there's one near you. One hostess, whose dining room is white with vivid green and blue draperies, hung the ceiling with fish-shaped Japanese kites painted blue and green. This had a further point as it was a birthday party for her husband, whose zodiac sign was Aquarius.

If you live in the country try simple decoration from the garden: sprays of greens, autumn leaves, or flowering shrubs, depending on the season. They can be simply attached to lighting fixtures or curtains, or massed on the window sills.

Should your dance be a costume party, the room needs less work, as guests themselves are the decoration. Costume parties are fun, every so often, but if there are many men in your circle who disagree, a *bal de tête*, to which everyone is asked to wear a hat or headdress on some theme, is a good substitute.

Time Schedule for the Dance

Now back to practical matters. The invitations are out, you have (or have not) hired a helper. You have settled on the music, decided what food and liquor will be served, and where. You have ordered it all. You have dreamed up decorations and bought what you need. Here is a suggested schedule for the final pre-party mechanics:

On the morning of the day before the party set the scene. Clear the dining room. It looks nicer to remove the rug entirely, but if you can't face that effort, roll it up. If you have a leggy sideboard, leave it in the room and slide the rolled-up rug between the legs to prevent dancers from running into it. Move as many chairs as possible into another room, to make more places to sit, and put others in the garage or basement. Nice as it is to leave a few chairs against the walls, ballroom-fashion, you probably can't afford the space.

After the rug is up there will be sweeping to do, and you may decide also to polish the floor. It is not necessary from the dancers' standpoint for it to have a high polish since they are not as particular as Fred Astaire might be. However, you may want to give it a quick once-over for looks and its own protection.

When furniture has been moved, do the decorating. Hanging things from the walls and ceiling takes time and energy that are best spent a day ahead. Not feeling pressed, you will do a better job. You can blow up balloons, too, and put them in laundry bags or cartons, ready to be "floated" up to the ceiling on the afternoon of the party. Balloons that will be tied in place can be put up a day ahead.

Another day-before chore: set up the hall with the serving table or tables, glasses, plates, and napkins. Get out liquor, soft drinks, and bar equipment. Arrange any greens or flowers. Start on the food. Most casseroles taste better reheated after a night in the refrigerator, and most cocktail party food can be prepared ahead too.

An alternate schedule is to reserve the morning of the party for doing the food. Since guests won't arrive until ten or after, there is not the same urgency as for a seven o'clock dinner. At any rate, on the morning of the dance, check your list. You may want to make calls to the iceman, the maid, or the musician, to make sure each remembers that he is expected. Clear a closet for coats or tidy things up in the room in which coats will be laid.

With this much out of the way by the afternoon, you have plenty of time to rest, wash your hair, or attend to a few non-party chores. What's left to do? Put out cigarettes and matches, and piles of extra ashtrays. Air the room. Check the bathrooms for necessaries.

Now, if you have decided not to accept an invitation for dinner, the schedule goes like this: At seven or so, have a simple supper. And a cup of good strong coffee. Plan to be dressed by nine. In the final hour before the party, light the house. If you've hired a maid, make sure she knows what her duties will be. Open liquor, and the first bottles of soda and tonic. Get out any food you plan to have on hand for the entire evening. If you are planning a casserole supper, light the oven, turn it to a low temperature, and put the casserole in. Or tell the maid what time she should do this. Load the record player.

If you have been persuaded to go out for dinner, the schedule will be tighter, and you will have to arrange for someone to be home while you are out. If you have children the sitter can take messages, but otherwise a maid should be there. She can keep busy getting out the cigarettes, filling the ice bucket, lighting the house. Just be sure before you leave to tell her what you want done.

Then dress, go to dinner, and enjoy yourself—until nine-thirty. At that moment, even if it is the middle of dinner, make tracks for home to be sure of being there before anyone else. Arriving at nine forty-five gives you time to make a final check on things, refresh your make-up, get out food platters, and open bottles.

At ten o'clock turn on the record player. It doesn't matter if no one's there to hear it; you want it going when the first guests arrive.

If a musician has been hired, he need not play until guests come, but should strike up as soon as the doorbell rings—an example of perfectly timed party sound effects.

During the Party

At the beginning you, as hostess, do just as you would at any other party: introduce people and see that they have company and refreshments. It is probably better not to dance until almost everyone has arrived; you will have to stop to greet people, for new arrivals mustn't comb the party for the hostess. Later, dance as often as you please. A hostess may politely refuse invitations to dance if she is needed elsewhere, and would be wrong to dance continuously, because she couldn't help missing opportunities to look out for guests. As at all other parties, hosts should watch for those who may be stuck with one partner—either dancing or in conversation—and they should try to mix groups and see that a man and wife are not left to entertain each other.

The host's part in a dance is important. Any woman, including the hostess, is naturally diffident about trying to get men to dance. So the host should be his own floor committee of one, cutting in on a couple who have danced together a long time, and mixing seated groups by asking one of the women to dance, and returning her to a different group when they stop. An unmarried hostess should appoint a man "host" of her party to do these things.

How does the host keep from getting stuck himself? Very simple. He is the host, and no woman will expect him to devote himself to her. After she has taken a few turns of the room with him she will probably say, "I'm dying of thirst. I'd love to get a drink and sit for a while." If she does not give him this easy out he simply makes an excuse—"Must check the ice supply" or something—and takes her to a seat, preferably where there are more men than women.

This brings up a point about other men's manners. When a group sits out and there are more women than men, it is rude for all the men to take partners and go to the dance floor. And it is worse if a man does this when he is alone with two women, since the one he does not invite to dance is left high and dry. Many women have the aplomb to cope with this: there is always the dressing-room ploy, or they look for their husbands or dates, or go over to another group. But this doesn't make the man in question any less rude.

When a man finds himself alone with two women and sees no hope of being joined by more men, he can take polite steps. He might excuse himself to get fresh drinks and, when he is at the bar, ask another man to join him. They return to the women as soon as possible. Or he can simply suggest that they all go to the bar or join another group. This ploy seems obvious. It is, but not impolite, since the man has done nothing to show that he dislikes the women's company. Rather, he wants to find better entertainment for them. The women, feeling stuck themselves, will surely go along.

The main thing for both men and women guests is to be co-operative. Men should try to dance with several women. They should not vanish to the sun porch or den for talk, unless women are with them. They should look for chances to keep the party well mixed. Women should do this, too, and should make a point of helping the hostess with any person who does not appear to be having a good time.

It is not necessary for all the men to dance with the hostess. If the evening is suddenly over, and a man has not done his duty dance, he just tells the hostess how disappointed he is. By the same token, the host need not dance with every woman. He also has good intentions, but he may miss out on a few. To each of these, as she leaves, he might mention his bad luck. That's good enough. Some of the gaiety may leave a party if people feel tightly bound to dancing-school etiquette.

Ending the Dance

If you have an orchestra this is easy. You have engaged it from ten to . . . one-thirty? Two? Two-thirty? When the hour comes, they play "Good Night, Ladies," to signal that the party is about over. They usually play one quick encore, then a final few bars of "Good Night, Ladies," and that's it. At subscription dances where people pay their own way, a hat is sometimes passed by late-stayers to keep the band for another hour or half hour. This should not happen at a private party. The hosts have made their own plans and guests should not change them. After "Good Night, Ladies," the dance is over. Period. Guests stay to finish their drinks or suppers, but then they should go.

When the dance music is recorded, ending the party gracefully may be more difficult. Why not just load up the machine and continue? There is no reason why not, for one or two records, if that seems to be the will of the majority. Some hostesses, definitely against an all-night party, make the point clear on the invitation by saying "from 10 to 2." But if you haven't done this, and a few stragglers stay on and on, just flick off the record player when the time seems right, and offer everyone a nightcap—a hospitable way to indicate that the end of the party is near.

While dinners should wind up around midnight, or well before that on weekdays, a dance is essentially a late party. It begins late, and the last guest probably won't be out before three in the morning. With this in mind, have your dance on a weekend or holiday evening. The wee hours are no time for you to start moving furniture back in place. It is better just to air out, put away leftovers, and sink into bed. Let the do-it-yourself cleanup take place next day.

CHAPTER *7*

Parties Out of Doors

Everybody loves outdoor parties. Just being in the open helps a party's spirit. People relax quickly and enjoy one another. The food always tastes marvelous.

There are two types of outdoor parties: the lunch or dinner that could just as well be served inside, and the picnic. The first is usually at home, the picnic more often away. Both can, and should, be planned as carefully as any indoor party but it always seems easier.

THE OUTDOOR PARTY AT HOME

This might be a small seated meal or a big buffet lunch or supper. Many hostesses who dislike big cocktail parties feel that an outdoor buffet in summer is not *that* much more trouble and is a more complimentary way to return a winter's worth of obligations. Small outdoor parties you can easily do by yourself. A big one requires at least one person to help with serving and cleaning up.

Invitations and What to Wear

Give the same invitations for the same hour that you would for a indoor lunch or dinner. But let women have some idea of what to wear. Men's clothes vary little for any outdoor party; sport coat, shirt, and tie are always right. But if you were having a barbecue on the lawn, tell women to dress more simply than for dinner on a stone terrace. Flat heels, which can't sink into the grass, and an easy skirt are right for the lawn, especially if some people will have to sit on the grass. No woman can sit there comfortably in a narrow skirt. If you plan to wear long pants or shorts, say so. Most women won't wear them unless specifically told that it is all right. Others might wear them and be embarrassed to find themselves too casually dressed.

Furniture and Fireplace Arrangements

Comfort is a big factor in the success of an outdoor party. When it's at home, have enough chairs and benches, or at least extra pillows, for people to sit on. Since smoke in your eyes is romantic only in song, be sure that the fire isn't located where it will disturb the guests. Before a party in a new location, have a dry run to see if prevailing winds work for or against comfort. By all means experiment before building a permanent outdoor fireplace.

Neatness Made Easy

Spread lots of ashtrays about to prevent a guest having to get up each time he finishes a cigarette—and to prevent a strewn lawn. Deep heavy ones are best for tables; the breeze can't scatter the ashes. You might also put small flower pots, half filled with sand, on the ground. Have a central place for all the drinkables, a table or terrace wall, from which cocktails, wine or beer, and coffee all will be served. Put glasses and cups here. Then have a separate place for serving the food. This is especially helpful at a self-service party; guests see at a glance where things are.

Cleaning Up

Decide on a system for cleaning up, especially if you're giving a big party; in no time the garden can become as littered as Main Street after a parade. Guests will co-operate if you make it easy for them. One hostess suggests a big straw hamper with a lid. After the first course, guests are asked to lay in plates and cutlery, and then it's closed. Beside it she puts a cylindrical umbrella stand for napkins and other debris. She collects glasses on a big tray.

Another hostess reserves a table for debris. Guests are asked to stack plates, cutlery, and glasses on it and to throw napkins into a big wastebasket underneath. Set up this table where guests won't have to stare at it; or, after it's full, cover it with a checkered cloth until the party ends.

Since, no matter what the forecast, skies sometimes open in midparty, have the house in order. At the first drop of rain ask each guest to take his plate and glass inside—you scurry to save the food. No need for full cigarette boxes and flower arrangements indoors, just neatness.

Cooking and Serving

Unless you are having a small party—eight people, say, who will skewer their own shish kebabs and broil them the way they prefer—it is best never to let guests cook. It may seem polite if you are having individual steaks or chops, which some people like rare and others well done, but it slows things down and can disorganize the party. People hang back politely waiting for someone else to have first turn at the fire. Then, when several do begin to cook, they get in one another's way.

If guests will not be seated at tables, don't set groups of chairs too far from each other. A little clutch of chairs under a tree across a garden may look inviting, but those who sit there in effect drop out of the party.

Food Planning

As with all other parties, try to do most of the cooking before guests arrive to save treks to the kitchen after the party begins. As dinnertime nears, slip in to make sure that simmering dishes are hot, heat the rolls, toss the salad. Or, if you have a helper, let her cope. Even without help a well-thought-out menu can mean only one trip to the kitchen per course. One hostess simplifies serving small outdoor parties like this: She has a dozen straw trays set and waiting in the kitchen. At dinnertime she serves the main course, then each guest comes to pick up his tray. All are encouraged to go back for second helpings. Then, while her husband carries in the trays, the hostess brings out dessert and coffee.

The Menu

How many courses for an outdoor dinner? At a small one, particularly if it is served at table, three courses are pleasant and need not be difficult. You might have jars of cold soup in an ice bucket set out beforehand, and soup cups, to be filled at dinnertime, already laid. An easy-to-serve salad course which guests pass around could begin the meal. At a big party a first course is too much trouble; have filling hors d'oeuvre instead.

Decorations

Part of the charm of an outdoor party lies in where it is and how it looks; if the visual appeal is high, the simplest meal can seem epicurean. Decorating an outdoor party can be fun and not very expensive. You already have the yard or garden itself as a backdrop. Take it from there.

Lighting

For an evening party, first think about lighting. Hostesses who give many outdoor parties often have permanent floodlights fixed to the house or trees. There is a year-round plus in this: even in dead of winter a house lighted outside sets a cheerful mood for arriving guests. Lighting should be diffused, not concentrated. Lights secured to tree trunks and beamed upward into the leaves, or placed high in trees, so the leaves act as a filter, are attractive. Should a wall enclose the garden, you might light it from behind to give an indirect glow. And you can always fix permanent lights along the eaves of the house or behind low shrubs.

If you seldom entertain outdoors, lighting need not be permanent and can be simple. One hostess simply twines chains of outdoor Christmas lights with white bulbs in the trees surrounding her patio. As she says, "The wires don't look very pretty in daylight, but by the time everyone arrives the dusk hides them and the effect is magical." It is even simpler to run a length of outdoor wire with a floodlight up a tree trunk. Another hostess borrows sand from the children's sandbox, fills brown paper bags half full, and sticks a candle in each. These "lanterns" border her garden and driveway simply and prettily.

Many people use tall torches stuck in the ground. This can be very dramatic, and in a mosquito-threatened community, torches flaming with liquid bug repellent add comfort as well as eye appeal. Big hurricane lamps can be put on the edges of the party area and on the buffet table, small ones on the small tables. Most ten-cent stores have good-looking hurricane lamps made of wrought iron. Small kerosene lamps, twentieth-century versions of Aladdin's, with a wick coming from a spout, might be put on all tables, on low walls. These are also convenient for lighting steps. For attractive bargain lighting you might buy tiny hanging lanterns from the toy or garden store. One hostess hangs these at random from the lower branches of the trees surrounding the deck where she gives her summer parties. Another, with a single dogwood in her yard, uses them as she would baubles on a Christmas tree.

Water—anything from a bird bath to a swimming pool—suggests wonderful lighting possibilities. Buy floating candles or use life preservers as the base for a lighting arrangement. A girl who was giving a birthday party bought a paper cake "model" from the pastry shop, stuck candles in it, and floated it on a life preserver in her fishpond. Another hostess always fills two big Italian pottery urns with water, has flowers and a few floating candles in the shape of water lilies on the surface.

Table Settings

Have some fun with the table settings. Paper plates and napkins, right for outdoor parties, come in delightful designs and colors. If you do much entertaining out of doors, build a collection of pottery, non-silver cutlery, and mats, cloths, and napkins whose colors complement the rest of the equipment. One hostess, who often has seated dinners for six or eight on a small terrace, began with aquamarine—chairs, cushions, and a wrought-iron table. Her stainless steel flat service goes with anything, and she has collected pottery cups, plates, and soup bowls, some French, some Italian, some Mexican, all harmonizing with aquamarine. From time to time she adds to her supply of mats and napkins, always choosing colors that mix well—yellow, lime, deep blue, bottle green—and can be rotated to suit her mood of the moment.

A Delaware hostess flagged a small area of lawn off her living room with stone and made a "ceiling" above this of redwood slats. They don't keep out rain but do break the sun's rays. She uses a redwood table for serving and has redwood chairs with pillows covered in oranges, yellows, rust, and turquoise. Although in Delaware, there is a definite Southwestern feeling. Flowered Italian pottery didn't seem right, and Mexican or Indian things seemed overdone for Delaware. The hostess found black was the answer, and now has a soup-to-dessert service in that color—some oriental lacquer, some sturdy pottery, black metal candlesticks, black trays and tables—everything black but the glassware and silver.

Colors in nature, the blues of sky and water, the greens of trees and grass, the browns and blacks of tree trunks, and the yellows and oranges of the sun, are sure-fire, but not the only possibilities. Pink awnings and chair seats look lovely against white, gray, green, or black. White bamboo or wrought-iron chairs look well upholstered in lavender denim. Purple can look right in a sandy beach setting, and beiges, grays, and cream colors in the woods. One of the best outdoor color schemes we've seen *seems* out of character: black bamboo chairs with cushions of fake leopard in a stone-paved, ivy-covered courtyard—in Westchester, not Kenya. Here, on a mustard-colored tile table, the hostess sets spanking-white pottery or glass. It's perfect.

Every day new things in plastic, wood, paper, and straw turn up in the stores. Since outdoor party things are not supposed to be conventional, you can improvise to your heart's content. Just pick something that goes with the setting and isn't "cute"—like the gnomes and bobbing storks at roadside stores. If you want to use a washtub as a punch bowl or mattress ticking as a tablecloth, go ahead. And of course it's fine to use indoor things if you're not worried about damage.

For table centerpieces, try what's growing in the garden—fruit or vegetables that can be eaten after the party. One Southern hostess lays round tables, seating six, with circles of green felt covered with smaller circles of white linen. In the center of each she simply puts a bowl of lemons and limes. Her children "drink up" the centerpieces during the week. A Massachusetts hostess always has a big arrangement of whatever vegetables are available: corn, tomatoes, peppers, squash. She says, "And there's nothing like that marvelous dark purple of eggplant to set the whole thing off." You can get the same effect with fruit: pineapple, pears, peaches, melons, apricots, grapes, and so on. Going further with food centerpieces, one Minnesota hostess made a hit when she had a lobster dinner. (These days Maine lobsters can be flown almost anywhere and, miraculously, arrive on time and alive.) She set her long outdoor table with straw mats, hurricane lamps, and ordinary glasses. When the lobsters came off the fire she simply put them on trays down the center. "There were many ohs and ahs," she reports, "and it did look wonderful!" Practical, too, because to eat lobsters, big in themselves, you need lots of room. Additional decorations would only have added clutter.

How about trying one of these on the table? Goldfish in glass bowls. Dried flowers. Dried gourds, polished up with a little salad oil. Candles sunk in tumblers or goblets of colored glass. Or stuck in the leafy ends of pineapples. Typical Japanese lanterns or, for a twist, trainmen's lanterns from the hardware store. Why not? At dusk before one party, a hostess set her children to catching fireflies, which is easy and fun to do. They collected them in colored jars which the mother sealed with gauze. As darkness came on, guests enjoyed watching the flies blinking on and off. Of course, other lights were needed but, as the hostess said, "When anyone speaks of getting the most out of natural resources, I challenge him to top this one."

In her city back yard, where there is less natural setting to start, one hostess gets a handsome effect by bringing out one or two big formal arrangements of cut flowers. Another cheated a bit for her one money-no-object party: buying potted flowers, she "planted" them, pots and all, amidst the ivy ground cover bordering the brick yard. Deliberately fake flowers are also entertaining in back yards.

Anything goes, as long as you make sure that decorations and lighting effects won't go awry or topple in the breeze.

PICNICS

Enjoyable because they break dull routine, picnics almost always take place because of some special event—a ball game, a country fair, the Fourth of July. You decide to spend an evening on the beach, take a hike, or go fishing. Even city dwellers often take a picnic along when they go for a row on the park lake.

What is it about picnics? Open air, certainly. And variety. It appears that any kind of picnic can give the ultimate in pleasure as long as weather and food are good. Asking for descriptions of memorable picnics, we received such replies as these:

"The picnic I most admired took place before a play at a summer theater on the Connecticut shore. The hostess went all out: cocktails, then cold borsch, hot chicken in wine, molded salad, chocolate mousse. Ice-cold chablis, too, and espresso. She brought along glass and china for the liquids, and served the food on blue and white Salem print paper plates. We sat at a permanent picnic table on the edge of the water and the sunset was spectacular. But it was really the 'unsandwichy' meal that made it an enchanted evening."

Another favorite picnic was "at a football game in November. I loathe football and loathed the thought of shivering over cold fried chicken in the stadium parking space with everyone in a rah-rah spirit, except myself. I was pleasantly surprised to be offered a cocktail with a plate of sliced cheeses, followed by steaming ham and pea soup. There was fried chicken, as predicted, but it was wrapped in foil and heated up over a little hibachi set on the lowered tail gate of the car. The hosts *apologized* for not broiling a steak on a grill as others in the parking lot were doing! After the chicken came hot coffee and brownies. We didn't need a plate or a fork for the entire meal, yet it was delicious. Since then, even football games are bearable if the picnic is good."

A third young woman wrote, "My picnic to beat all picnics was in France. Four of us drove out from Paris for a day's sight-seeing. We had planned to go to a café somewhere for lunch, but at midday a picnic suddenly seemed better. We stopped in a little town and bought the ingredients of a French picnic. Fun to do. Everything is sold in a different shop. We split up, one of us buying butter and cheese, another bread, still warm at the bakery. Another bought four cheap glasses and the one utensil we needed: a knife to cut fruit and cheese, and to spread butter. The fourth member of the party found the fruit and a bottle of wine, which he had uncorked in the shop. There never was a simpler, more delicious picnic, nor a more beautiful one. We went into the park of a château, with lawns and woods as far as the eye could see, and ate on the edge of a lake. Swans, willows, birdcalls, a fairy tale. There was a sign, of course, saying 'Picnicking Prohibited' but, since it was in France, when the park keeper bicycled by he just waved at us."

Sometimes picnics become summer routine. A young woman who lives in farm country told us, "We almost always have a picnic Saturday noon. My husband makes a stew and he and the children get out early to pick the vegetables and start cooking. We have a permanent picnic table and benches on a slope overlooking the farm, with a bunkhouse nearby. The stew is cooked there over a kerosene stove, and when it's done one of the children comes to get me. I drive over with milk, coffee, dessert and, if we are having guests, cocktails, ice, and wine as well. Perhaps, also, a fancy cold soup or a salad. Sometimes the meal gets as elaborate as an English picnic, the only thing missing being the butler to serve us. Not 'just a picnic,' this is our party specialty. Our friends never seem to tire of it and neither do we."

People who live near water often have a favorite kind of picnic too—beach picnics with everything from grilled hamburgers for six to clambakes for fifty. Where boat picnics prevail, most people, even those with stoves on board, find it easier to cook at home. One hostess keeps food hot by packing it with heated bricks. Another has vacuum jugs for everything. She aims for simplicity on her boating parties. "Excuse the pun," she said, "but many people here go overboard about equipment. I do it all with a couple of vacuum jugs and some tin cups. Our standard picnic is cocktails, with a couple of jars of nuts or pumpkin seeds. Then clams on the half shell which I buy just before we weigh anchor. I bring along forks but we serve the clams right from the boxes they come in, and throw the shells in the water. We have a corn and lobster chowder or some other filling soup in vacuum bottles. Enameled tin cups for that. Assorted crackers from a cake tin, and finally, my big display, a straw tray filled with fruit, cheeses, and a few communal knives. If we have wine that needs chilling, I decant it into a big bottle with a screw top and plant it in the ice hamper."

Picnic Equipment

If you customarily give clambakes, Texas barbecues, or Western chuck-wagon luncheons, you no doubt know, and have, what you need. But for sporadic picnickers we offer a few suggestions:

First, though attractive, it is not necessary to have elaborate picnic equipment, hampers fitted with plates and silver, or leather-bound bottle bags. That picnic in France, for which one knife and four glasses sufficed, shows that equipment counts for little. There's something amateurish about too perfect equipment, as there is about matching suitcases; *experienced* travelers rarely have them. Luckily, today, all that anyone, including a gourmet, might need for a picnic can be bought at a five-and-ten. Practical indoor equipment—the ice bucket or baby's bottle toter—also serves.

Among special conveniences are wide-mouthed vacuum bottles— wide-mouthed because neither ice cubes nor hot stews go into a bottle with a standard-sized opening. Plastic cups are also nice. No more trouble to pack than paper ones, they make anything from a daiquiri to a demitasse pleasanter to drink. Get good plastic that won't be affected by hot liquids. Metal cutlery, easier to use than paper or plastic, is sold inexpensively at ten-cent or hardware stores.

Always use paper plates; carrying other kinds makes the basket too heavy. Always pack double the amount of paper napkins you think you will need. If you are not picnicking where you can get water, include a box of the individually packaged moist paper towels that people use for traveling. They will refresh face and hands, especially after a picnic at which all the food is eaten with the fingers.

For frying fish or hamburgers, a heavy pan from your own kitchen will do, but you might buy one with an extra-long handle designed for open-fire cooking. Also from your own kitchen comes a long-handled fork or turner, and plastic freezer containers, which are good for toting butter, cottage cheese, or anything you plan to use in the cooking, such as sliced potatoes or onions. Salad is best packed in plastic bags. Keep it cool in the ice bucket, serve it from a light unbreakable bowl.

Two big straw baskets with handles will hold a lot of picnic things. Some come partitioned for carrying bottles and jars. The lightness of the straw is a great asset if you have to walk any distance to the picnic site.

Where there is no permanent picnic table, bring along some sort of "surface" for the spread. An unscratchy blanket or tarpaulin works perfectly well, but a colored or checkered plastic cloth is prettier. In Europe folding tables and chairs are standard *pique-nique* equipment. Driving along, you see other motorists ceremoniously sitting down to a cloth-covered table, as if the roadside were their private dining room. Chairs do seem too much, but a table and a few pillows to sit on can make serving easier and eating more comfortable.

No matter what your picnic menu is, do not forget the following:

Knife
Corkscrew or bottle opener
Salt and pepper
Sugar
Napkins
Implements for cooking and serving
Matches or fluid for lighting charcoal or wood quickly
In buggy country, a can of repellent

This little list includes the most obvious things—the most often forgotten, too. It ruins the hoped-for effect to bring wine stew and forget the ladle, or to cool a dozen bottles of beer in a stream and then go thirsty for want of an opener.

The last word about picnics is also obvious, but worth repeating, perhaps. Fires must be totally extinguished before picnickers leave, and this means *totally*. Embers often stay alive beneath the surface of a fire, so kick away ashes and stamp them out. Finally, good public manners include leaving a picnic site as litter-free as the West Point parade ground.

8

When It's a Family
Affair

It's a week or two before Thanksgiving, Christmas, or Easter and your turn to have the family for lunch on the day. The whole idea sounded wonderful when you decided to do it, but now you are not so sure. Thirteen grownups, nine children, and a baby: an Invasion, not a party! And you think that if it turns out to *be* a party it will be in spite of tedious Uncle George, vague Cousin Lucy, and your mother's poorly disguised criticisms of the children's behavior.

A few ideas can help make the party a success for others and fun for you in spite of Cousin Lucy and the home truths that may fly about like angry wasps.

First, just as for any other party, plan ahead. You have virtually no control over the guest list—family parties usually consist of people who cannot be left out, rather than those you'd like to include. But you may decide to ask one or two people not in the family. No invitation is more gratefully received than that to a single person who might otherwise spend the holiday alone. Having one or two extras will not be that much more trouble and will cushion the party against any sharp points of all-family discussion. Grappling with family matters on holidays isn't very festive.

Timing and Planning the Meal

If children will be there, the hour you set should coincide as nearly as possible with their regular mealtimes. A midday meal could be for one or one-thirty. Or you might invite everyone for four o'clock and plan to eat at five or so. Children, having had a light lunch, would be more or less on schedule, and the grownups might have late breakfast and skip lunch.

Holiday parties today are usually given without outside help. Most part-time helpers have their own holiday plans or their fee can double on holidays, so most hostesses do it alone. This means a self-service meal with most of the cooking done ahead of time, and a lot of washing up afterward.

Fortunately, most of the traditional American holiday food can be prepared the day before. Sweet potatoes, cranberry sauce, corn pudding, pies, and all other baking can be made ready for cooking or cooked and reheated. You might have everything done except the roast well ahead of the guests' arrival, even setting the table the day before.

While it may not be possible for everyone to eat at a table, or at several small ones, it is a good safety measure for each child to sit down somewhere and be served. In a small apartment, seat children on the floor around the coffee table or spread a plastic cloth on the rug and serve them there. A big plate of holiday food is just too much for the young to manage on laps or small folding tables. If you can seat everyone in the same room by using your regular table and one or two small ones, do so. It's more fun if everyone can be together at the feast.

Seating probably won't work out perfectly. There are usually too many women, and young children should be seated beside their mothers for help with the food. The oldest family members get the preferred seats, and we think it is a nice idea—training for the hosts and hostesses of the future—to seat children who are old enough to eat by themselves with older people, not all together at one table. Use place cards if they will be helpful—and if you can find cards decorated with the holiday theme, so much the better. Try to have something on each table suggestive of the holiday.

If you have drinks before dinner, make "cocktails" of ginger ale or sweet cider for the children. If it is to be a long cocktail hour, also have games or puzzles on hand to keep children amused. About three quarters of an hour before mealtime, ask the baby's mother if she would like to feed him, let her warm up his food, and show her where he's to have his nap.

Having no maid at this dinner, you can ask one or two of the younger adults to help. Assign a brother to make cocktails or a sister to pass appetizers while you are in the kitchen. Have trays available for clearing cocktail glasses when dinner is served. Refuse offers of assistance from the older generation. It doesn't look right for your mother or mother-in-law to work because she is willing and knows the house when your contemporaries are around.

Serving

The service of this dinner is a replica of the seated buffet described in Chapter 5. If you have a first course, put it on the table before guests come in, and ask one or two grownups to help clear it. Then bring the main course to the sideboard, and when enough has been carved for the first few people, begin to serve. With the aid of one or two others, everyone else can remain seated. It is definitely a good idea to serve small children. They may spill, and certainly will get in the way if they get up for their own plates. You and your lieutenants clear the main course. Dessert is put on the sideboard and all but the children might serve themselves. Since most people have two or more desserts at a big holiday meal, older guests will probably want to get up and take their choice, or a little of each.

If dinner has been eaten in a dining room, close the doors and forget the debris until everyone has gone. Serve coffee in the living room. When dinner is served in a dining area, clear plates and glasses, for looks, but save washing up for later.

After Dinner

Since children are often tired by the long meal and the excitement of being at a grown-up party, you might offer beds for naps after dinner. Or, if part of the children's holiday treat is to be let off from naps, have something planned for them to do while the grownups sit and talk. If you have a yard and weather permits, they can play outside—members of your own generation may want to work off lunch by joining in. If all else fails, let the children watch television or play games, preferably in another room. There will be noise, of course, and you will be called in to arbitrate disagreements and decide whose turn it is. That's what family parties are, and always will be.

You might have some sort of after-luncheon program. At Christmas there is carol singing. At Easter the egg hunt is a natural.

For children beyond infancy and not yet in embarrassed adolescence you might arrange an informal show. More often than not each child will have a turn he can perform: a piano piece he has learned, more or less well, a poem to recite, or an acrobatic feat he is dying to demonstrate. Simple pleasures? Yes, very simple, but each child will leave the party glowing with accomplishment. As long as the turns are kept short, grownups can fairly be asked to watch. You might have a "prize" for each child, or none at all; Susie's handstand cannot be fairly compared to Tony's unique rendition of the Minute Waltz.

If the family group is more or less the same each year, even though you may not always be the hostess, you might suggest this game: Before the party think up a few questions about the future in current events, sports, or some local issues. Give a pad and pencil to each person, including all children who know how to write. Thanks to TV, it is surprising how aware they are of what's happening in the world. Someone reads the questions and everybody writes down an answer. Next year the papers are pulled out and read aloud. There are bound to be laughs over the predictions— whose was right and whose wrong—especially when children have been included in the game. If you all know each other well enough, it's also fun to read off one set of answers at a time, and see if people can guess who wrote it.

The point of games is to keep all ages entertained, so that the party is truly a family affair. Never have games at any party if they are a desperation attempt to unify it.

How to Get the Most Out of Holiday Parties

Fortunately, at least for those who give holiday parties, each comes only once a year. Exhaustion looms, for on top of the work of the actual party you usually have a crowded calendar before and after. Try to reserve time for an unrushed cleanup, and do not impulsively get involved in giving more than one party in any one holiday period. You have done your bit and more. And if you give the family Thanksgiving dinner, count on someone else at Christmas. Or have a Christmas party with only your immediate family present.

Some people give an annual Christmas Eve supper or New Year's Day open house, or "always have everybody on both sides of the family" for a meal on one of the big holidays. Building up a tradition contributes to spirit and family unity, and it is pleasant to count on a holiday party year after year. But it has hazards. You may tire of Easter dinner always being "yours," and yet feel you must not disappoint others. Or perhaps, during a particularly busy year, doing *anything* special, including going to other family parties, will make you feel overworked. When this happens, don't go. If your relatives won't understand your taking a year off, they have been taking you for granted. And when your party includes friends as well as relatives, remember that anticipation results in a better party when they say to themselves, "We hope the Nelsons are going to invite us again this year," instead of, "We always go to the Nelsons'," and assume that they always will.

More philosophy on this, aimed particularly at the youngest, or recently married, readers of this book: your holidays can be ruined if you try to be all things to all people on a given day. If you are married, it is assumed that your husband's family wants to see him and your family wants to see you, but if it doesn't work easily, be tough about it. We know people who have had Christmas lunch in Philadelphia and broken speed limits to have Christmas supper in New Haven, dragging along exhausted children who would rather be at home with their new toys. Next day the parents, worn out, feel glad only because they did not crack up on the highway.

When a parent is going to be totally alone, you'd be unkind if you didn't try to do something about it. Aside from that, do what appeals to you. Undertake as much as you can, but make a schedule that keeps it a holiday, not an endurance test.

Traditions are all very well, but you have every right to start your own and to announce, "I always expect to stay right here on ——" If you are not ready to commit yourself to your own "tradition," let it be known that you *always* plan to make up your mind about each holiday invitation as it comes along, and not sign up for a lifetime schedule. Choosing one of these alternatives, you won't be a candidate for the "Christmas syndrome" psychologists write about each December. Your holiday spirit will come forth on cue, and the family parties *you* give, at least, can be fun for all.

SPECIAL NOTES ON CHILDREN'S PARTIES

Invitations

Verbal invitations may be given child to child, face to face, or on the telephone, as soon as the child can be understood. Many mothers feel this is important training even though they must hover in the background to discuss time, place, dress, and transportation among themselves. One mother told us, "I have always given my children the *impression* that they made their own dates. Not only good training, it's more fun for them. At first I'd help them make the calls or fill out invitations, and would always get in touch with the mothers later, so that they would know what was afoot and would know that I did too."

By the time a child is nine or ten there is less worry about confusion. The child asks permission to invite friends or to go to see them and the mother becomes involved automatically, if only as chauffeur.

Written invitations may be sent by children as soon as they can write clearly. Little girls enjoy filling out the balloon and lollipop variety; boys more often let their mothers do these. All children love receiving party invitations; replies should be supervised by mothers of young children, or made for them, mother to mother.

By the age of ten any child should have learned to take responsibility for inviting and replying after getting his mother's permission. There is usually no problem about inviting: Bill knows absolutely that he wants to ask John, Sabina, Becky, Robin, and Jake, or the whole class. In replying, children answer by telephone or letter depending on the way the invitation was given. Replies to invitations to teen-age dances which are written in the third person should be written by the child, dictated perhaps by his mother until he learns the correct wording. After sixteen years, all children should handle invitations as adults do, replying promptly, making a note of the date, and arriving where they are expected on time.

Addressing envelopes. Girls of any age are addressed as "Miss ——" A boy is addressed as "Master ——" up to the age of twelve or so, and then becomes merely "John Rodney Layton" or "James Brown, Jr." until he is of college age and considered old enough to be called "Mr. ——"

Manners

Learning good behavior *young* is a person's greatest asset as he grows up. Manners learned early more easily become second nature, and the child isn't inhibited at the party by having to remember please and thank you and how to behave at table. Thanking the host or hostess (and the mother) when he leaves is basic, as is a bread-and-butter letter to the mother when a child has been a house guest for any length of time. No matter how short, badly spelled or worded, a letter in his own hand, not dictated by a parent, is right.

On being introduced, a child should be taught (or ordered or bribed, if necessary) to look the person in the eye as he says hello and to call the person by name. While boys may always call a man "Sir" instead of "Mr. X," girls never do this. Girls, until the age of thirteen or so, who make a bobbing curtsy to older people always look especially attractive. Boys, no longer expected to bow, still get credit for a firm handshake and straight posture when being introduced.

Children's Party Decorations

Young children, particularly, like the party shop favors—snappers, paper hats, napkins, plates, and cups—available anywhere. These are often a boon to mothers who don't want good linen and china exposed to young treatment. After a child is eight or nine such set party props may lose their magic. Although a Jack Horner pie, a specially decorated cake, balloons, or other simple decoration will continue to please, something created by the mother (or the child) or nothing at all is equally good. One mother reported, "I've given up decorations at parties for my ten- and eight-year-olds. They don't seem to miss them, and their friends seem to prefer one fairly nice favor—a small game, a paperback book—to take home instead of crepe paper gimmicks." Children's party settings, we feel, should not be elaborate; the "program" for the party—games, a home movie, or whatever—should be the main feature. Extravagance is inappropriate; the classic example is the young mother who told us of going to a Hollywood birthday party as a child, where she was given a lovebird in a cage, was frightened by the chimpanzee act, and wept because she was "the only one there who didn't have a bodyguard."

Going and Coming

Parties for babies are really just parties for the parents or grand-parents and should be small. If you're having a baby birthday party keep the food simple and the afternoon short. Ask each mother to stay and attend to her own child. You might serve children at table if you have enough telephone books and dictionaries to prop them up. You could also serve them on a sheet on the floor, but not, as one mother cautioned, if you have a bounding dog that might run through, overturning children, plates, and glasses.

When children over four years old go to a party mothers leave them off and return when told to call for them, unless specifically asked to stay and help. Picking up your child promptly is appreciated. Nothing is *over*, when it's over, more than a children's party.

CHAPTER 9

Tea and Coffee Parties

TEA PARTIES

Tea for a handful of people is little trouble, but let's say that you have offered to let the Charity Ball Committee meet at your house. About twenty-five will come. You begin to think of the detail in a tea party and a normal reaction is "What got into me?" But it's too late now. You are having a tea for twenty-five women, most of whom, no doubt, would just as soon skip it (and concomitant calories) and get home earlier. But as you realize this you also realize that you *want* to give a good party; when people are coming you do your best, nothing less.

The main problem is equipment, unless your grandmother left it to you. You need a big old-fashioned tea service, twenty-five cups, saucers, spoons, tea plates. Twenty-five napkins and a tablecloth. If you should also serve chocolate or coffee you'll need a big pot or urn.

The temptation is to rent everything you don't own. But wouldn't it be better to donate the cost to the charity? Certainly. Start telephoning relatives and friends to see what you can borrow. You may be able to borrow the whole works from one source, right down to lace-fringed tea napkins. From two or three friends you can surely rustle up some sort of adequate tea service and enough china and silver. Napkins and tea plates, after all, could be normal luncheon napkins and dessert plates.

Equipment

The standard tea service consists of a tray, a hot-water kettle over a spirit lamp, a teapot, cream pitcher, sugar bowl, tea strainer, and what is indelicately but accurately called a slop bowl—into which the remains of a first cup of tea are poured before serving someone a second. Many old-fashioned tea services also have a coffee or chocolate pot.

If you cannot borrow a tea service—even by pleading with the banquet manager of the local club or hotel—make one up. Don't worry about things not matching. The tray could be any big one of tole, wood, or metal that you happen to own. The hot-water kettle could be a big coffeepot that you place on an electric hot tray or on a stand heated by a candle. And since tea is considered at its best when steeped in a crockery pot, any good-sized one will do. Use your regular sugar bowl and cream pitcher—even for twenty-five you don't need outsize ones—and the slop bowl could be any round china or silver sauce bowl you happen to have. You will also need a tea strainer, a dish for lemon slices—a bread and butter plate will do nicely—and a small fork or pick to spear them. You must have twenty-five forks, too, if cake is being served. But why add to your burdens and the guests'? It will be easier for everyone to have food that can be eaten with the fingers.

Arranging a Tea

Tea is traditionally served by the hostess or one of her friends in the room in which people will drink it. For your charity meeting you will probably use the living room, and plan to serve tea in the dining room or alcove. There is no rule about this. If you have a big living room, and a big enough table for all the equipment, serve tea there. But don't begin until the meeting is over. It's hard to run a good meeting with plates clattering and people tiptoeing to and from the table.

Let's say you plan to use your dining room or alcove, and like the idea of serving hot chocolate as well as tea. Here is the setup:

Lay the dining table with a pretty cloth. This could be anything from a pastel luncheon cloth to an all-lace dinner one. It needn't fit the table—a small square cloth may be laid so that its points hang over the center of the sides and ends of the table. Remove all chairs, except one at each end. In front of one chair goes the tea tray, in front of the other the tray for hot chocolate. On either side of each tray place cups and saucers and spoons. If borrowing has resulted in an assortment of china, group it by patterns. Divide cups evenly at either end of the table. If more people take tea than chocolate, they can simply pick up a cup from the chocolate end. Place the appropriate number of napkins near each group of cups, or put the plates for food under each teacup and saucer with the napkin in between. This is neat and convenient, but since many women on eternal diets won't need plates, it's simpler to put them near the food, to be used or not. Do not pile up more than five at a time; they look too stacked.

On the long sides of the table put food platters with, perhaps, duplicate platters on each side of the table for those few women who simply must jostle around the table "to try one of those delicious-looking sandwiches over there."

Tea Party Food

Tea party food is always fattening and more than anyone needs to eat, but since you're having it, make it tempting. Have something sweet and something not. We think the best choices are the traditional ones: cinnamon toast; Boston brown bread with cream cheese; nut, date, or orange bread, lightly buttered; small squares of pound or raisin cake; individual pastries or iced cakes. None of these requires a fork. Non-sweet food could include small cocktail party sandwiches, made with crustless bread slices cut into fours, filled with water cress, pimiento, cucumber, avocado, chopped chicken, egg, or whatever appeals to you. Ham paste is good. So is smoked salmon—good, and expensive. Sardine spread and anchovy paste are too fishy, and cheeses, except for cream cheese, go better with cocktails than tea.

For twenty-five people you should have about seventy-five individual pieces of food. If you are having mostly sandwiches, allow a

couple of hours to make them; cover them and store in the refrigerator. Arrange the less perishable cakes or cookies any time. Just before the meeting bring out the sandwiches, arrange them, and put
all the food on the dining table. Also bring in the lemon slices and
the milk—it won't sour during the meeting.

All that's easy. But cinnamon toast, to be good, must be served
hot, and will keep you in the kitchen a few minutes longer at the
end of the meeting than it takes to make the tea. (We shall come
to the tea operation shortly.) While preparing the other food, cut
toasted bread slices into squares or oblongs. Spread them with a
lavish mixture of sugar, cinnamon, and butter, and put them on
cookie sheets. Light the oven before the meeting. Then when you
go out to make the tea, pop cookie sheets in the oven. By the time
you have carried in tea and chocolate the toast may be ready. If it's
not, it will be in a minute or two, and the guests have the other
platters to sample while you wait. Marmalade toast—buttered toast
spread with orange marmalade and heated to bubbling in the oven
—is no less delectable than cinnamon toast and can be prepared
ahead in the same way.

The English consider white bread and butter a perfect complement to a good tea, and they're right in England where you can get
bread that tastes homemade in any store, unsliced, and firm enough
to slice paper-thin. If you know of a good bakery, or bake bread
yourself, you might serve it at the tea. Before slicing, spread with
softened butter. Then cut each slice diagonally. Leave crusts on.
Don't try this with "thin-sliced" supermarket bread; it's twice the
thickness you are after.

If making sandwiches and hot things is too much trouble, just
have cookies, plain or fancy, or brownies, cut small, or macaroons,
which are especially good with tea. Scotch shortbread must have
been invented to accompany tea, and any of the famous English
cookie brands—such as Carr's, Peek-Frean, and Huntley & Palmer—
have assortments that, though far from homemade, taste special
with tea. For simple non-sweet food, butter squares of raisin bread,
or sliced brioches, or fill a platter with assorted sherry crackers.
These, while not sugarless, are only faintly sweet compared to other
cookies.

For eye appeal, slice lemons thin and arrange them neatly. You
might score the lemon before slicing so that each piece will have a

fluted edge. Or cut four wedges out of the whole lemon, to make a Maltese cross of each slice. Or simply peel the lemon before slicing. A tiny leaf of parsley or a clove looks nice in the center. The parsley won't hurt the taste of the tea, and the clove will enhance it.

Check List for a Tea Party

Tea tray
Cups, saucers, and spoons
Napkins
Teapot
Hot-water kettle
Spirit lamp or candle warmer
Cream pitcher, sugar bowl, sugar tongs
Slop bowl
Tea strainer
Dish for lemon slices, with small fork
Tablecloth
Candles (optional)
Carafe of rum (optional)

If also serving hot chocolate:
Tray
Chocolate pot and warmer
Bowl and ladle for whipped cream

If also serving coffee:
Tray
Coffeepot and warmer
Cream pitcher, sugar bowl, sugar tongs

For the food:
Tea or dessert plates
Forks if having a big cake or pastries
Platters

Serving the Tea

Before the meeting you might ask four close friends, or two friends and two of the group's ranking women, to pour the tea and chocolate. Pick two to pour first and arrange for them to be spelled by the other two halfway through the party. Pouring tea is work, and though it is considered an honor to be asked to do it, no one person should "have the duty" for the whole party.

Now, how to have the tea ready the moment the meeting adjourns? All the food, milk, sugar, and lemon are ready in the dining room. Make the chocolate ahead of time. Leave it on the stove with an asbestos pad between pot and burner, and turn the heat to its lowest point. The chocolate will stay hot but won't burn. Just before the meeting make the whipped cream for the chocolate and put it in the refrigerator in the bowl you'll serve it from. It will stay fluffy enough for an hour or so.

Now the tea: the correct way to make it is to rinse the teapot with hot water, then put in the leaves and bring the pot to the kettle of water just coming to a boil on the stove. This insures getting the hottest possible water over the tea leaves—a must for really good tea. Since you will be in the living room until the last moment, put the leaves in the pot ahead of time and place it on the stove as near as you can to the heating water. During the meeting the pot will pick up some warmth. Since you need lots of hot water, have two big kettles or stew pans filled and simmering before the meeting. Then, when teatime comes, turn up the flames and bring the water to the boil quickly while pouring the chocolate into the pot. Don't use a whistling hot-water kettle. It always blasts off just as the chairman comes to her main point, and you have to dash out and turn it down.

When the meeting begins to wind up, slip out and as you pass the tea table light the spirit lamp or plug in hot trays. If you have set the table with candles—they're attractive in winter—light these too. First task in the kitchen: turn up the hot water. Then put cinnamon toast in the oven. Decant the chocolate into its pot. If the water is boiling by then, pour some of it over the tea leaves and fill the hot-water kettle. Now take the chocolate pot and whipped cream to the table while the tea steeps a little. Returning to the kitchen, put a fresh batch of water on to boil (high flame this time), check what's in the oven, and carry out the teapot and kettle. You're ready in less than five minutes. Announce that tea is served, and corral the first flight of pourers. By this time the toast should be sizzling and you go out to the kitchen to get it.

Once every guest has been served to tea or chocolate, watch for pots that need refilling. When the teapot is empty, take it out and make fresh tea. Although some people pour boiling water over the same tea leaves, this violates the rules, and you may end up with tannic acid or a very bitter brew. Instead, rinse used leaves from the pot and start over.

Loose tea or tea bags? It's up to you. Rinsing the pot of loose leaves takes extra time so you may decide to use tea bags. But, whatever the ads say, you will get better tea from loose leaves. Remember the English butler beginning his first job in America? "I would have had tea ready faster, madam, but it took time to get the leaves out of those charming little bags."

There is tea and tea. Everyday tea is all right, but for a party you might consider something special or aromatic. Standard "exotic" teas, available almost anywhere, include China teas such as Keemun, Lapsang souchong, Formosa oolong, India teas such as Darjeeling and Queen Elizabeth's, and the blend of China and India teas known as Earl Grey. Many English tea firms have the whole array and export them to supermarkets everywhere. Any one of these will be *good* tea, but if you are in doubt about which you would prefer, buy a small "tea sampler," a package of several different teas in small amounts. Have a private tea tasting before you order a big tin for the party.

Pouring Tea

It is not done with the ritual of the Japanese tea ceremony, but there is a system to it. First you ask, "How do you take your tea?" Weak, strong, or medium are the standard replies, and of course the amount of hot water you need to add varies with the strength of the tea. A bourbon-whisky color is strong enough for a "black" tea.

"Green" tea will never get that dark. As you pour with the tea strainer over the cup, the guest will indicate when to stop and add hot water. Lift off the strainer and pour in hot water. Then you ask, "Sugar? Milk or lemon?" These go in after you pour the tea. Note "milk" instead of "cream." Many people feel that milk is best for tea, because the fat content of cream smothers the tea's flavor.

When a person comes back for a second cup, pour in a little hot water and swish it around. Then dump it, along with lemon and sugar remains, into the slop bowl. Now start over. You will be a memory wizard if you can repeat the first orders of each person, so you simply resume with "Weak or strong?" It is not very fascinating conversation, which is another reason not to have one person pour for the whole time.

A nice extra on the tea tray, especially in winter, is a small carafe of light rum. It goes well with any tea and particularly perks up a bland one. The rum is poured in after the tea and hot water. Just a teaspoon or so; the idea is to give the tea spirited flavor, not to make a hot toddy.

Spring and Summer Teas

English colonials who have lived in the tropics will tell you that there is nothing more cooling in hot weather than piping-hot tea. But Americans like iced drinks at any time, and in the warm months iced tea is much easier to serve. All you do is make a big batch on the morning of the party, put the pitchers in the refrigerator, set out tall glasses and a full ice bucket, and when teatime comes bring on the pitchers and pour. No trouble about borrowing equipment and asking friends to help. Little trouble about food either, since cookies are all you need.

When you serve iced tea, try to make it really tasty. Never a purist's invention, it improves with the addition of fresh mint, orange or lemon juice, ginger ale, or whatever sounds good to you. And since it clouds up when made ahead it will look better with something added. Don't make it too sweet. Many people dislike sweet drinks, and a bowl of granulated sugar takes care of those who don't. Have out a few long spoons or stirrers.

COFFEE PARTIES

A fairly new entertainment, the coffee party has come in because it is inexpensive and simple to prepare and equip. There are three types: morning, afternoon, and evening.

The Morning Coffee Party

No one seriously calls anything before lunchtime a party. (Brunch is just a luncheon with food more commonly eaten at breakfast.) Like teas, morning coffee parties usually come about because of good works; there's a meeting, or a group gets together at someone's dining table to address envelopes for a community appeal. The person who loans her house wants to offer refreshment, and coffee is the obvious choice.

If the meeting is going to be fairly early, organize the night before. Set out coffee cups, a tray, hot plate, cream pitcher, and sugar bowl. At breakfast time make a lot of coffee and keep it hot. Before the group arrives, fill the cream pitcher and bring a full pot of coffee to the hot plate. People serve themselves at will during the course of the morning. Have cigarettes around, and keep the coffee-pot full. If you care to, you might also offer a pitcher of orange juice with small tumblers.

Food is not necessary. Presumably, everyone will have eaten breakfast. But probably most hostesses would feel that coffee alone was not hospitable enough. If so, a couple of platters of breakfast breads, such as coffee or crumb cake, cinnamon rolls, or sliced and buttered biscuits, can be put on the sideboard. Have anything that is easy to pick up and does not have to be cut or buttered. Extra butter, plates, and knives are too much of a production for a work session. Have napkins if any food at all is on the scene.

The Afternoon Coffee Party

This could top off a meeting, just like a tea, but is often more of a social occasion for housewives. Many women today keep so busy that lunch or tea parties are too much effort except for special events. Also, women who cannot crowd in parties at lunchtime or after-school hours may have time for cards or just visiting in the early afternoon. The party *begins* with coffee and a dessert, and everyone arrives home early enough to start dinner without dashing to the kitchen and paring vegetables with her coat on.

The setup is the same as that for a morning coffee party. The coffee equipment and food are out beforehand, with forks and plates for the dessert. As people arrive you show them where everything is and they serve themselves. Some will take only a cup of black coffee, others will have skipped lunch at the prospect of pastries. Some people will take nothing at all, yet there will be a party spirit to the afternoon.

The Evening Coffee Party

The evening party has the same components—coffee and something in the way of dessert. We question the idea of such a party, in itself. To bring people out in the evening for fun, shouldn't you go all the way and give them a simple dinner? Or shouldn't you arrange a late evening supper, with beer or long drinks, a casserole or scrambled eggs and sausages, or cocktail party food: hard-boiled eggs, a cheese tray, some cold cuts? We think so.

But if the point of getting together is work, not entertainment, proceed as before. Have lots of good hot coffee. You might have espresso, too, and decaffeinated coffee for wakeful friends. Two or more choices of cake or cookies would be nice.

Set out both demitasse and regular coffee cups, and have dessert plates, forks, and napkins for the food. Plan to use all your small tables. It's impossible to manage a coffee cup and napkin while eating a slice of cake, and men, especially, hate balancing acts. Everything should be ready when people arrive. They are served then, and when the meeting is over they should go. If you think many night owls will linger, and you don't mind, prepare for long drinks and have some popcorn or potato chips on hand. If you want everyone to leave, offer nothing.

Check List for a Coffee Party

Big coffeepot
Big tray
Warmer, if available
Cream pitcher, sugar bowl, sugar tongs
Coffee or teacups
Demitasse cups
Spoons—teaspoons and demitasse spoons
Napkins

Optional:
Extra pots for espresso or caffeine-free coffee
Trays for each extra pot
Warmers, if available

For the food:
Plates
Forks
Platters
Small folding tables, if available

CHAPTER 10

When a Lion Comes to Dinner — The Formal Party

Since life is full of surprises, you may be faced sometime with giving a party for someone who deserves the full treatment—a formal dinner. A distinguished citizen might swoop down, or someone important to your husband's business, whom he wants to impress. Or, later, your "lion" might be your own child, and the dinner in honor of his engagement, or for bride and groom on the eve of the wedding.

Today, virtually no one gives a formal dinner without a special reason, except those who entertain officially in Washington or at the United Nations. One explanation is that servants, more than guests, make a formal dinner: the serving follows a prescribed ritual. Basically an informal people, we prefer parties with less system and more swing. Dining rooms today, where they exist at all, often house piano, television, or bookshelves, as well as the dining table. A formal dinner would be out of keeping in such a room, equally so in a dining alcove or a single girl's apartment. Finally, there's the expense. Even with enough servants and space, the bills for formal parties are formidable. Without regular help, they are enormous.

The dinner that follows is expensive. To come off as it should, it must be.

Now here is a plot: Let's say your husband has just been made head of his political party's campaign committee and one of your senators and his wife are coming to discuss the campaign in your town. Your husband wants to give the dinner at home, so that the senator can discuss strategy and fund raising in an unofficial way.

Yet he also feels that the senator, in his twenty-fourth year on Capitol Hill, would not be especially comfortable at your usual self-service suppers. He tells you to go all out and he will worry about the bills.

Guest List and Invitations

You decide there are six men in town, all married, who should be asked. You assume all will accept, making a dinner of sixteen with yourselves and the guests of honor. You decide that, by moving out the sideboard and hiring small tables, you could fit twenty-two into the dining room, which would allow for six friends to lard the group.

In picking extra people for a party with a political slant avoid firebrands and people whose main interests do not include politics. Also pass over way-out friends who only like to sit around in stretch pants and discuss life.

Invitations to a formal party are always written and answered in the third person. Use either the plain white cardboard cards that are half engraved (see sample following) or your own writing paper.

The half-engraved card comes in two forms, one saying, "request the pleasure of your company," and the other, "request the pleasure of Mr. & Mrs. X's company," like this:

Mr. and Mrs. James Macmillan
request the pleasure of
Mr. and Mrs. Smiths **company**

at dinner in honor of
Senator and Mrs. John Resolution
on Friday, the fifteenth of June
at eight

R.S.V.P.
68 Lake Drive   Black tie

Note: You do not write in Mr. and Mrs. Smith's full name.

Use the same wording when writing the whole invitation by hand. Either a single or a double sheet of writing paper is fine; so is paper with your monogram or home address. Do not use paper with your full name or telephone number on it. Your name is redundant as it will be repeated in the actual invitation, and the telephone number not pertinent, as everyone should reply in writing.

When writing out the whole invitation, line it up like the engraved form. Do not write "Mr. and Mrs. James Bruce MacMillan request the pleasure of your company, etc.," all on one line.

The invitations should go out, if possible, about three weeks ahead. But don't mail them until you are positive the senator can come. Nothing takes the stuffing out of a party more than asking people to meet a "lion" and not having him show up.

In setting the date you probably will have invited the senator and his wife by a regular letter. When they accept, send them the same invitation you are sending to the others as a reminder, and put "To remind" in place of R.s.v.p.

An acceptance to a formal dinner invitation is written thus:

Mr. and Mrs. Michael Wright
accept with pleasure
the kind invitation of
Mr. and Mrs. MacMillan
to dinner on Friday, the fifteenth of June
at eight o'clock

OR:

Mr. and Mrs. Michael Wright
accept with pleasure
Mr. and Mrs. MacMillan's
kind invitation to dinner
on Friday, the fifteenth of June
at eight o'clock

It is not necessary to say, "in honor of Senator and Mrs. Resolution."

A regret reads:

Miss Virginia Wright
regrets that she is unable to accept
the kind invitation of
Mr. and Mrs. MacMillan
to dinner on Friday, the fifteenth of June
owing to absence from town

OR:

Mr. and Mrs. Michael Wright
greatly regret that a previous engagement
prevents their accepting
Mr. and Mrs. MacMillan's
kind invitation to dinner
on Friday, the fifteenth of June

Planning the Meal

In the past, the menu could have any number of courses. Queen Victoria, even when roughing it in Scotland, sat down to a formal dinner of eight courses every night. More recently, courses have been cut to five: soup, fish, meat, salad, and dessert; and signs suggest that four courses will soon be in, at least among hostesses who think about waistlines. Four courses could be soup *or* fish, meat, salad, and dessert, or soup, fish (with some sort of salad-like accompaniment such as sliced tomatoes and cucumbers), meat, and dessert.

Equipment and Help

Perhaps you have or can borrow enough extra silver and china, tables and linen to take care of twenty-two at dinner. If so, fine. But the amount is pretty staggering. A five-course dinner with two wines for twenty-two people takes a minimum of 88 glasses, including cocktail glasses, plus 44 more for liqueurs and highball glasses. You will need 154 plates, not counting platters and serving china, but including after-dinner coffee cups and saucers. Exclusive of serving forks and spoons, you could work up to 218 pieces of silver if you had a fish course and a salad with cheese for which knives would be needed. Grand total of basic table equipment: 494 separate items.

There should be one waitress or butler for every six or eight people. During a formal dinner, you don't lift a finger. You *could* do the cooking—making the soup, or a cold fish course, and a dessert beforehand, and relying on helpers to supervise the main course as it cooks and to toss the salad. But isn't this perhaps time to let a caterer do the lion's share of a "lion's" dinner? We think so. You won't lose control of your party. A good caterer merely helps produce whatever you want, with a staff who work well together and usually know the ritual of formal dinner service.

If you decide to have a caterer, ask him to come in and go over everything, right down to the last coffee spoon. He may have suggestions about the best use of space, and will need to see the kitchen and the layout of the house.

Have a tentative menu in mind and discuss it with him. Be guided by his ideas if he is to be responsible for the food. Only he knows what his cook does best.

Make everything as clear as you can in your first talk. The best way to get an intelligent estimate of the cost, this also helps ensure a smoothly run party. It should not turn into a surprise party for the caterer at the eleventh hour, even though most good ones can scramble through in emergencies.

Ask the caterer as many questions as you can. Do his personnel expect tips? They usually do. If so, how much? Will he add tips to the bill so that you don't have to remember them during the party? What about after midnight? Do the rates for his service go up? Should one butler or maid stay on in case the party lasts into the small hours? If the dinner is going to be cooked ahead and brought in, who sees that it is hot when it comes into the dining room? The caterer may suggest having a kitchen helper for this. She will also arrange food on platters and attend to used plates as they come back to the kitchen. It's an extra expense, but the other helpers really don't have time for kitchen work during dinner, and may cause clatter if they have to do it.

A good caterer is something like an obstetrician. When you are having a baby you go to your doctor, discuss every detail, and ask all the questions on your mind. This is comforting and tells him what you hope he will do. From then on, unless there are complications, he merely reassures, and on the big day he sees you through.

In the same way, a caterer delivers a party. You and he discuss preliminaries thoroughly. When interim questions arise you call him. (Will he bring a big coffeepot? Is ice his responsibility or yours? And so on.) He will have all the answers and a calming bedside manner. On the big night, though it will still be *your* party (as the baby is *your* baby), there's comfort in having had his professional help from the beginning.

Setting the Table

A good caterer's crew should know this cold, but in case they don't, here is a quick check list:

Tables should be laid with white cloths, underlined by a felt or mat of some sort.

The cutlery is laid as usual, in the order in which it is to be used. Dessert forks and spoons are passed with dessert plates.

Place plates are on the table and the first course will be passed after the guests come into the dining room. Butter plates are not in order but finger bowls are. They used to be passed after dessert plates had been taken away. But this requires bowls with saucers underneath—no dish for liquid, whether it be soup, sauces, or a finger bowl, is ever passed or laid without a plate beneath. These days, most people have finger bowls passed, with a doily underneath, on the dessert plates. Guests put the doily above the plate and the finger bowl on the doily.

At a formal dinner there might be two or even three wines. In the old days four was the rule: sherry with soup, white wine with fish, red wine with meat, champagne with dessert. Nowadays most people skip the sherry or one of the wines. Champagne is still considered right for a formal meal. Since it can be served with anything, the two wines might be a white with the fish and then champagne with the meat course through dessert. When the main course is chicken you could have the same white wine for the fish and chicken, followed by champagne, or have white wine with the fish only and start champagne with the chicken. At a dinner of soup, main course of meat, salad course, and dessert, you would have red wine with the main course, then follow with champagne.

Glasses are laid in order of use: water glass, and to its right the champagne glass, then in front of and a little to the right, the wineglass or -glasses. The servants should remove the wineglass that goes with a course when the course is finished, so that finally all that remains is the water goblet and champagne glass.

Nut dishes are traditional but expendable in the interests of an uncluttered table. If you include nuts they may be passed in a bowl with a spoon during the soup. They are put right on the cloth, as are the soup crackers and later the unbuttered rolls. If you have individual nut dishes they are removed when the table is crumbed after the salad.

Place cards are always used. They go on the center of the napkin, which is laid on the service plate. The cards are always written "Senator Resolution," "Mrs. Resolution," "Miss Hughes" and "Mr. Brown," even though you call everyone by his first name. Should there be two Mr. Browns, distinguish between them by writing "Mr. James Brown" and "Mr. Robert Brown." No nicknames.

Candles are a must. How many to use depends on table space and how the room is lighted. With twenty-two for dinner, you might have a table of ten and two tables of six. If there is other lighting in the room, four candlesticks on the main table and two on each of the smaller ones is enough. But if you want only candlelight, the experts say one candle per person, which in this case would mean: four candles on each of the small tables, and sixteen on the big table! Well, it *could* be done, with four three-branch candelabra and four single candles. Or you could put some candles elsewhere in the room. Discuss this with the caterer and see what he has in supply. Experts notwithstanding, it would seem that two or three candles on the small tables and six or eight on the big one would be bright enough.

A centerpiece is also a must. Flowers are the best choice, lending uniformity to the three tables. On a long main table you might have one big center arrangement and two smaller ones at either end, or three arrangements of the same size running down the length of the table, with a single bowl on each of the small tables. Sometimes a single arrangement of flowers is put in the center of a long table and compotiers filled with candy at either end. On the table throughout dinner, more for decoration than for eating (though they are often passed after dessert), the candy should look pretty. Pastel mints, candied violets, or marzipan in fruit and flower shapes are good choices.

Arrival of Guests

Guests should make a point of arriving promptly at eight o'clock. The senator and his lady will be no more than five minutes late and must not walk into an empty room.

After offering them a cocktail, you might escort the Resolutions around and introduce them to everyone as at any other dinner, or you and the Resolutions might form a casual receiving line near the living-room door. The other guests then come up to be introduced. With prompt guests, introductions will soon be over and you can turn the senator loose to win friends and influence people.

When introducing the senator to a woman, say, "Mrs. Wilson, may I introduce Senator Resolution." To a man you say, "Senator Resolution, this is Mr. Wilson" or "Senator Resolution, may I introduce Mr. Wilson." Always say Senator Resolution (or Mayor Patronage, or Bishop Benign). "The Senator from Michigan" is correct only on the floor of the Senate, and whatever the person's title, in an introduction it is always accompanied by his name. Later, in conversation, one may say "Mr. Senator" or "Mr. Mayor."

Going in to Dinner

Within twenty minutes to half an hour after the guests of honor have arrived—but no later—dinner is announced. If a couple of guests have not shown up, you go in to dinner without them, and they are served whatever the rest of you are eating when they come in (they are not served courses they have missed). Latecomers are not introduced. They say good evening to you quickly and go to their places.

When dinner is announced the host goes up to the woman guest of honor, offers his arm, and takes her in to dinner. Traditionally, the hostess at a formal dinner goes into the dining room last with the man who will sit on her left, and the man guest of honor escorts the woman who will sit at his right. You would be correct in following this order, but you may feel it is nicer if you and the senator go in together—again etiquette adjusts to the spirit of the occasion.

The other guests *can* come in helter-skelter, but there are tried and true ways to make the procession run smoothly. One is a seating chart, with each guest's name written in. This can be left on a hall table for guests to look over as they arrive. When dinner is announced each has a general idea where he's sitting.

A chart will work well for a dinner of twenty-two, but it is less efficient than the take-you-in card. As each man arrives a butler hands him an envelope with his name on it. In the envelope is a card on which is written the name of the woman he is to take in to dinner. Often a sketch of the table or tables is also on the card with an "X" to give him an idea where their seats are. During cocktails the man locates the woman he's to escort and when dinner is announced he goes to her. While this seems awfully elaborate, at very big parties it works well. Using a plain fold-over card, such as a prop-up place card, simplifies it. The man's name is written on the front with the woman's name and table diagrams inside.

Menu Cards

The forks, knives, and wineglasses give guests a good idea of the size of the meal, but menu cards are also often used. The four or five courses, but none of the extras—olives, nuts, rolls—are written on cards placed at intervals around the table. A guest who doesn't care for fish dabbles with that course, knowing that his favorite rack of lamb is coming next. Good stationers have these heavy white cards, and little clip stands to hold them. You might have just one menu card in front of the guest of honor. A nice touch for even the most casual party, it looks well planned and always makes a hit, especially if you invent your own titles for each dish. It's a conversation piece, if nothing else.

Serving a Formal Dinner

The two rules are these: No plate, except the soup plate, is ever put down with food already on it; and there is a clean plate ready to receive the next course at each place at all times. It is as if the servants were playing gin rummy. Each time they pick up a plate they "discard" a fresh one at each place.

Here is the "hand" for a five-course dinner of soup, fish, meat, salad, and dessert.

Place plates are on the table when the guests enter the dining room. Servants pass filled soup plates, which are put on the place plates.

Soup and place plates are removed together and fish plates are laid at the same time. Or the soup plates are removed alone and the butler exchanges the place plate for the fish plate on his next trip.

Then the fish is passed. When this course is finished each plate is replaced by a dinner plate. Then the meat course is passed, and so on with the salad and dessert.

At a formal dinner you would have two or more platters of each dish, with enough food for every six to eight persons passed around simultaneously, starting with the woman guest of honor.

Wine is not put on the table and is poured by the servants. It may be in carafes but is more often served from the bottle or from wine baskets. White wine or champagne that has just come out of the ice bucket is wrapped with a napkin to absorb the dew. Incidentally, champagne is never decanted, even if the other wines are.

While a course is being eaten you might ask one of the helpers to stay in the dining room. (If you have an electric buzzer under the table you can signal the kitchen, but a table bell does not appear at a formal dinner.) Directions to servants should be inconspicuous. When you have a request give it briefly in a low voice. Sometimes a gesture minus dialogue is enough.

Ordinarily no course is offered twice at a formal dinner—how could anyone take second helpings of all that food? But if the guest of honor compliments you on something, naturally you offer him a second helping, and if he accepts you signal one of the servants. Everyone else is then offered a second helping, too.

When salad plates are cleared, the servants also remove salt, pepper, and nut dishes. They exchange used ashtrays for clean ones and the table is crumbed. The dessert plates with forks, spoons, and finger bowls, filled a quarter to a third full of cold water, are laid. To make a charming thing of it, you might have a sprig of lemon verbena, a few violets, rose petals, or a single daisy in each one. Lemon slices are only put in finger bowls passed after lobster.

Toasts always add something to a party. One of those best-foot-forward touches, a toast can make the simplest supper seem like a special occasion. At informal dinners, anyone can make the first toast—one of the men might rise to toast you or one of the guests. In Scandinavia there is a nice custom of toasting the food which many a hostess here would appreciate. At a formal dinner, the host opens the proceedings by making a short speech to the guests of honor. The man guest of honor responds to this as soon as he can. Not to respond is no less rude than a slap in the face. We have no worries that a senator will not return a toast—he will seize any opportunity to endear himself—but we mention it because we have often seen someone toasted sit mute for the rest of the dinner. Since a toast is not a speech and *should* be brief, people who are nervous about speaking on their feet can simply stand up, raise a glass, and say, "Thank you," in response.

The time for the first toast is determined by the wine you have. If you are having champagne with dessert it can be served just before the salad course is cleared. Then the host can make his toast between salad and dessert. If you are having champagne throughout dinner a toast at any time is all right, but most men usually wait until after the main course; starting earlier interrupts conversation.

After the host and guest of honor have spoken it is open season for anyone else. Both men and women who have something to say simply rise to get the floor. If silence is long in coming someone usually taps a spoon on a glass and everyone stops talking.

All guests stand at the end of the "official" toasts, but if many speeches are being made (by each of the ushers at a wedding dinner, for instance) the person who is speaking can say, "This will be a seated toast," and no one stands except him—a relief to women who must scramble for napkin, gloves, and handbag each time they rise, and still have one hand free for the wineglass.

If you do not drink, raise your water glass or an empty wineglass. A toast, an all-for-one gesture, loses its point if everyone doesn't join in.

After leaving the dining room the procedure is the same as for dinners described elsewhere in this book, except that the men *always* separate from the women for coffee and liqueurs and are offered cigars.

The men join the women after a fairly short interval, and water, soda, or tall drinks are offered.

The time to leave is no longer bound by rules, but any guests of honor wise to the ways of protocol will leave first, probably half an hour after the men have joined the women. After they go, others may leave immediately or stay until they have finished their drinks. No one lingers at a formal dinner. Perhaps the best argument for formality is that there *are* rules of service, of timing; everybody knows what is expected of him and the party is not affected by people having to make on-the-spot decisions about right and wrong.

Menus for a Formal Dinner

Whether you decide on four or five courses, the big thing is to have a well-balanced meal. So much has been written about this that little more need be said. Remember the all-red dinner in Chapter 1? Balance colors and richness; follow up a fairly heavy course with something light and refreshing.

Here is a bad menu:

Oysters or Clams on the Half Shell
Consommé with Sherry
Breast of Chicken in Cream with Rice and Peas
Salad
Vanilla Ice Cream with Strawberries

Everything on it is good party food, yet it is too light, watery, and monotone in color.

Another bad example:

Cream of Mushroom Soup
Crab Meat au Gratin
Roast Pheasant or Squab with Bread Sauce, Jelly, and Wild Rice
Salad
Profiteroles with Chocolate Sauce

That one, of course, is too heavy, but having a clear soup, or a poached fish after the mushroom soup, could make it perfect. Though desserts should always be sweet and caloric, after such a dinner a simple fruit tart or sherbet seems more appetizing and digestible.

In the chapter on menus and recipes we list many well-balanced meals, only a few of thousands of possible combinations. Here, just to give you an idea, are three to illustrate that the framework of a good dinner is really very simple food, with perhaps one creation, such as a creamed fish or a rich dessert.

Bouquet of Shrimp on Lettuce—Herbed Mayonnaise
Clear Turtle Soup
Roast Young Chicken—String Beans, Shoestring Potatoes
Mixed Green Salad—Brie or Camembert
Soufflé Grand Marnier

Clear Tomato Soup
Grilled Sole with Lemon Butter
Sliced Filet of Beef—Whole Mushrooms in Cream and Soufflé
  Potatoes
Apple Tart with Cream

Chicken Consommé
Crab Meat au Gratin
Roast Mutton Chops—Tomatoes Stuffed with Peas, New Potatoes
Green Salad with Avocado and Grapefruit
Crème Brûlée

Accompaniments to a formal dinner menu are fairly standard. Crackers, cheese straws, or tartines (small bread and butter sandwiches) are always passed with the soup, and unbuttered dinner rolls with the main course. Salad, when it is served with cheese, also calls for crackers. To accompany desserts having no pastry, such as ice cream or fruit, there might be chocolate leaves, cookies, or some light cake. Nuts, as we have said, may or may not appear, but celery, olives, and radishes are usually passed with the soup.

That about does it, except for the bill. Don't blanch when you hear the grand total. If you have had a caterer, his bill may be bigger than the estimate, and you may regret such expense for a fling that lasted such a short while. Before becoming too depressed, divide the cost by the number of guests. Compare that figure to what you think the cost per person might have been had you given the party at the best restaurant in town. You may be pleasantly surprised. But even if the cost is about the same, remember the *priceless* aspect to the party: it was much more complimentary and memorable to have it at home. And there's the satisfaction of looking back and saying to yourself, "*I* did it, and I did it *right*."

Part Two

THE INDISPENSABLE
INGREDIENTS

CHAPTER **11**

The Manners of the
Host and Hostess

Good manners are indispensable to good parties.
And the manners of the hosts are most important. Remember Eliza
Doolittle's line in *Pygmalion?* "The difference between a lady and
a flower girl is not how she behaves but how she's treated." The
better the hosts' manners, the better the guests'—and the better the
party. Most people have instinctive good manners born of friendly
consideration for others. And most readers of this book, we feel
sure, know their manners well. Here we merely underline a few
rules that are particularly pertinent to parties, and add some suggestions about handling certain situations as politely as possible.

The Basic Rule

From the moment guests arrive until they leave, think of nothing
but them. All the traditional rules of etiquette, and our own ideas
about manners *today*, come to nothing more than this: your
thought of others, *in action*.

Arrival of Guests

Since it is not polite to make guests wait while you put finishing touches on the dinner—or an elaborate hair-do—arrange your time so that you are in the living room ahead of the first arrivals. Get up to greet each new arrival. Calling, "Hi, glad to see you," on your way to baste the roast is not enough; first, make introductions.

Introductions

At a small cocktail party or dinner everyone should be introduced to everyone else. Even though many people could not repeat the names ten seconds later, not to introduce a guest implies that you don't care whether or not he is there.

At a big party, when you must stay near the door greeting people, introduce arrivals to those nearest you. Later, when the rush is over, keep making introductions as you move around.

Introducing is easy for some and difficult for others. Many people in a crowd forget the names of their best friends. It is nothing new. Two thousand years ago in Rome, citizens brought with them to the Forum slaves called nomenclators whose job was to whisper to their owners the names of approaching friends. In more recent times major-domos stood at doorways and called out the name of each new guest, which not only reminded a busy hostess but helped other guests to get the names.

Not having these props today, if you sometimes forget names, look over the guest list just before the party. If you really study it, visualizing faces to go with names, you won't look blankly at new arrivals as if you hadn't expected them.

Sometimes mental crutches help: the boss's wife's name is Sybil, and your fate is in her hands, or some such aid to memory. But don't lean on a mental crutch too heavily, like the golfer who tried to remember the name of the pro, Mr. Hummock. He would say "Hummock-Stomach" over to himself and then always call the man Mr. Kelly.

The etiquette of introductions goes this way: a man should always be introduced to a woman (even if he is seventy and she is twenty-two), and young women should be introduced to older ones. (There is only one exception to this rule: everyone, male or female, young or old, is introduced *to* the President, royalty, or a high church dignitary.)

Nowadays everyone uses first names so soon after meeting that to introduce Mr. This to Miss That sounds stuffy at a young party. But be sure to give the last names: "Susan, this is Charlie Price. Susan Andrews." To say only, "Susan, this is Charlie," to people who have not met before sounds like kindergarten.

"Debby, you know Roger Martin," is all right too. An introduction at its briefest, saying nothing between the names, will not sound as hasty as it seems if you pause and speak with exclamation points: "Debby Palmer! . . . Roger Martin!"

Introducing a woman to a mixed group is easy if you keep thinking "ladies first." "Mary, I'd like to introduce everyone here." Give the women's names first, indicating by a look or a gesture which one you mean: "Peggy Mathews, Jane O'Brien." And then, "Bob Walker and George Metcalf. Mary Chapman."

A relative should be introduced as "My brother-in-law, Fred Cavanaugh," or "My sister Jane's husband, Fred Cavanaugh." When you introduce a relative whose surname is different: "I'd like you to meet my mother, Mrs. Hamilton," or "My brother, Paul Hamilton." When your surnames are the same, "My father-in-law," or "My brother-in-law, Jack," is enough.

It is nice to identify relatives, but don't qualify other people: "My friend, Susan Bridges," implies that Susan is a better friend than the person being introduced. And to say, "This is Paul Williams, *the* movie critic" (or *the* something), looks as if you felt having just *friends* at the party wasn't good enough. If you feel you must tell what a person does to avoid a boner, make the introduction and then say, "George, I loved your book." Or turn to the other person and say, "Tom is one of the architects who did our new concert hall." Then you are not guilty of trying to impress, only helping two strangers begin a conversation.

One time a hostess can properly qualify an introduction is when someone new to the group needs help getting started. "Mary, this is an old friend of ours from Detroit, Frank Patterson, who has just arrived in town." Mary will know that you are really saying, "He knows no one here. Help me take care of him."

After the Introductions

The next step is to see that guests have something to drink and someone to talk to. Try never to leave a husband and wife talking together or to let single guests pioneer on their own. Knowing one or two people at a party, new arrivals fall easily into conversation, but you may have to help total strangers:

"Bess, please tell George about your trip."

"Susan, I know you'd love to hear about Bill's new boat so come over and sit next to him."

While these remarks sound strained out of context, they merely help to start people off. Please note: Bess is talking to George and Susan to Bill. The good hostess does not let all the men collect on one side of the room and the women on the other. It happens often enough in America to make one wonder what the sexes are coming to. At parties in Latin countries men more or less avoid each other, and women do not shimmer in to talk to other women. Each sex seeks out the other, and the talk entertains both—current events, politics, or frivolities that make up in amusement for what they lack in importance. It's a party after all!

If your party's opening line-up looks like the girls against the boys, it is your fault. Go right to work. Break into a knot of men and guide one or two over to some women. Move women around the same way until you have the party mixed. As in cooking, don't "stir vigorously," but "gently fold in the ingredients."

Now the party has started, you become a sort of one-man band, calling the tune, conducting, and improvising—with conversation, and with people who look bored or ill at ease. In the back of your head you think of the hour, the dinner on the stove. Before you are glasses that need refilling, appetizers to be passed, and noses to be counted. "Are we all here? No. No Wilsons. Perhaps they've forgotten. Shall I call them?" you wonder. (Yes. It's better than worrying, if they are really late.) At this point you cannot let anyone monopolize you—you're too busy. Yet you should *seem* willing to

talk and to listen to everyone. The etiquette here? Simply, keep at
it. And try, even though totally involved with others, to keep looking at the party as if from the wrong end of binoculars. It will help
you to see where you are needed most, and if you look and sound
enthusiastic, no one will notice how busy you are.

Announcing Dinner

When it is time for dinner the hostess or maid announces, "Dinner is served." People are usually ready for food by dinnertime but
tend to hang back when it is announced. After a few minutes you
might say, "Shall we begin?" and get the show on the road. Today it
is considered all right (except at a formal dinner) for a guest to take
an unfinished cocktail to table, but only if the hostess suggests it.
When wine accompanies dinner, this seems unnecessary. Half-
empty cocktail glasses don't improve the looks of the table, either.

Seating

At a seated meal, to plot out the dinner partners each guest
would most enjoy can be great fun and is vital to the success of the
evening. Since it is the only time you have complete control of those
you have brought together, make good use of the opportunity.
Draw a sketch of the table, mark off the number of places, and play
around with the guest list.

The rules of etiquette present few problems. The couple who are
guests of honor sit at the right of the host and hostess. Technically,
the guest of honor is always the woman (even if her husband has
just won the Nobel prize). Therefore, if you have two tables, one
smaller than the other, you sit at the smaller so that the woman
guest of honor will be at the "main" table.

When the party is being given for no one in particular, pre-
cedence goes to the oldest people there. Sitting at the right is
their "right of seniority." If no appreciably older people are coming, give the honor places to a couple who have never before had
dinner at your house.

If your guest list includes both bona fide guests of honor (people around whom you planned the party) *and* an older couple, you might divide the honors. Put the woman guest of honor on your husband's right and the older woman on his left. At your end of the table, if it works well with the rest of the seating plan, you might put the older man on your right and the guest of honor on your left. In any case an older woman, unless she is a close relative, should always sit on one side of the host.

With guests of honor and newcomers at the same party, the guests of honor go at the right, the newcomers at the left.

A single person, unless he or she is the reason for the party or, again, an older woman, traditionally gets the worst place. A nice way to make a single person seem special is to seat him or her next to the guest of honor of the opposite sex. If several or all of the guests are unmarried give the best seats to those whom you know least well or whom you have never entertained before.

Separate families of course, and watch out for any obvious oil-and-water mixtures among the list. Gone are the days, we keep telling ourselves, when people have uncontrollable feelings about religion or politics. But don't believe this totally; keep some distance between the girl who's a volunteer at the local Democratic Club and the man whose Republicanism shakes the rafters at unpredictable moments.

A good idea is to seat dull people together. They usually get along well with each other, feeling safer together and sometimes brightening each other up beyond your—and their—wildest hopes. Everyone at the party, and especially you, will have to make extra efforts with the dull and shy throughout the evening, but, at table particularly, do not let them become granite burdens on others.

Most of the time at a well-planned party you won't have more than one or two dull people—any more than you will have more than one or two sparklers. Most people are just pleasantly average. If a single very shy or dull person is coming, put a chatterbox next to him, or some good friend who can be counted on, at least during dinner, not to give up easily in the tiring work of "making conversation." Next time your good Samaritan comes you can repay her efforts by giving her the most entertaining dinner partners there.

While it is wise to put dull people together when possible, it can be disastrous to seat two wits cheek by jowl. Each needs an audience and will have a better time if he doesn't have to struggle for the floor. Make the most of them, your trump cards.

At a dinner of eight, twelve, or any number divisible by four, a man has to sit opposite the host to keep the man-woman-man-woman arrangement working. In this case the hostess takes the chair one place to the left of her usual one, so that the honor man at her right will be "chairman" of his end of the board. Since there is no rule of etiquette about this, the hostess could as well sit on the right side of the table if it will make the serving easier by putting her nearer kitchen or sideboard. However, the married hostess always takes the place on the side; her husband always stays at the head of the table. The unmarried hostess stays at the head and puts another woman opposite her.

When you have several small tables, you can cover only one, so when you do the seating try to place some girl who strikes you as a good hostess at each of the others. The table will "go" with her help.

Place Cards

There is no etiquette about place cards. Use them any time you feel like it. An attractive addition to a table setting, they also make the party look well planned.

At a small dinner you will probably have no trouble memorizing the seating. If you can't depend on your memory amid the other distractions, write the plan on a scrap of paper and slip it under your plate before dinner. What matters is being able to direct people accurately. "Now let's see, how am I going to do this?" as people come to table sounds as if you didn't care enough about who would enjoy whom.

A great help at any big dinner, place cards are absolutely necessary when you have more than one table. Since you will probably have a general idea where people belong, stand at the door of the dining room and direct traffic. Simpler yet, make a seating chart. On a big piece of paper, draw the tables as they stand in the dining room. Write people's names in big letters and leave the chart where they can see it easily. This will head them in the right direction.

Turning the Table

In young circles, you never see the hostess pointedly turning from the man at her right to the man at her left halfway through dinner. Dinner parties today are not so ritualized. A conversation that begins as a twosome becomes a threesome or joins the talk across the table. But the idea behind "turning the table," that everyone should have a chance to talk to both dinner partners, is a good one.

If you notice someone who looks stuck or a couple making labored conversation, that's the time to turn the table. The old-fashioned way was to turn to the man on your left and say, "Now I'm going to talk to you." He stopped talking to the girl on his left, she started with the man on hers, and the switch was on. A more subtle approach accomplishes the same thing. You have been talking to the man on your right. Now bring the woman on his right into your own conversation. They will get going together, and then you can turn to your other partner.

Interruptions during Dinner

Depending on how it is served, you may have to get up during the meal, leaving your dinner partners dangling for a few moments. Just say, "Excuse me," and get up. Do not let your dinner partners follow you, and refuse all offers of help from other men and women. They are very polite to offer, but the polite hostess, we feel, turns them down. No guest should have to work at a party. Without servants, the hosts should do all the work. When you are a guest, it is your turn to sit. This seems sensible; if we all helped at every party, there would never be a party at which anyone could enjoy being waited on and having no responsibility for the mechanics.

The telephone can be disruptive at a party. The hostess may be tempted to turn it off, but she can't, when guests have left her number with sitters or the office. When the hostess is telephoned, she should say that she will call back next day. (She'd better make a note of it, too, since her mind is on the party, not the message.)

When Dinner Is Over

After everyone has finished dessert the hostess catches the eye of one of the other women or, if she is married, signals her husband, and gets up. Everyone follows suit. When things are going swimmingly you might delay getting up for a few minutes, but don't linger too long. It slows the pace of a party—and the coffee may be getting cold.

Serving Coffee

If there is some reason for speed—if you are going on to a concert or play—coffee can be served right at table after the dessert, or even with it if the party is running late. If you are staying at home, it seems pleasanter to serve coffee away from the table.

After-dinner coffee is supposed to be served in small cups, but at a buffet supper cups of both sizes might be welcome. A thoughtful extra is to have a pot of decaffeinated coffee for guests who are kept awake by the real thing.

Separating after Dinner

The custom of separating after dinner came about because of smoking. Women didn't smoke and men "joined the ladies" when all the cigars and cigarettes were out. Nowadays many men still like time for all-male conversation and women a chance to powder their noses and put on fresh lipstick. The coffee break takes care of this nicely but is not mandatory. Separating seems artificial at a buffet supper or in a house where the dining area is part of the living room. At a small party or a family meal it's more natural for all to have coffee together.

When you decide that the men and women will separate for coffee, women can go into the living room and men can stay at the table. Or men can take the living room and women go to your bedroom.

The Men Return

If the men have coffee alone they must not be allowed to forget to join the women. At a mixed party women may enjoy half an hour or so of exclusively female companionship. But when it lasts much longer they begin to feel slighted, especially when bursts of baritone laughter echo from the inner sanctum.

You should not have to burst in and drag them out, or wave frantically from the door. One good reason for women to have coffee in the bedroom is that *they* can join the *men*. Or just before the party starts, firmly tell your husband (if you are unmarried, the man you've appointed as host), "Watch the time and join us at the first lull in conversation after half an hour. No matter if you are discussing the quantum theory or how you can make a million dollars."

The End of the Evening

This is often the best time. People have become acquainted, have discovered whom they would most like to talk to or whom they would still like a chance to know. A good hostess simply helps them by rearranging chairs, by seeing that all the women, if the men have left them after dinner, do not stay seated together. There may be many small groups, or general conversation. If the latter happens, let it. Sometimes a party gets exciting when all start giving views on a single subject, when there are debates, "speeches," or when one person spellbinds the rest with an "inside story." You cannot make this happen, though it has been tried.

A well-known hostess in New York, who had a genius for collecting interesting and famous people, ruined her parties by trying to control their talk. After dinner she would seat herself at a small table, rap a gavel (yes, really!), and announce, "Now we will have general conversation. Ambassador A (or Senator B or Judge C), we are all most interested to hear your opinion of the President's State of the Union speech." At any other time most people would be fascinated to hear A, B, or C on this subject. But not necessarily at a party. Even the speaker was given no choice, and the other guests had to be quiet until he had finished singing for his supper. Then someone else would be called on, sometimes a celebrity, but often a young unknown not particularly anxious to air half-formed opinions with experts present.

The moral of this story: a hostess controls her party subtly, not blatantly. In mid-evening she goes along with any turn in the tide, always watching out, of course, for those who seem isolated or not to be having fun. She also makes a point of speaking to guests with whom she hasn't talked earlier. She may politely leave one group by saying, "I must go over there. I haven't had a word with Tommy all evening." Or she may ask Tommy to come over to the group she is with, on the same pretext, if he would help the conversation along. "Good manners are made up of petty sacrifices," so Emerson tells us, and perhaps one of these is that hosts must avoid the temptation to talk mostly to their favorites.

When Guests Start to Leave

All of us say, "Oh no, must you? It's still early." Even if it isn't. But don't press the point. If you are really anxious for guests to stay, and they really want to, they will, but guests do have the right to leave when they think the time has come.

It's not necessary to leave the living room with the first people who go. Just get up and say "Good night, it was wonderful to see you," or whatever. If you are married, your husband might help with coats and show people to the front door or to the elevator. If you live in a house it is especially polite, when an older couple or single girl is leaving, for the host to show them to the car.

Single women should never leave alone, but if a girl has driven herself to the party there is no way of avoiding it. In a big city, even a girl who may have traveled the world over by herself should leave with an escort. If she comes with a man, naturally he takes her home (at whatever time she thinks is right, no matter how much he might want to stay). When she comes alone by bus or taxi, the hostess should ask another couple or one of the men to drop her off. If she meets a man she likes at the party—and what could be nicer?—she will probably arrange this for herself. All else failing, if you are married, your husband should at least offer to see her home. It seems an awful chore at the end of a busy evening, but the necessity comes up rarely. If it should, the girl will probably refuse the offer violently enough to make your husband feel he will ruin *her* evening if he does more than see her into a taxi.

If you are unmarried, and living alone, the man who balances you should leave with the last guests. Even though purely platonic, your relationship cannot help but appear otherwise if he lingers.

Guests Who Stay Too Late

A good party stimulates the host and hostess as it does the guests, and as the evening goes on they have more chance to relax and enjoy it. Therefore, late-staying guests seldom present problems. In fact hosts may feel let down when the last one has gone.

Other times, at even the most successful party, enough is enough, and one or two lingerers fail to realize it. (This inevitably happens on the eve of your mother's 7 A.M. arrival at the airport.)

Yawning is out at parties. Probably guests will leave before their yawns become uncontrollable, but a hostess, even at 4 A.M., must still control hers.

Examples sometimes help over difficult spots. When it's past one o'clock, you're worn out, and still the guests stay on, take a lesson from Queen Mary, who, when asked to describe royalty, once said, "We love to visit hospitals, and we are never tired." Straightening up and telling yourself, "I am *never* tired," works like a pep pill. Try it and see.

What polite steps can you take to end the party?

Step One: Do not keep refilling glasses. This usually works as effectively at home as it does in a night club when they close down the bar.

Step Two: Quiet down. At two in the morning there is no reason for you to effervesce the way you did hours earlier. Guests, sensing the party's change of pace, should recognize the signal that the evening is over.

Step Three: Now you are getting a little desperate. While you plow bravely on with the conversation, you might begin making post-party motions—emptying ashtrays, collecting glasses. This cannot be considered pointedly rude, because you are patently keeping the room attractive for the people who remain.

Step Four: So far you have said nothing to show that you think the party should end. Now it is time to speak up. Nothing you say need be rude.

Say to no one in particular, "I wonder how long I should allow to get to the airport. Mother's plane is due at seven this morning."

Or, if you are married, ask your husband, "What time is your meeting tomorrow?" Rest assured he will mention an early hour.

After remarks like these, lingerers shouldn't stay longer than it takes to snuff out their cigarettes. When they leap up and say, "Heavens, it's so late, we've got to go," let them.

A Word about Poise

No matter how well you, as hostess, cope with all this, neither our suggestions nor your decisions will make a party perfect. You will always think back on something that could have been better. When things go really wrong, as they sometimes will, roll with the punches. An overcooked roast or an unhappy mixing of guests demands a most important quality: poise.

What is poise? A manner that is unruffled, confident, relaxed. When a famous collector of porcelain, a guest having crashed his million-dollar vase on the floor, said, "Think nothing of it," he showed poise. When, a minute later, he fainted, he showed just the opposite.

Some people, born with poise, can remain imperturbable through almost anything. Others, not blessed with the gift, learn to assume it, as an actor assumes a role or a doctor his bedside manner. Say you forget something. Even with lists and well-laid plans you will occasionally. When you do, forget it again. You are not likely to omit the main elements of a party, and if you have forgotten some embellishment—crackers for the soup or cream for the dessert—it's not important. Your cry, "Heavens, I forgot . . ." shows lack of poise and calls attention to something guests will never miss.

When an emergency arises at a party, first try to ignore it. If that's not possible, attend to it quickly. If it is something you cannot fix, like a broken vase, or two guests at loggerheads, make light of it. Change the subject. Above all, poise is knowing when to speak out and when to hold your tongue. When in doubt, choose the latter.

The Uninvited Guest

It goes without saying that people with good manners do not turn up at parties uninvited. When guests ask if they may bring a friend along, and you say yes, it is especially polite to write or call the stranger and invite him personally unless it's an "open house." If your friends have not thought to ask ahead and just walk in with someone, no matter how you feel, greet the unexpected guest with enthusiasm. It is hard to believe that someone would bring an uninvited guest to a dinner, but it's been known to happen. When it does, the hostess either invites him to stay or, if there is not enough room or food, says frankly, "We'd love you to stay, but I'm terribly sorry, there just isn't enough food, or room at table. Please come back another time."

Gate crashers occasionally turn up at cocktail parties and dances in big cities. When this happens the host should go up to the crasher and say in his most polite tone, "Sorry, but this is a private party." There is absolutely no reason to allow a stranger to stay, and a firm but gentle approach from the host or some other man usually works.

The Role of the Host

Beyond the things already mentioned, what should a wife expect from her husband when she gives a party? In one sentence: a lot of moral support and very little work. She should expect enthusiasm and interest in the guest list and menu. His spirit will influence hers, and it won't be a good party without involvement on his part. She should consult him and conform somewhat to his ideas. If he turns thumbs down on friends she thought of inviting, she should go along with him to some extent. People often see their friends in very different lights. While a husband's lack of enthusiasm about a particular couple seems mistaken, it may still be better to leave them out than for him to feel hopeless about their fitting in.

When it comes to the menu, a wife shouldn't give in too easily. If her husband hates a generally accepted dish, she can include it every so often. But if he makes a pronouncement such as "No men like artichokes," it's best to save them for a women's luncheon, so that he will enjoy the prospect of the party.

Before the party, husbands can help in the brawn department, too. Carrying heavy trays, moving furniture, and laying fires are man's work. But a wife should expect little else. She really should see that rugs are vacuumed and tables polished. If her husband offers to help out, that's wonderful. If he doesn't, it's all right. A party, for him, should not be the end result of hours of housework.

When the party begins, the host helps the hostess to get the party mixed, makes introductions, and concentrates on the needs of all the guests. He makes cocktails and refills, and he might also pass appetizers and light women's cigarettes if he has a chance. If men but knew the hit this makes! At dinner, he should carve if necessary, and pour the wine.

Beyond these specific things—when the party is indoors—a husband should not be asked to do anything except in emergencies. It comes down to this: men look ridiculous doing women's work, and wives look rather charming playing second fiddle to husbands. What a wife gets him to do at other times is her business, but at parties, we say let him be half guest, half baronial lord. He looks better that way, and will act better too. His manners as a person, not as a functionary, count.

No wife should expect her husband to smile on flaws in service or the looks of the house. While he may have saintly forgiveness at other times, he wants things *right* at a party. This is for his own self-esteem, but it is also for hers. Men love their wives to do well and are usually free with praise.

If you are unmarried and appoint a bachelor to act as host, you should expect only help with drinks and general politeness to all. Don't expect him to carve and carry trays all evening. If a married man will be there it would be better to ask him to help you. He may be better at it, and it's better to avoid giving the impression, especially if you live alone, that the bachelor has the run of the place, even when your family is there. Especially when your family is there. When parents come for dinner and you ask a beau to make it a foursome, let your father be the host.

For a single young woman who lives alone the rules of etiquette have relaxed. She can now make up her own mind about entertaining, or being entertained by, a single man at home alone. The decision of course rests on the particular girl and the particular man, but we feel that "Avoid the appearance of evil" is still a good rule to follow—for the girl's reputation both in the eyes of the man in question and in the eyes of others.

CHAPTER 12

Being a Good Guest

Everything the polite guest should do is summed up in one word: co-operate. Hosts hope the party will give the guests pleasure. Guests respond by fitting in.

Being punctual comes first. From all parts of the country we hear complaints about lateness. Each year people grow more casual about arriving on time, which doesn't matter much at cocktail parties but is bad at dinners. Some hostesses report that the wait before dinner lasts as long as two hours, since they want to give every guest time for a drink and a chance to meet people. When people arrive—and many do—at eight or after for a seven o'clock party, this means planning dinner for nine, especially if the meal needs careful timing. It has been suggested that we should say, "Come any time after seven. We're eating at eight." Or in writing: "7:30 for 8:15" or "for" whatever hour we have planned to serve. It's not a bad idea. If enough of us stuck to our guns and served food at the stated time the trend might be reversed.

Until it does the good guest should try to be on time. If you know that an invitation for seven o'clock really means seven-thirty, well and good. But if you are in doubt, be punctual. When you know you are going to be late because of some emergency, telephone so that the hostess can adjust her cooking schedule and not worry that you may have forgotten.

Remembering names, when introduced, is a plus. People seldom fail to *hear* names, they fail to *listen* to them. Careful listeners get most of them, most of the time.

Talking to someone whose name they have missed embarrasses some people needlessly. "I'm so sorry, but I didn't hear your name" takes care of it. It's a help to the hostess to reintroduce yourself to strangers and to those you have met elsewhere who may have forgotten your name. Since you know them, probably they know you. But a person who really doesn't remember will bless you for repeating your name without being asked.

Helping the hostess. Especially at the start of a party the good guests think of this. While "taking one's social responsibility" sounds Victorian, it only means: help the hostess to make the party go by talking to strangers or to people who are momentarily alone. Hard as she tries, the hostess cannot be in more than one place at one time and will be grateful to guests who try to cover for her.

If you happen to be shy, helping to put others at ease is even more important; you'll forget yourself.

Following leads makes things easy. When dinner is announced, don't dawdle. Get up and go to the buffet or table. If it's a seated dinner try to find your place or wait for the hostess to direct you to it. (If a hostess hasn't thought out the seating beforehand a guest should not help her with it—even though he sees at a glance where everyone should fall in—because it will look as if he is trying to take over.)

Good Table Manners

The reason for good table manners is aesthetic: to make people look as attractive as possible when eating. Some of the finer points confuse people. Just for the record, here are our answers to the questions we most often hear:

Q: When should guests begin eating?

A: At a very small dinner they should wait until everyone is served, unless the hosts urge them to begin right away because food may get cold. At a seated dinner of ten or more they start as soon as those next to them have been served. At a buffet supper served at tables seating four or six people, wait until one or two others have sat down, not necessarily until the table is filled. At a buffet supper eaten on laps, everyone begins as soon as he finds a place to sit.

Q: What is the etiquette about drinking soup?

A: Soup is most often spooned with a backhand motion, and the soup plate tipped away from the drinker. Both gestures help to prevent spilling. Any soup served in a cup with handles may be drunk right from the cup.

When soup is finished the spoon is left *in* the soup bowl or *on* the saucer that goes under a soup cup.

Q: When are napkins completely unfolded, and when not?

A: At a luncheon napkins are completely unfolded. Dinner napkins, usually big linen squares, come folded in threes or fours and then are folded again to look pretty on the place plate. To keep them from slipping off laps, they are not completely unfolded, just opened out. A dinner napkin used at a supper eaten on laps might be completely unfolded to protect clothes and furniture.

At the end of the meal napkins are left as they are, not refolded, probably because refolding them might imply you expect them to be used again.

We would add, for women: try to control lipstick. Our generation copes with lipstick much better than our mothers'; many of us can finish a dinner with lipstick intact, especially if it's well blotted when first put on. Some lipstick always gets on the napkin, but the whole thing shouldn't be covered with red smudges.

Q: When is bread broken and when eaten whole?

A: Dinner rolls and slices of bread should be broken and buttered, one piece at a time. Biscuits or small triangles of bread, already buttered, may be broken or not, as you please. A small piece of bread can be used as a pusher, and eyebrows are no longer raised when bread, again in small pieces, is used to sop up gravy, as long as this is done with fork, not fingers.

Q: What is the correct way to get rid of bones in the month?

A: They are removed from the mouth by hand. Gristle and chewed food are removed by the fork; fruit pits, by the spoon.

Q: What is the correct way to eat asparagus, artichokes, corn on the cob, salad?

A: Begin asparagus with a fork, but it's all right to switch to fingers for the tougher ends of the stalks, unless they are dripping with sauce. Begin artichokes with the fingers, and use knife and fork for the heart. Eating corn on the cob is a totally hand-to-mouth operation. Butter only a couple of rows at a time and eat slowly.

Some people, men especially, run their teeth across the rows, munching for dear life, their hands acting like a conveyor belt to a grinding machine.

In most cases using only a fork for salad is possible, but it is now considered good manners, thank heavens, to use a knife for big or tough pieces. Hearts of lettuce make a knife essential, and the hostess will have knives when she serves salad cut this way.

Q: Why should you lay both spoons and forks for dessert?

A: Because it is a matter of convenience. People take their choice, or use both, as they probably would when eating ice cream and cake or a compote of whole fruit—spearing the fruit with the fork, cutting off pieces, and eating them with the spoon.

Q: People used to be taught to leave some food on the plate, but plates completely cleaned are often seen at parties. What is the etiquette here?

A: It is now correct to eat everything, but don't take more food than you think you can eat. It still is not considered good manners to take the last portion from the serving platter.

Q: What about putting elbows on the table?

A: We were all taught not to, but people do, and when a person is leaning across to speak to someone, or has finished eating, it looks comfortable and relaxed, as long as the person doesn't slump, or prop head in hand. Elbows stay off the table while eating, and the hand that isn't at work stays in the lap.

Q: What should I do with my handbag?

A: Leave it in the bedroom. Handbags lying all over the living room don't look very pretty, and since you comb hair and refresh make-up in the bedroom or bathroom, all you need in the living room is your handkerchief and, if you smoke, cigarettes. In a restaurant your handbag goes in your lap, on the chair or the floor, never on the table.

A guest who has doubts about eating etiquette can always watch what the host and hostess are doing. Their manners may not be perfect, but he won't offend if he copies them at their party. Such questions as which fork and knife to use present no problems if the table is set correctly. (See Chapter 4 for table setting.)

Some foods are trickier to eat than others, but none is very complicated if people take time to look it over and work out a neat approach. Food is there to be eaten, and a neat pile of bones on an empty plate is a pretty sight, to the eyes of the hostess.

The neatest approach to a small whole bird is to slice off the breast on one side, then cut off the wing, second joint, and drumstick. Any properly cooked bird carves and disjoints easily. It's polite to eat small wings and drumsticks with the fingers.

Fish vary greatly, but there is usually a main bone that can be taken out in one piece, and a pattern of small bones, which can be scraped away with knife and fork. With shellfish, the shell is held in one hand and the meat removed with a fork. Even a lobster can be eaten neatly if the big pieces of meat are removed intact and then cut up on the plate.

The Big Appetite and the Small

Need we say, moderation is part of good manners. If a favorite dish comes along, waiting for a second helping is more attractive than piling the plate at first. It's always polite to take a little helping of food you don't like and push it around the plate—a ploy as old as the first dinner party. If you are on a diet, no one minds if you say "No, thanks," to appetizers, bread, and potatoes. But don't sit with an empty plate, however fattening the menu. The implied "Look at me and my will power" may depress your dinner partners who want to enjoy the dinner *and* the calories.

Good Drinking Manners

Most hosts provide the mixings of standard drinks, but they shouldn't have to fill orders for unusual ones. A host who has prepared for whisky sours, Bloody Marys, or mint juleps will tell you so, and hope you'll take one.

At dinner, the good guest lets wine be poured in his glass only if he is going to drink it, and takes only as much as he thinks he will drink, indicating with a word or gesture when enough has been poured in the glass.

After the host has poured a small amount into his own glass and tasted it to see that it's all right, he fills the glasses of the women on either side and then goes on around the table, or asks one of the nearby men to pass the bottle around without getting up. People may start drinking wine as soon as those on either side of them have been offered some.

Before and after dinner and even at table, if there are coasters, *use them*. The hostess can only once, politely, put down a coaster and set the glass on it. Often people then put the glass to one side and use the coaster for cigarettes, olive pits, and toothpicks. Until we have coasters lettered, "This is a coaster; please use it!" guests should remember, or use cocktail napkins or their handkerchiefs to protect table tops.

It should go without saying that drinking too much is the end, as far as manners go. It is usually the end, too, of repeat invitations. People who have a drink or two can be more relaxed and extroverted, and this always helps the spirit of a party. But people who overdo are merely boring to the other guests and a trial to the hosts. Good guests know how much they can drink and *still be* good guests. They stop drinking when they near that point.

Good Smoking Manners

Every hostess expects people to smoke and puts cigarettes around. Pipe smokers today are welcome in mixed company, as is the rare cigar smoker. It still looks wrong to take a lighted cigarette to the table and to smoke straight through the meal. The true "chimney" should try to wait for his cigarette until after the meat course.

Again, neatness counts. If no ashtray is handy, smokers should ask for one, or go find one. They should watch the ashes and be careful where they put down a lighted cigarette. Pipe smokers should avoid spilling tobacco while filling or emptying their pipes. While we're at it, let's try to put an end to throwing matches and cigarettes into the fireplace. If the fireplace is empty, or laid just for looks, it is a terrible job to pick out the debris.

Basic Politeness at Dinner

The co-operative guest talks to everyone and looks as if he were enjoying it. If you run into someone you just don't like, perhaps you can dodge him before and after dinner, but if seated beside him try to act happy. Even if he does not respond to your best efforts (which isn't likely to happen), try to make a go of it.

During dinner conversation, guests should bring in a person nearby who is talking to no one. It is wrong to speak across a third person at any time, but especially at a seated dinner, because he cannot leave to look for more congenial company. This seems rudimentary, but we have often seen two women gabbling across a silent man, or two men talking shop over the head of a beautiful girl.

Also rudimentary, but worth mentioning because it *does* sometimes happen: at parties, husbands and wives should never discuss private problems, particularly when there is difference of opinion. Nothing disturbs others more than being pulled into, or even overhearing, a family squabble. If you run into one, try to change the subject. Failing that, get up and move. This works like cold water on angry dogs.

Another of our peeves is the guest who gives orders to the helper of the hostess. It is one thing when a maid asks if he would care for this or that, but another if he gives instructions or asks for something not in evidence. When the hosts' maid is your own regular party helper, it may seem unnatural not to ask her. But she does belong to *them* during *their* party.

Guests often cause telephone trouble. Many people, magnetically attracted to telephones, ask "Where's the telephone?" when they first arrive, and disappear for twenty minutes. When a guest must telephone he should keep the call short and make it from the bedroom or kitchen if possible so as not to inhibit other people's conversations.

A thoughtful hostess has a clean pad with pencil and an ashtray beside the guests' phone. A guest, on making a long-distance call, should ask for the charges and leave the money by the telephone without mentioning it. If it's mentioned the hosts will try to refuse it, which they shouldn't have to do.

The Good Guest after Dinner

After dinner you should try to talk to people you've missed earlier. Let the hostess draw you into different groups. She will do this only if she has a good reason—realizing you are not happy where you are, or needing you somewhere else in the room. It is bad manners for two guests to go off in a corner for an "exclusive little talk," particularly if both are of the same sex. The hostess will be grateful if you try to break it up.

If the subject of games comes up, be as co-operative as possible. A hostess senses when playing a game is a sound idea and won't press the point if her suggestion falls flat. But if most of the group is enthusiastic, always join in, unless it is a game in which not knowing the rules would ruin it for others. In this case it is *more* co-operative to say, "Sorry, I don't play." There is no fear of being left to your own devices; the hostess will never let this happen.

Perhaps someone plays guitar or piano. The hostess might ask him to play after dinner, but only if he *and* the other guests are willing. Everyone will enjoy a few numbers. The player should stop when he feels like it, and the other guests should not be expected to listen all evening. If the hostess is lucky enough to know someone who likes to play background music, singers and willing listeners can gather around him, while others go on talking at the other end of the room.

When to Leave?

At a luncheon, present rules are fairly stringent. It is right to leave twenty minutes to half an hour after the meal, and wrong to stay more than an hour, the supposition being that the hosts have afternoon plans which should not be thrown off by lingerers.

At evening parties it used to be that guests of honor—if any—left first and the rest followed shortly. But today it is more natural to do whatever suits you, with an emphasis on politeness.

If you should *have* to leave the moment dinner is over, tell the hostess earlier in the evening and slip out without calling attention by saying good-by. If you have to leave in mid-evening, say good night to the hosts, and also to any V.I.P. or older person there, mentioning why you have to leave early. Saying good-by to everyone else may break up the party.

When the clock passes midnight at a dinner party that started at seven or eight, the party may be picking up or it may be slowing down. It's not hard to sense the difference. If it is picking up, stay as long as you feel in the mood. If it is slowing down, go.

Perhaps this bears repeating: having decided to leave, leave. Don't keep host and hostess lingering in the hall listening to effusive thanks, especially when other guests are still in the living room. "Thank you very much, we had a wonderful evening," is enough for now.

Thanking the Hostess

The day after the party, or within a few days, try to say thank you again. We say "try" because we realize that it is often hard to find time to go to a party, much less follow up with special thanks. But a short letter, a few words on your visiting card ("Mary, it was wonderful! Thank you from us both"), or a telephone call takes very little time. Most important of all, it is the hostess' great reward. Somehow, even though she could see what fun you had, hearing from you later makes her feel good. Whether you had the time of your life or just a pleasant evening, thanking is polite. If the party was a frost, the hostess knows it and will not be comforted by gushing protestations. But you can still applaud the food, the flowers, or her.

In Praise of Plain Talk

We all want to put best foot forward at parties. Manners and rules of etiquette help, because they come mostly from a common-sense approach to living with one another. But sometimes, in trying hard to be polite, people overdo, become artificial. This is almost as bad as no manners, destroying the give-and-take needed for good parties.

Examples? The quirked little finger, the self-conscious facial expression, the artificial accent or tone of voice. And especially the use of words.

There are some words that are considered nicer to use than others. Classic examples are "curtains" or "draperies" instead of "drapes," "evening dress" instead of "formal," "dinner jacket" or "black tie" instead of "tuxedo." Though a speaker begins with "Ladies and Gentlemen" and we say "Ladies' Room" and "Ladies' Day" at the golf club or ball park, and though no man objects to being called "an officer and a gentleman," the experts say that ladies should be called women and gentlemen men. In conversation, at least. We are also supposed to say, "Please come to my *house* for dinner," and never "The Browns have a lovely *home*."

Is there some sense in these preferences? Yes. Perhaps it is gilding the lily to call a woman a lady and a man a gentleman, because it is unnecessary. Perhaps "home" is bad usage because a *house* is where you live and a *home* is what your house becomes through your spirit and values. To say "Let's go home" is approved because you are not really referring to the bricks and mortar.

"Wealthy" and "drapes" are taboo possibly because "rich" and "curtains" are simpler—a matter of calling a spade a spade. Words considered good usage are those that are simple, straightforward, and not spoken out of a desire to impress.

The use of foreign words is an even better illustration. "Serviette" and "boudoir" are bad because they are French words for which perfectly good English ones ("napkin" and "dressing room") exist. Many French words are members in good standing of American and English vocabularies because we took them over and haven't come up with our own substitutes: garage, chauffeur, valet, maître d'hôtel (not mayter-dee!). Some French words we say exactly as pronounced in French: *crème brûlée, soufflé*, Camembert, Port de Salut. But since others have become so Anglicized it sounds stilted to pronounce them the way you would in Paris: we say "foy-err" or "foy-ay" for the Parisian's "fwa-yay." Charles Boyer understands this.

Because languages are constantly evolving and there is no over-all rule to count on, our suggestion for use of English is this: conform to the best local usage. For using foreign words: *don't*, unless absolutely necessary, or you'll seem as ludicrous as the social-climbing "lady and gentleman" who asked people over for "potluck, *chez nous*." When you must use foreign words, do say them as pronounced in America. If people are linguists their friends know it, and it's ridiculous to say *"succès fou"* and *"quelle horreur,"* when "wild success" and "how horrible" serve the purpose. Most genuine linguists stick to one language at a time.

The Virtues of Imitation for Both Hosts and Guests

Imitation, reputedly the sincerest form of flattery, is also the best way to develop party prowess and good manners. When someone puts on a great party, try to analyze what made it so. The people? The dinner? A perfect host and hostess? We should always do things our own way, but we can become more versatile by borrowing ideas and adapting them.

This is especially true of manners. Even though we always keep manners in mind there may be room for improvement. In your town, perhaps there is a woman whom you particularly admire for her manners. Copy her courtesies to others, her dignity, her ready smile, her patience, her posture. These attributes, and many others, can be imitated naturally. And there is always room for one more like her!

CHAPTER 13

Dressing for Parties

Being correctly dressed at work, at home, at parties is important to you; it makes you feel better and act better. At a party your good appearance is also important to everyone else. It is a politeness to your hosts, showing that their party means something to you. Looking your best also affects your relationship with other guests. Among those you meet may be some who have the time and inclination to discover the real you that lies beneath your looks. But most people don't. They form their impressions of the outer you from your manners, your face and hair, your clothes, your look. What they think of you, especially at first, is greatly influenced by what they see, even though you have marvelous inner qualities.

Dressing in Fashion

Looking your best at parties means, to some extent, looking your up-to-date best, wearing the best that fashion produces for you— clothes that are simple, unstartling, but contemporary and beautiful. Luckily, today, every woman can find something becoming at a price she wants to pay. Some women who are always fashionably dressed at parties buy only inexpensive clothes, imaginatively put together. Others buy few new things in a given season but always look up to date by the way they adjust what they have to a new turn in fashion: adding a newly popular accessory, "this year's" hat or shoes, or altering hems. (Everyone's eye, including men's, becomes quickly accustomed to the "new" length, and nothing looks dowdier than "last year's" hemline, if there has been a change.)

Wearing the Right Dress to Parties

Be *appropriately* dressed for each occasion. No matter how fashionable, you don't want to be the sore thumb at parties. Study the prevailing currents of dressiness in the community for each sort of party. With a when-in-Rome attitude you cannot go far wrong.

In most communities daytime party clothes are the same: for a luncheon or tea, a simple dress or suit, in a material appropriate to the climate. But later in the day there is more variety around the country in degrees of dressiness. In some places elegant fabrics appear earlier in the day and are worn more often to little parties.

Keeping an Open Mind

Whatever the local party clothes customs are, it is best to follow them, but not at a total sacrifice of your likes and dislikes and your feeling for individuality. Keep an open mind about color, fashion changes, and the look you have adopted as your own. It is very difficult to see yourself as others see you. It is even more difficult to see the possibilities in a change in look, but you can experiment at your favorite stores.

By the time a girl is eighteen she is pretty certain what she dislikes and what doesn't look well on her. But if you never try a new line, never buy this material or that color, it's time for re-evaluation. When you are out after something different, take along a friend who will give a frank opinion. Or, if you are married, get help from your husband. Few husbands willingly shop for dresses, but perhaps you can do the groundwork and then get him into the store to approve the final choices. Or bring home the new-you dress; if he moans, return it next day.

Every woman should consider the clothes likes and dislikes of the man in her life. Some men have good taste, some do not. Most, alas, take to a fashion change only when they get good and used to it. But if you buy something a man can't stand, it will rarely leave the closet; if you buy something he compliments, you will wear it to shreds, even if you yourself are not so sure it's right.

Dressing Your Age

We see twenty-five-year-olds at parties dressed as if they were forty, thirty-year-olds who think they are still nineteen, and women of any age who dress *old*, by default. They can't look at themselves objectively—hard to do, but possible—and don't realize that they have a long way to go before they need stop trying to look young, up to date, and attractive.

Dressing with Taste

Most women understand the elements of what we call *safe* taste —unstartling colors, good materials, plain cut—but that's not necessarily knowing the art of dressing well, which is good taste: a balance between the drab and the dramatic, the trite and the becoming original. Good taste certainly involves a form of simplicity; a dress may be cloth of gold or embroidered with pearls, but the cut can be uncontrived, really unnoticeable, or noticeable only *after* you see the wearer. A dress in good taste can be any color or combination of colors—even an unlikely one—as long as it suits the wearer. As one Paris designer has said, no mistakes are possible if you stick to black, white, and red. But it's not bad taste to wear purple with yellow, or pink with orange. Good taste also involves understatement, which is not quite the same as simplicity. Matching shoes, bag, and gloves might be simplicity but not understatement. An elusive thing, it comes from being able to decide between what adds character or only clutter, in knowing what to omit, what not to add. The unusual belt, the outsize pin, the novel shoe shape may be in fashion and in good taste by themselves, but as part of a whole look they can be overdone. And that's bad taste.

Figure and Fit

These are basic considerations. No dress, however well designed, becoming in color, and tasteful, is going to look right if it doesn't suit your figure or fit correctly. Have alterations made when you buy a dress, and if they aren't right keep going back until they are. Or learn to tackle them at home. The essentials of fit are simple: a neckline that stays in place, shoulders that don't pull, a back without wrinkles, straight seams, skirts that aren't too loose or too tight, so that they ride up or bind when you walk.

When altering, it's unwise for one to make basic changes in a dress. Superficial ones, such as discarding a self-belt for a leather one, or sewing on handsomer buttons, often improve things, but don't tamper with the designer's intention by chopping off sleeves or taking inches out of a skirt. The end result may be a hodgepodge.

Poor posture is the worst figure fault. There isn't a designer in the world with the genius to disguise it. Breaking a bad posture habit is do-it-yourself work. For inspiration, there is this: poor posture only makes other figure problems look worse; the heavy bust looks more so if you stoop in a futile effort to cover it up. A plump tummy sticks out more if you bend from the waist and let shoulders fall forward.

When You Aren't Sure What to Wear

Hostesses usually give a clue when they give the invitation. If you're in doubt about what to wear, even though you have been to the house a hundred times, call and check. Or, if you don't want to telephone, try to remember back to the last party at that particular house. Or try to think what the hostess usually wears when she comes to yours. When still in doubt, underdress. You will he happier; no one feels as comfortable overdressed as she does slightly underdressed, except at a formal party.

At parties to which men wear black tie, a short dress in an evening material is almost certain to be right, no matter where the party or who gives it. In some circles and some years long dinner dresses are routine, or worn just as often as short ones.

However simple and sure this all sounds, if a night comes when you make the wrong choice, forget it. Forget yourself and enjoy the party.

How a Hostess Should Dress

Whether it is an outdoor barbecue or a dress-to-the-nines dinner, the clothes of the hostess help to set the tone of the party.

At a luncheon the hostess should wear a simple dress. Suits are all right, too, but seem better for going out than staying in. If your best lunchtime choice is a suit, you might wear it without a blouse and button up the jacket so that it looks all of a piece. Or if you wear a blouse you might leave off the jacket, or take it off before you eat. The idea is to look *at home*. For a Sunday or holiday luncheon the hostess might wear a dress of wool or linen, depending on the season, but a dressed-down silk would be fine too, as long as the cut is simple and covered.

At a tea, the same applies. A tea should be a dressed-down occasion, but because it is later in the day the hostess would be right to wear a dress of some silky material, such as jersey or crepe, perhaps, but not velvet, damask, or any other specifically late-day fabric. She might wear one good piece of jewelry—a clip or necklace—plus earrings, but not jewelry that she would wear at a cocktail party or later.

A *small dinner or buffet supper* suggests these choices to the hostess: a cocktail dress or something in a dressy material with a distinctly evening look—neckline or back lower than one would wear in the afternoon. It should be a dress that looks especially well in your own setting. Why wear Kelly green when your living room is a mixture of subtler green shades?

Other choices for dinners at home are, not surprisingly, at-home clothes. Many a hostess knows the joy—in look and comfort—of the long skirt with blouse or the one-piece tea gown, as our mothers called it. These clothes are easy to move in—important for a hostess who must be in constant motion in the living room and kitchen.

Black-tie dinners and dances. Since these are specifically dressed-up occasions, the hostess should dress as she would for another person's party. At a dance she wears her very best evening dress. For a black-tie dinner at which she will help serve the food she might wear her prettiest (but easy-to-manage) at-home outfit.

At a formal party, that night when a V.I.P. comes to dinner, the hostess' uniform is the most beautiful evening dress she has, preferably full length, and her best jewelry.

Economical Dressing for Parties

The first suggestion: don't buy a dress the day before a party. You might in haste choose something not quite right. It's new, so you think it will do. That's a non sequitur. While it may "do" for the party at hand, it rarely "does" again, and a not-quite-right dress is simply wrong, an expensive mistake that could wreck the clothes budget for a year.

The most economical way to be always well dressed for parties is to make a list twice a year of what you have and what you think needs replacing. Do this six weeks or so before the end of a season to prevent impulse buying at the first change in the weather. Most of us need few new clothes at one time. The maximum might be a nice dress for afternoon parties and small dinners, plus one daytime suit or dress, for church, Sunday lunches, or meetings, which is better than your everyday clothes. If it's a dressy community you may need something new for dress-up dinners; or, if it's not, perhaps new separates for supper parties, indoors or out.

Think hard before deciding whether there is a gap in your wardrobe. Every woman wants new party clothes, but a realistic closet canvass may prove that all you need, for practical reasons, is a new pair of pumps, and they might be enough to provide that nice sense of starting a season with something new.

The next step is to shop. Go when you have time and the determination not to buy something that isn't what you need, just because it's there and it's pretty. If you don't need new separates, steer clear of separates departments. There's nothing wrong with separates from the fashion standpoint, but if the point is economy, they can trap you. Thinking, "Oh, this blouse is only eleven dollars, so I may as well get it," or, "Here's a party skirt for twenty-five that looks like a hundred," can make separates, separately not very expensive, come to a total that could prevent buying a party dress next time you need one. On the other hand, separates carefully chosen with a plan can give you great variety.

Accessories

The very word "accessories" seems to imply "lots of," and "lots of" always means dollars. To be well dressed for parties you should have the right accessories, but they need not always be expensive, nor do you need many.

The well-made shoe and bag, the spotless glove, the carefully chosen clip or earrings, are important; even the most expensive costume suffers without them. The economical solution is always to watch for what you need, resist buying on impulse, and limit yourself to things simple enough to go with many outfits. Become a collector. It's possible because accessories do not change as fast as other fashions. It is better to have one beautiful beaded evening bag that goes with everything than a whole drawer of rayon satin envelopes. A fifty-dollar leather bag that you will carry proudly for three years is better than a ten-dollar one that can look worn after a month or two.

In city life gloves are the finishing touch. Have a couple of pairs of good gloves for daytime (black, gray, or brown suede or leather), to wear on special occasions. For afternoon and evening, build a collection of white kid or washable doeskin in different lengths. Since they must be spotless, white kid gloves involve endless cleaning expense, but there is some comfort in summer, when washable white cotton is correct with almost everything, day and evening.

Time was when women (and men, too) always wore gloves at evening parties and on the dance floor as a point of etiquette. For better or worse, this custom has gone out. But women who look well turned out still wear gloves for formal dances. Rings or bracelets should never be worn outside a glove, and no one should smoke or drink with a gloved hand.

Jewelry is never *economical* but has *economics* of its own: real or fake, it's a loss unless it goes with most of your party clothes. When buying costume jewelry, choose only well-made, fairly expensive pieces, not because you are trying to pretend they are real, but to be sure that they will retain freshness after months of wearing. Good costume jewelry can usually be cleaned easily.

Pearls are always a good buy. An inexpensive fake string with a simple clasp can be indistinguishable from a better one. But count on replacing cheap pearls every so often—if worn constantly, they can look "tired" fairly fast. The alternatives are to buy an *expensive* fake necklace (each strand may be ten dollars or more) or to save up for cultured pearls. Since these last forever, pick a shade that is becoming to your skin.

Taking Care of Party Clothes

Cleaning. For keeping party clothes up to the mark, your best friend is a good dry cleaner. Top-quality dry cleaning is expensive, but with party clothes it's senseless to look for bargains. When a dress is returned limp and old-looking, from a dollar job at Kwickie Kleeners, you may have lost the whole price of the dress. Or you will think twice about wearing it again to a party. A whacking five or ten dollars to keep a good dress new-looking is a sound investment.

Things should be cleaned only when absolutely necessary—not just because of the cost but because many materials, especially fragile evening ones, lose a little of their body each time they are cleaned.

If you return from a party with a couple of small spots on the dress you may be able to get them out with a favorite cleaning fluid or French chalk. If you are uncertain, don't tamper; you might permanently discolor the material. It's better to call the dry cleaner. Pin a note on the dress telling what caused the spots, as far as you know. Different stains are often attacked differently. You can probably handle smudges of dust around the hem or shoulders of a dress, by following the directions that come with the cleaning fluid and working gently. Never worry about a little dirt on the hem of a long dress. If there is no other soil, wear the dress one more time; hem smudges are rarely noticeable after a long dress is on.

Pressing. Press clothes as little as possible. Many materials hang out beautifully between wearings. You may erase wrinkles in other materials by hanging them on the shower rod, turning on the hot faucet in the tub, closing the door, and giving them a good steam. (Allow a few hours for them to dry out.)

When you have to press, be as light-handed as possible. Use a pressing cloth (dampened, if necessary), and always iron on the wrong side of the dress. Be especially gentle around the hem to avoid its showing in a ridge around the outside of the skirt. Send such things as a knife-pleated skirt or a ruffled blouse, which seem beyond amateur capacities, to a pro *before* you tackle them. It's much easier for the cleaner if he does not have to begin by pressing out your mistakes.

The closet. No party clothes are helped by being jammed together with everyday things. If you have an unused closet somewhere, use it for your party clothes, or use plastic dress bags, which will keep them clean and unwrinkled as things worn more often go in and out of the closet. If you have a long evening dress that is worn only once or twice a year, it may best be kept in a box, since it will inevitably lose some freshness just hanging month after month, especially if it is organdy or another delicate material, or jersey or chiffon, which sags if hung for long stretches.

Keep the closet fresh. After a long evening at a smoke-filled party, hang your dress outside the closet until morning—or longer if it still smells of smoke. If you should notice that the closet smells smoky or dank the time has come to take out everything, air clothes and closet, and spray the latter with a deodorizing mist. Sachets can be a help too. Spicy ones are ideal for closets.

Try to take care of each party clothes problem as it comes up. Don't let food stains sink in any longer than necessary. When a hem, a snap, or a button is loose try to sew it right away. Repair needlework is boring, but prompt care is good for clothes, and you'll be ready for any party at any time, without hectic last-minute repairs. You can go to a party in a wondrous construction of hidden safety pins, but you won't feel your best if you do.

Men's Party Clothes

Never let it be thought that men care less than women about looking well. Have you ever watched a man pick out his morning tie or heard him ask, "I think these new socks look terrific with this suit, don't you?" Have you ever complimented men on their clothes at a party? They beam like debutantes. They are interested in how they look all the time, except when puttering in backyard privacy or on those Sundays when they take a holiday from shaving and make a wife wonder whether that spectacle reading the sports news could possibly be the man she loves.

Since this is a women's book, let's throw a bouquet at ourselves and say that an important prop of the well-dressed man is a good wife who attends to his laundry and pressing. Regularly. She may do it in the house or send it out, but he always has at least one pressed suit, one pressed pair of slacks, and several sets of clean linen—shirts, underwear, and handkerchiefs. Bachelors seem to cope nicely with their clothes, how we do not know. It's the saintly wife who checks her husband's closet once a week. Why go looking for trouble? But as husbands call only as they rush out the door that this or that needs attention, most wives become part-time valets by default.

A man is in fine shape for parties with only a few clothes. His mainstay is a good dark suit, navy blue or very dark gray, which is right for almost any party. He also needs one "best" pair of slacks, not worn to mow the lawn, and one or two fairly new odd jackets. If he has only one, it should be lightweight wool that will do for all seasons. With two, one could be winter tweed and the other a cool cotton madras, plain linen, or denim. If he lives in or near a big city he also needs a dinner suit. Black and midnight blue are the standard colors, considered better taste than the bright or patterned jacket materials sometimes seen. With one or two good white shirts, one pair of fairly new black oxfords, and patent-leather shoes or opera pumps for his dinner clothes, he is all set. In the past, evening shirts were always starched, but today a soft cotton shirt with pleated front, a plain silk shirt, or an everyday white shirt (not button-down) is suitable.

For cocktail parties, buffet suppers, or informal dinners a man should wear his good dark suit. For midday parties indoors, slacks and an odd jacket are usually right except for big-city or holiday luncheons. For an outdoor party it's best for man to wear the same thing—slacks, sport coat, shirt, and tie, unless he knows for sure that old Levi's and an open-necked shirt are the approved uniform. Ar-

riving at a party where everyone turns out to be dressed in garden-
ing clothes, a man can always take off his tie, roll up shirtsleeves,
and leave his jacket in the car.

We have noticed a trend among men—even some who otherwise
dress like bankers—to wear patched-elbow sport jackets, sloppy
sweaters, or worn-down moccasins to country parties. It's as if they
thought: "I'm so well dressed at other times that I can come as a
scarecrow to cookouts." They *can*, but they are getting away with
murder. While we can give a *little* on aesthetic points, the messy
look, plus hair emerging from a man's collar, and socks crumpled
around his ankles, are not appealing at parties—or anywhere else.

A man should wear what matches the woman's clothes in degree
of dressiness. If the woman wears a late-day dress, the man wears
his good dark suit, not slacks and a fuzzy tweed jacket. When at a
country lunch she wears a simple day dress or suit, he wears slacks
and tweed jacket, not a short-sleeved polo shirt. This seems obvious
but we often see couples looking as if they were going to different
parties instead of the same one.

Our last word on dressing has nothing to do with parties per se,
but we think married women should dress for dinner every night.
"Horrors," you say. "After the days I put in?" Yes, you should dress
for dinner every night except when children are sick or an emergency arises. Dinner at home with your husband is not the same as
a single girl's restaurant date, but there is a little ceremony to it.
The chat before dinner with or without a drink, watching the news
on TV, or reading with the children, followed by a good meal, is
modest ceremony to be sure, but it can be vastly improved by how
you look. "Dressing" need only be putting on a fresh blouse or a
negligee, or changing from wrinkled pants to a pretty skirt, plus
fresh lipstick and a squirt of cologne. This will cheer *you* up, which
can make a great difference to a man who has no doubt put in
quite a day himself. Never think a husband doesn't notice. He
may not seem to see and may never comment, but in his mind's
eye rests an *impression* of some sort. It might as well be a good
one.

CHAPTER 14

The House That Lends Itself to Entertaining

Your house or apartment may be two rooms or twelve, in need of vast improvements, or freshly done up; an old barn remodeled or a brand-new "compact" in a development. As far as parties go, the setting matters little. Every place has defects, and guests are much less conscious of them than the owners. Since people come to see you, not to take a house tour, the aim is an impression that is pleasing to the casual eye, and a welcoming and comfortable atmosphere.

Neatness

Since it's obvious that disorder gives a bad impression, we all try to make the house neat for a party. We straighten up books, pictures, the family desk, and put things where they belong.

But are we right about where things belong? Not always. Next time you plan a party, go through the house and pretend you are seeing it as an arriving guest. Do all those magazines belong in the rack and all those pictures on the piano? Do you need two ashtrays on every table? Do those antique cups belong together or apart? Or do they both belong in the cellar?

In the bedroom, does the knitting bag, just for tonight, need to hang on the bedpost? Does your collection of perfume bottles (or elephants or pillboxes) do anything for the bureau? Do you need to have every one of those cosmetics on display?

While all these things make a house look lived in, they do not add to the look you want for a party. It is surprising how a sort of organized emptiness can make a room look new and ready for a party, even though it may need complete redecorating.

Don't overlook the bathroom. Make sure it is spotless and that all the essentials are there. There is no need for fancy hand lotion and cologne (though these make nice additions). Nor is there any need for grubby soap or crumpled towels.

Cleaning

This goes hand in hand with neatness. A party suffers in an unclean house. People can sense a difference between a house that is really clean and one that has just been swished up for the occasion.

Keeping a clean house, as if anyone needed to be told, is a treadmill: when curtains are clean, windows need washing. Then it's time to clear kitchen shelves and swab them down. There is always something to do. Books. Woodwork. Clothes closets. Polishing.

In big cities you have to clean thoroughly every day or so. In the country you may get away with a lot less. But since the outdoors has a way of getting indoors, you won't be idle long.

Keeping a house or even a one-room apartment clean is easier if you have a routine. An unpressed dress or dusty glasses won't suffer much if left untouched until the next party. But when you let basic house cleaning go, it seems to double and takes extra hours when you finally attack it.

For everyday purposes you probably have a routine that works. We can only encourage you to stick to it. Here, for party purposes, are uncomplicated ways of coping with other things that need attention.

Cleaning bibelots and bric-a-brac. These are often overlooked, even in houses where every table and floor shines like a mirror. For fear of disaster, you steer the cleaning woman *away* from family treasures, china and glass figurines. Pictures, clock faces, and the TV screen may also pile up dust until the day when, looked at from a certain angle, they appear to have the first stages of penicillin fuzz.

Let's take the treasures first. The best way to "dust" objects of glass or china is to wash them. If you do not have a rubber or plastic sink liner, lay a dishcloth smoothly in the sink first, to avoid chipping the bases. Use warm water and detergent suds. If the piece is very dirty you may have to soak it awhile and get at dirt in ridges with cotton on a toothpick or a soft toothbrush. Otherwise, simply scoop the soapy water over with your hands. To rinse, scoop up clear water by hand again, or use a cup, or the spray attachment on the sink if you have one. Do not pick up the figurine and hold it under the tap. It may slip from your hand, or you may hit one part on the sink while rinsing another. To dry, set the piece on toweling to sop up moisture on the base, and let the air do the rest. Trouble, yes. But the difference you notice afterward will seem worth it.

Pictures on tables and walls, clock faces, mirrors, and the TV screen often get overlooked because glass that can be seen through doesn't look dirty. Don't be too sure. Run a wet finger over it. When there is dirt, wipe the glass with a dampened sponge—not a soaking-wet one. To dry the glass without smudges, use crumpled tissue paper, newspaper, or any paper that won't shred when damp. Moistened tissue paper is just as good as a sponge for the washing.

If you have oil paintings, get a feather duster and use it fairly frequently. Save it for this one job. The duster will get rid of all surface dust. Do not, however, try to *clean* paintings yourself. That's a job for experts.

Well-polished tables and floors bring an especially pleasing look to a house. Polishing is work, but a little regular effort goes a long way if one has the right equipment.

Always begin with a clean surface. Let's say you are doing a table. First dust it thoroughly. Remove smudges with warm water with a little vinegar in it. Dry the table and put on a small amount of polish. Most of the infinite varieties of furniture polish—waxes, liquids, creams—are good. We like liquid polish because it is easier to spread just a little. But whatever you use, be sparing. Have two cloths, never used for anything else, which are soft and lintless— worn-out sheets or threadbare flannel. Apply polish with one. Then, with the second, rub, rub, rub. Always rub in the same back-and-forth direction, *with* the grain of the wood, until all the polish is off. How can you tell? When you run a finger across the table and no mark appears. Electric polishers with small buffers are labor savers but hand polishing is not exhausting if you don't apply too much polish. (*Note:* On contemporary teak or walnut oil-finished pieces, use one of the polishes specially manufactured for them.)

Floor polishing is the same. Floors must be clean, then covered with a thin layer of polish, then rubbed until it is gone. There are now many "self-polishing" floor polishes that don't have to be rubbed off. But to build up a good patina and preserve your floors, polish or wax that requires rubbing is better.

With a lot of open floor, the maidless hostess owes herself an electric polisher. You still have to clean and put on polish, but the machine does the rest. Well-polished floors, dusted regularly, need the whole process fairly seldom—buffing between times keeps them looking up to scratch. Scratch! Horrid word. But scratches do occur. For scratches on a dark wood table or floor one home remedy is to paint them with a little iodine before you apply polish. After a time the scratch usually blends in. On lighter woods be more careful. Probably a few fairly heavy applications of your regular polish just on the scratch will cover it, or you might use one of the special polishes for light woods. When in doubt ask a cabinetmaker.

Polishing silver. If you want your silver to look as it did in the store you need a good polish, chamois, a bar of jeweler's rouge, and some brushes and cloths. Polish alone *will* give a decent shine. First wash the silver in detergent or ammonia and water, then put polish on and rub it off. But we asked a silver expert how to keep it really beautiful and she said:

"Start by washing the silver well. Sponge on polish. Then remove it by running hot water over it or, if it has dried, wipe it off with a soft towel. Go at tarnished crevices with an old toothbrush, and clean fork tines and silver that has raised designs with one of those banana-shaped brushes designed for the purpose. Now take your rouge. Moisten it with a little denatured alcohol or kerosene, and with a soft cloth or cotton wool rub it into the silver. You can't really rub it *in*, but rub as if you thought you could! Then remove the rouge with a soft cloth, or brush it out of ridges with the silver brush. Now take the chamois and start buffing. Keep it up until the silver has a 'white' shine—no cast of gray, yellow, or blue."

Our expert continued, "It is important to have hospital-clean cloths, without a trace of grease on them. Never wet the chamois. When you set aside time for rouging, put on gloves. Rouge powder penetrates the skin."

This sounds like a tiresome process but, as in all cases of doing things right, there is an advantage: silver you use regularly, if kept well buffed with the chamois, will stay beautiful for a long time without polish or rouge. Another good tip is to buff silver right after you have used it, *before* putting it back in its chest or flannel bags. You may find you have no polishing to do before the next party, or that a quick rub with your chamois will be enough.

The silver expert also told us, "When you get out silver for a short-notice party and it looks yellowish, just wash it in detergent and water. Let it dry and buff it once over lightly with your chamois. No need to polish." She also said, "I must admit, too, that those treated flannel silver cloths can make smudged silver presentable in emergencies."

Brasses. There are no tricks about cleaning brass. Just make good use of your favorite polish. But be sure to get all the brass done at once. You may do the front doorknob and letter slot as a matter of course, but what about fire tongs, table legs, indoor doorknobs, light-switch plaques? If they are not lacquered, polishing them brightens the look of the whole house.

Windows are frustrating because it never fails to rain just after they are washed. Actually most windows aren't noticed at parties. But if you have one whose curtains are never drawn because it's a feature of the living room—overlooking a city view or a garden—it should probably be washed before a party. If it is not, the smudges will blur the view in daylight, and if it is newly washed the window after dark will gleam like onyx and be an attractive element of the room.

Smudged woodwork and upholstery cast shadows on an otherwise clean room. If you have small children you have your work cut out. But woodwork can usually be cleaned quite easily with a sponge dipped in one of the all-purpose liquid cleaners on the market. Follow the directions for diluting. These cleaners are also excellent for sponging down a whole wall. However, a whole wall in need of washing shows less in a room brightly lit for a party. Really tough marks around the baseboards or doorjambs may need a cleaner with an abrasive in it. But use it sparingly. It is better to leave a few marks than remove some of the paint.

A good upholstery cleaner is a great help for chair arms and spots on sofa cushions. Use it well enough ahead of the party to keep the house from smelling like a dry cleaner's. If several big pieces of furniture need to be completely cleaned, you may decide to call in a professional cleaner who will arrive with special soaps and sponges and who usually knows how to erase dirt from various kinds of material.

Curtains. Taking down curtains and shaking them out is a big job in itself and it is often difficult to rehang them right. Every few years they probably should be taken down, dry-cleaned, and rehung by a professional. In the intervals, the brush attachment on the vacuum cleaner draws much dust from the folds. This brush is also good for venetian blinds.

Glass curtains are no problem if they are nylon or Dacron that can be washed and hung up wet if need be; in any case they require only the slightest pressing with a cool iron. When curtains of man-made fibers turn yellowish after a few washings, check the bleach bottle for the right solution to bring back their whiteness.

Rugs. Vacuum cleaning is probably a part of your usual routine, with an occasional once-over-lightly with the carpet sweeper when necessary. If the whole rug is dirty send it out to be washed or give it a shampoo yourself. This is a big job but some of the labor has been eased by the electric shampooing attachments available for many vacuum cleaners. For a spot here and there, or an area darkened by frequent tramping, sponging with detergent suds and rubbing hard works pretty well if you keep people out of the room until the rug is dry. When a rug is brightly colored, attacking stains with strong cleaning fluid or detergent may permanently discolor the area.

Inevitably a rug you have had for years will get a few spots that just won't come out, no matter what you do. Unless these are very large or eye-catching, don't worry about them. They are part of the lived-in look that guests rarely notice.

Emergency cleaning. The cleaning ideas above are for parties planned in advance. When an emergency party comes up you must concentrate on the guest list and a good meal, and save energy for being a good hostess. On a day's notice, get things as clean as quick dusting and vacuuming can make them. Have the bathroom spotless, the table silver shining, and let everything else go. It just isn't that important.

If people call and say they would like to come in half an hour, cleaning is out. You have just time to make yourself presentable and get out refreshments. You might copy the technique of a New York wife whose husband likes to bring people home on the spur of the moment: in the broom closet she keeps a straw flower basket with a duster in it. When her husband calls she grabs the basket, flies around the living room dusting table tops and gathering up children's toys and other clutter that makes any room look messy. "These are times," she says, "when there simply isn't time to put everything where it belongs, so I just throw it all in my basket and replace it neatly next day." She has real understanding of what makes a house ready for entertaining: more than cleaning, more than polish, a look of order is what counts on short notice.

Lighting

Try for a middle way between glare and gloom. Each room has its own lighting problems, depending on size, shape, color scheme, and so on. But here are some things to guard against as a general rule: never have lamps whose bulbs are exposed. Make sure the shades are deep enough to prevent a person's eye from meeting the bulb when he is sitting as well as standing. Avoid dark lamp shades. While they may be beautiful in themselves they tend to create tight little islands of light instead of diffused glow. If the main source of light is centrally located, diffuse it by placing lamps in the corners. Be willing to experiment with lighting, and use up "wrong" bulbs elsewhere. When you plan structural changes in a room, think of lighting first. It may be that indirect lighting would do more for the scene than many another improvement.

Have extra bulbs and fuses on hand at all times, especially if you live in a place with antique wiring. One usually puts on all the lights at parties—the perfect setup for overloaded fuses and total blackout.

The Kitchen That Lends Itself to Entertaining

The fortress of the good hostess, the kitchen, is perhaps the most important room to keep in perfect condition. Surely it is a good place to spend improvement dollars as long as the rest of the house or apartment is in reasonably good shape. The ideal kitchen is well lighted, airy, and uncluttered, making it easy to keep clean. Big enough for the necessities, it is not so big that you wear yourself out whirling from refrigerator to stove to sink to closets.

If your kitchen does not now seem well organized, don't ignore it because you feel the answer is to rip out the whole works and build a new one. You may be able to make immediate improvements that cost nothing.

Where do you prepare vegetables? At the sink? At a cutting board? Then knives and parers belong in a drawer near at hand. Cooking ladles, basters, turning forks, and tongs belong near the stove. Measuring cups and mixing bowls should be stored under the counter where you normally prepare a recipe. The pots and pans most often used should be the easiest to reach; relegate those for special dishes to the back of the closet. The garbage can should be near where you work with food, to avoid leaving a trail of onion skin and carrot tops when you clean up. Have an extra garbage box (a grocer's carton perhaps) on hand for parties.

Herbs frequently used probably belong with the salt and pepper beside the stove, with others out of the way in the closet. The constantly used toaster or blender should be out all the time; other electric appliances can be shelved until needed. Store everyday china and silver near the sink or dishwasher so that it can be put away with the least effort. Party plates can be stacked on higher shelves.

Here is a system one young hostess—with a dream bank account —dreamed up. It works well for every aspect of modern parties: cooking, serving, and party atmosphere. She and her husband moved into an old New York brownstone that needed top-to-bottom reconstruction. And since this girl rightly considers cooking her own fine art, and never wanted to be dependent on party help, she decided to have a kitchen and dining room in one. Don't misunderstand: this is not a kitchen with an eating area separated by a counter, or a dining room with a kitchen alcove. It is a beautiful dining room that happens also to be the kitchen. In the center of a polished brick floor (pretty enough for a dining room, but practical for a kitchen) stands the round dining table and eight armchairs. Two sides of the room hold the usual modern kitchen paraphernalia; counters, built-in stove, wall oven, and dishwasher, under cabinets picked to look un-kitchen-like. The third side of the room has a handsome sideboard and an oil painting, and the fourth side has windows with pretty curtains, and a french door leading out to the garden.

One great virtue is that the room is correctly lighted; guests are hardly conscious of stove, sink, and so on. Also correctly ventilated, it isn't full of cooking smells as you walk in. But, to the hostess, the room's greatest virtue is that she can cook under conditions that are ideal for her, both for the family and for parties. To guests, the charm of a party here is, first, the small group of people all seated comfortably. Then the delicious food; besides being prepared by an expert, it never leaves the stove until the ideal moment. And because the hostess doesn't keep jumping up and disappearing, everyone feels relaxed.

This arrangement is made to order for someone lucky enough to build from the ground up, according to her own fancy. But it also illustrates the importance of trying to use your own kitchen as an effective tool for good parties, making it a place where you are glad to be when doing party work.

Household Gadgets

Some gadgets are indispensable for taking work out of parties. Others, bought on impulse, collect dust and take up space, like expensive toys.

Almost everyone enjoys the meat thermometer, the giant eye dropper for basting, an egg slicer, a bean stringer, and that dime-store gadget that scrapes potatoes, carrots, and asparagus more easily than the best knife. Most people probably have a favorite gadget that they wouldn't be without—anything from a pressure cooker to an electric frying pan or can opener. Here are a few others, both cheap and expensive, that we think deserve house-room.

In the kitchen, first on our list is poultry shears. They cut any poultry, cooked or raw, neatly and with little effort. They also take the trauma out of opening and disjointing lobsters. Two French gadgets are next: a wire sauce whisk, easier than anything else for smoothing gravies, folding in egg whites, stirring soups and purées. The other is a garlic crusher, a few cents' worth of metal that mashes the garlic into the pot, not under your fingernails.

Another blessing is a collapsible vegetable steamer that fits any pot and has legs that extend to different heights, depending on the amount of water you need below. It works well for many vegetables (there is satisfaction in knowing that the vitamins have not boiled away) and it is also good for small fish and steamed puddings.

Have two pairs of scissors that never leave the kitchen. One pair of average size is for cutting cheese cloth, opening frozen food packages, snipping string from roasts. A smaller pair is ideal for recipes that say "parsley, finely chopped." Cut some parsley, put it in a cup, and, holding scissors with points down, snip away. It is fast and neat; the parsley stays put the way it never does on a board.

Among electric gadgets there is nothing like a blender. Besides the speed with which it purées and blends, it also simplifies concocting sauces—hollandaise and mayonnaise are a matter of minutes. And with some liquid added, you can chop many raw vegetables in exactly one second.

An electric egg beater saves time and energy in beating eggs, whipping cream or butter, and is also a help for beating thick cake batter and pâtés. The elaborate electric mixers with rotating bowls and many attachments are wonderful, but a simple hand model is an excellent substitute. It is much less expensive and fits in a drawer or hangs on the wall.

Bar equipment is discussed in Chapter 3, on cocktail parties, but here are some further suggestions. Your bar may be a permanent part of your living room or set up for special occasions. Either way, keep it uncomplicated.

Most bar gadgets turn up under the Christmas tree and get thrown out a year later. Exceptions are the versatile electric blender, which is great for certain drinks, and a good ice crusher. A cup for measuring the ingredients of a complicated cocktail can be helpful too, but it looks miserly to measure simple on-the-rocks drinks and everyday cocktails as if they were priceless chemicals.

Ice tongs seem to have gone out. We haven't seen one in years. People must be less squeamish about germs, or they assume alcohol will kill them. Hands, plus a bar knife or ice pick to separate cubes, are easier, anyway.

The secret to easy bartending is a cocktail shaker that doesn't drip. Find one with a tight-fitting top or a spout for pouring. A pitcher with a closed lip to hold back the ice is best for martinis.

Bitters bottles, bowls for lemon peel and cherries, lime squeezers may be useful but essential is a sturdy bottle opener with enough weight and length for good leverage, which can double as a weapon for blasting ice cubes apart. Many big ones also have a beer-can opener. Also essential is a good corkscrew. If you don't already have one you swear by, try the kind headwaiters use. You simply screw it in, lower the lever against the bottle, and ease out the cork. This professional gadget, which costs a dollar or so, also has a small knife in the handle for cutting off foil around the bottle tops.

Not essential but useful are permanent bottle caps, sold at any five-and-ten, that preserve half-empty bottles of soda. An old sugar sifter or salt shaker makes a tidy container for the sugar used in mixed drinks.

Furniture Arrangement

A big living room can be more complicated to arrange than a small one. Too often in a big room there is a great expanse of open rug with chairs running around the edges, almost like a ballroom set up for dancing school. In an attempt to fill it up, another big room may be so crammed that it looks like a furniture showroom.

The solution to both extremes is to divide the room into two or three units that balance each other and are balanced within themselves. A fireplace and a big window might each make the center of a unit. And within each unit individual pieces of furniture should balance: overstuffed chairs near a straight-backed settee, straight chairs or low benches next to a deep heavy sofa.

In small living rooms where there is usually room for only one unit, the rule of centering and balancing holds. If there is a fireplace the big sofa probably belongs opposite. Easy chairs go beside the fireplace and straight chairs on either side of the sofa. This makes a regulated look at the start of the party and later, if need be, guests can bring the light chairs from the borders of the room.

Dining rooms, as such, present few arrangement problems, but in contemporary houses they have shrunk to alcoves or ells off the living room, or don't exist at all. It is still best if dining furniture can be arranged as a separate unit (with a carry-over, perhaps, of the living room décor). In a small apartment where this is impossible, double-duty furniture—the expansible side table to eat or serve from, the chest that becomes a party sideboard—can work well in the basic arrangement.

To arrive at a good room plan, apply the primary rules of arrangement, taking into account the proportions of your own furniture and your own habits. Chronic card players probably always want a table and four chairs permanently in the plan, and this makes sense because of convenience even though it unbalances the room a little. Many rooms are successfully arranged around an outsize desk, breakfront, or grand piano which, no matter what a decorator would say, is too beautiful or useful to leave out of the scheme. Take what you have. Move it around until the room seems most right to you.

The Single Girl's Apartment

While we won't make strong statements about color schemes and furniture styles for married people—it's up to each couple and what they have to work with—we do have this suggestion for the single girl who lives alone or with a roommate: don't have your apartment too feminine. No one objects to soft colors and flowery materials if that's what you like, but keep the over-all look tailored and unfussy. Without a man around, an apartment may become too much like a bedroom. Then when men come for a party it looks overly girlish, not to say suggestive.

The Party Capacity of Your House

Only you can decide the capacity of your house, or its potential capacity if you remove or rearrange furniture. If a meal is to be served there should be enough room for everyone to sit comfortably, before and during the meal. Cocktail and tea parties may be much more crowded, because a slight crush gives an aura of success. For dinner parties, try to arrange small units. Avoid a big circle of chairs and don't let one form after the party starts. When the first arrivals take the sofa, and the next take the chairs alongside, it can soon look like a game of pass the thimble.

At a dinner table, people must have room to wield knife and fork. Twenty inches per person is the absolute minimum. If you can't manage that, have two tables, or a buffet supper—or fewer guests.

To make people comfortable at a meal-less party, think about obvious stumbling blocks: the coffee table, or chairs and sofas that crowd doorways or interrupt the sweep of the room. Plan to get people into the dining area. If you have a separate dining room, pick out three or four friends to go there as front runners; others will follow shortly.

The easiest way to take care of a big crowd is out of doors. But since weather is such a fair-weather friend it is not a good idea to ask more people to an outdoor party than you can handle indoors with some crowding. Under the circumstances a traffic jam is forgivable.

CHAPTER 15

Your Party "Staff" — Part-Time Helpers and What to Expect of Them

On this subject, first a little philosophy: the word "servant" is almost obsolete in America. Though we constantly hear about the difficulty of getting help, we seem bothered, even guilty, by class connotations.

There is less and less domestic help, and more and more of us are proficient in doing, with pleasure, the "gracious living" things that used to be servants' duties. But probably at some time or other we will have help—from a cleaning woman, mother's helper, waiter or waitress, or a caterer's crew. And there is no reason to feel that it is undemocratic. Domestic workers choose their jobs themselves and earn not only fair pay but respect—not as *servants*, but for the *services* they offer.

But they are, being in your house, personal employees. Emotions naturally enter in that seldom occur in an office because the nature of the work is emotional: the everyday effort involves trying to keep a house attractive (not just running) or children well and happy (not just washed and fed). When a party comes along— something to be done in the name of pleasure—how you and your employee react to one another is especially important.

To make things between you go smoothly, at parties or any time, always treat an employee as you would like to be treated, asking nothing of him that you would not willingly do if he weren't there, or that you wouldn't willingly do if you could—like fixing the TV set or carrying a rug. The second rule is: *explain* what you want done. The woman who says, "I could never give orders to anyone," probably runs her house badly and gives slipshod parties.

There is a world of difference between "giving orders" and explaining. "Please leave the soup on the stove until the last minute" is not like saying, "Have the soup hot." And "Did you have a chance to polish the cocktail shaker?" calls forth a better reaction than "You've forgotten it again, Alice." Manners again. Your manners.

You have a right to expect helpers to have good manners too, and to be neat in appearance and willing to work. They should be reliable, come on time, and call when they cannot come. But you should not expect them to do in an hour what would take you half a day, or to do special things that you have not gone over together in advance. No one can read your mind and know that you want the pie warmed up or the cheese at room temperature. You must say so. Remember, too, praise for a job well done is often better incentive than a raise in salary.

How to Direct Party Helpers

Fortunately, in most communities there are still enough experienced party helpers to go around. They know their basic tasks and are efficient, careful of your things, and willing to do things *the way you want them done*. They probably don't have to be told about table setting, serving, or the little details, such as emptying ashtrays and refilling the ice bucket. They do need, each time they come, a full explanation of the party. Let's say you are engaging a waitress for a small dinner. When you call her, give as much preliminary information as you can: the approximate number of people coming, how many courses you plan to have. Make the date, and the hour she should come definite. If you will have cooked the dinner but would like her to make appetizers or set the table, say so. She'll do better without last-minute surprises. If you do not know her fee, bring this up too. If there is any doubt in your mind, ask if she has the proper uniform. (More about uniforms later.)

Always have a helper come early enough for a complete explanation of the party details. If she has never been in your house before, a good start is to take her around, showing where coats are to go and which bathroom will be used. Then return to the kitchen and go over the whole dinner together. Point out the food in the refrigerator, the food on the stove, the serving things. You may have set the table and got out everything down to the last coffee spoon before the maid comes—a wise plan if she is new to your house. If you haven't done this, you will have to locate everything for her. It takes time.

Whether or not she knows your house, it's always good insurance to make a couple of lists. One list is simply the menu. Start with the appetizers and include every dish. It might read as follows:

Guests invited for 7:30
With cocktails:
    Crab meat canapés on white bread
    Bowl of mixed nuts
Dinner to be served at 8:15
    Cold soup—Assorted crackers
    Hot beef tongue—Bowl of mustard sauce
        Creamed spinach
        New potatoes
        Toasted rolls
    Baked mixed fruits, served hot
        Bowl of sour cream
        Cookies
After dinner: Coffee in the living room

As you go over this with the maid it will help you remember to point out all food and equipment, and later, when you cannot be in the kitchen, the waitress uses the menu as a reminder.

The other list, more detailed, is *your* mental crutch for more things to tell the maid, and *hers* for the sequence of events and what she will do on her own when the party begins. Using the same menu, List 2 might read:

At 7:30:

    Start heating main course—tongue needs half an hour more simmering.

    Heat mustard sauce in double boiler; and vegetables in dutch ovens on top of stove over low heat.

    Preheat oven to 300°.

At 8:15 announce dinner.

    During soup, toast rolls in oven.

    When main course has been served put dessert in oven.

    During dessert, make coffee.

This gives the waitress an easy-to-follow time schedule and will remind you of what you may want to check on or do after the party has started. With the menu above, your last-minute job might be to skin and carve the tongue and arrange it on a hot platter.

The more food you have ready in the dishes in which they will appear at table, the easier it is for the waitress. With this menu the cold soup could be in cups in the refrigerator. You have the crackers arranged on a plate. The dessert is baking in the dish from which it will be served, and the cookies are on a serving plate. During the meal, all the maid needs to transfer to dining-table equipment are the meat, the sauce and rolls, and after dinner she pours the coffee into your party coffeepot.

For an experienced waitress, information such as this is probably more than enough, especially if you have worked together before. But let's imagine that you are giving the same dinner with the help of someone who has little or no training. The first list—the menu—stays the same, but the second list should be much more detailed. Go over it with the maid carefully, pointing out each piece of equipment.

At 7:30 start heating vegetables and sauce.

At 8:15 I will carve tongue.

At 8:15 bring soup cups from refrigerator to table.

Then announce dinner.

When guests are seated, pass plate of soup crackers.

Then bring vegetable casseroles—with covers on—to sideboard.

Then bring sauce and heated dinner plates. Heat rolls.

Clear soup plates. Bring meat to sideboard.

I will dish main course.

Pass plates around to guests, starting with woman on host's right. Pass rolls.

During main course, take tray and clean ashtrays to living room, collect cocktail glasses, appetizer trays. Put out clean ashtrays. Plump sofa cushions and open window.

I will offer second helpings. Help to serve these.

Check on dessert in oven. Get out sour cream.

When main course is finished, clear dinner plates and bring dessert plates to sideboard. Remove salts and peppers. Crumb the table.

Bring dessert and sour cream to sideboard. I will serve it from there. Pass dessert to guests. Pass cookies.

At end of dinner, fill coffeepot and bring to tray in living room. I will pour coffee. After fifteen minutes refill coffeepot. Check ashtrays and ice bucket.

Many of these things are obvious, and you will sense whether your helper needs all of them in writing. Others, such as airing the living room or removing the salts after the main course, are details a novice may need to be told. You can also direct the maid during the course of the evening, but it is better to do as little as possible after guests arrive. It makes you less able to concentrate on your friends. Perhaps even more important, the inexperienced maid is apt to get rattled when you interrupt her with requests and reminders.

Urge helpers to ask questions before the party, and during it if necessary. Tell them anything special about cleaning up, too. If your glasses should not go in the dishwasher, say so. When a helper is new to your house, it is probably easier to have her put nothing away and for you to do it next morning. It may take half an hour, which is better than spending half a day rearranging misplaced equipment.

To help prepare a completely untrained maid, here are a few basic rules for serving.

Order of service: everything is offered first to the woman on the right of the host, then the man on her right is served, and so on around the table with the host served last.

Platters and plates are handed at the left of the person being served. Plates may be cleared one at a time from right or left, though the right side is conventional.

Pass dinner plates one at a time, from the left.

Soup and dessert plates may be laid and taken away two at a time if the maid can manage this without spilling.

A course is cleared when everyone has finished eating it.

Water and wineglasses are filled from the right, of course. Water glasses are filled almost full, wineglasses about half.

How to Speak to Helpers and Vice Versa

Maids and cooks are called by their first names with the exception of an older married woman coming to "help out" who may prefer to be called "Mrs. Accommodate." Men helpers, traditionally called by last names, are often called by their given names, today. Nicknames are too casual—call the bartender "Robert" unless he insists on "Bob."

That's simple. More complicated with today's informality is to have helpers address *you* correctly. In most parts of the country "Sir" is still used but "Madam" has been replaced by "Mrs. Last Name." "Ma'am" still goes in the South.

Experienced helpers know that they should speak as little as possible, stay out of conversation, and pretend not to hear even the most hilarious remarks. An inexperienced person usually has enough sense of fitness to do the same. But not always. One hostess says her cleaning woman, when she first helped at a party, could not resist crooning, "Enjoy, enjoy," to each guest as she served. Another part-time waitress keeps up a running conversation with herself: "Oh, Lord, I burned the rolls. Mustn't forget the sauce. Mercy on us, the candle grease!" The meal is eaten in an atmosphere of impending doom. Faced with similar distractions, you have to be blunt beforehand: "Grace, it would be better if you didn't talk during dinner." To shut up a compulsive talker, you might tell her that when dinner is served she should just catch your eye. You will be watching out for her and will know that it's time to eat. Speaking to a helper in whispers is always a good idea; she will usually whisper back automatically.

"Dinner is served" is the correct line for a maid to announce dinner, and "Hello" is the best way for her to answer the telephone. "Mrs. X's residence," frowned on in the past, is sometimes used and does make more sense today when you have only a part-time helper. If she says "Hello," the caller, not hearing your voice, may think he's got the wrong number.

When You Have More Than One Helper

When more than one person helps at a party, the main thing is division of labor.

At a cocktail party the division is clear. The bartender makes the drinks, the waitress or waitresses serve drinks and food, empty ashtrays, and so on. All help with cleaning up.

At a dinner party with a butler and maid, this might be a good division of labor: The butler helps make and serve cocktails, and passes appetizers. The maid oversees things in the kitchen. During dinner the butler takes the lead, passing the soup to most of the guests. The maid follows along with the remaining soup plates, then attends to things in the kitchen while he passes crackers. A butler probably passes the meat course (it is usually the heaviest platter, anyway) while the maid follows with the sauce. They alternate serving vegetables and rolls, and the butler pours the wine. They each do about half the clearing and after dinner probably take turns serving coffee and liqueurs, or the butler does this alone while the maid begins cleaning up the dining room and kitchen. When coffee and liqueurs have been cleared and the ice bucket filled, the butler helps wash up.

When two maids serve, both may want to help in the living room before dinner, but one should be assigned to watch the stove. If one maid is familiar with your house and the other is less so, or not at all, you might suggest that the first take the lead and let the other be guided by her.

The more help you have, the better it is to make lists to save time being wasted in the kitchen over discussion as to what comes next and who does what.

For a very big party, when more than two helpers are needed, the solution is often a team from a caterer. They usually know one another and have a system worked out. The hostess explains any special wishes, and each helper does what falls into his particular area. This is not to say that the work will be evenly divided. A waiter may make only the grand gestures—pouring wine, carrying in the roast, serving after-dinner drinks—while waitresses bustle in a hot kitchen. Or one waitress may become a self-appointed, and unnecessary, cocktail attendant while another is left to do more than her share of kitchen work. When someone is idling the hostess should suggest a specific task or ask the idler to lend a hand to the others. Rightly or wrongly, there is a double standard in party service. Waiters make more money than waitresses. So do cooks. Yet waitresses are often busiest for the longest length of time. The good helper, no matter what his job or pay, will usually help others if he has time.

Many hostesses have told us that in their communities a caterer has the party business sewed up. He won't send them a helper or a team unless they buy the food from him too. Or he sends second-string people to chastise the hostess for doing her own cooking. "My cooking is cheaper and, I think, better than the caterer's," one hostess wrote. "Also, everyone uses him, so the menus are the same all over town. For small dinners I can get along without anyone, but for our annual Fourth of July party I need three good helpers and this means that guests arrive resigned to another stereotyped buffet supper, which they may have eaten three nights before somewhere else."

One hostess gets around the problem this way: "For our occasional big parties, I act as contractor, using two or three sources. A bartender from my husband's club, two maids I sometimes use separately, main course bought at the local gourmet kitchen, dessert from a good pastry shop I know." As long as the helpers work well together and the hostess doesn't mind the trouble of assembling food, it's a good solution. Or one might do part of the cooking: make the soup and dessert at home and have the caterer supply the main course. Or make the cocktail appetizers and a special homemade salad. "Bought" appetizers are rarely as appealing as homemade ones, and few caterers do anything exciting in the salad line.

About Uniforms

Part-time helpers bring their own uniforms, but if they ask what you want them to wear, here are today's approved outfits:

Women helpers. Waitresses should wear black dresses with long sleeves, high V-necklines, with collars and cuffs of white linen, organdy, or lace. Beige collars and cuffs are sometimes worn instead of white. Simple black shoes, normal nylons, and a spotless apron complete the costume. The apron most often matches the collars and cuffs, though a few part-time waitresses wear the black taffeta apron that used to be an insignia of a lady's maid. While you cannot forbid part-time waitresses to wear colors other than black, you can discourage it. Black is always right. Pale colors, such as gray, mauve, yellow, green, or blue, are appropriate at lunch or outdoors, or for your regular part-time housekeeper.

Although caps have long since gone out, women helpers with a sense of fitness have neat, short hair-dos. And though they pass up bright nail polish, heavy make-up, and perfume, powder and lipstick are now part of the "uniform."

Men helpers. The uniform most often worn today is a replica of any man's black-tie dinner suit: black jacket with silk or satin revers, black bow tie, and white shirt, which some waiters still have starched. The only difference between this outfit and a regular dinner suit is that the trousers do not have braid down the sides, and a waiter wears black calf shoes instead of patent leather.

Some caterers' waiters wear old-time butler's evening dress: black swallow-tail coat, black trousers, stiff-bosomed white shirt with wing collar. With this, to make a distinction between butler and guests, a black waistcoat or a black bow tie would be worn, instead of all white. Appropriate for a formal party, this is too dressed up for the informal parties most people give today.

A bartender can correctly wear a white duck coat or mess jacket with black bow tie, white shirt, and black trousers—as long as he sticks to bartending. If he helps to serve dinner he looks less like a restaurant waiter if he wears a black jacket. At lunch or any outdoor party the white duck jacket is fine.

Some helpers arrive in uniform, others expect to change after they come. In either case, it is a good idea to assign them a room, or at least a bathroom, where they may change or leave their overcoats. Remember to put out coat hangers.

The Troublesome Helper

When you sense a bad attitude in a hired hand before the party, first try a little psychology. Is he feeling well? Is he minus some equipment he needs? Does he have any questions to ask? A diplomatic approach may improve his manner. But if it doesn't, pay him off and let him go. It is better for you to pinch-hit than to cope with someone who is rude or begrudgingly helpful.

If things go wrong during the party you can only feel your way. It is best to overlook rudeness and laziness; you make a mental note not to engage the person again. If worse trouble occurs, you may decide to ask him to leave immediately. A helper who argues with you or another helper, or who has been drinking, does the party more damage by staying than by leaving.

Naturally you never engage a troublemaker again. If he has come from an agency or caterer, report what went wrong, not to assassinate his character, only to show concern for the agency's reputation and the next hostess who might get stuck. When a person has done especially well it is nice to report that too. If you hand on your helpers to other hostesses, it's good to describe their special fortes, and what, as far as you know, they do less well. Also, always tell the truth about what you pay. If you give a tip, say how much. This sort of fair employment practice makes life simpler for everyone and keeps party standards high.

When helpers come from an agency or caterer, a bill is usually sent later, after they have reported the hours put in. If you want to add a tip you can ask the agency to put it on the bill, or give it to each employee during the evening. Most seem to prefer this. When you hire helpers direct, have their pay ready for them and deal out the envelopes before the party begins—it's a detail not worth trying to remember later on, and they'll be glad to know that you haven't forgotten. Extra cash for bus fare, or taxi fare in case the weather turns bad, may come in handy.

CHAPTER 16

Party Food and Drink

If people are the most important party ingredients, what you give them runs a close second. A party will not necessarily suffer from mediocre food and drink, but offering your best always improves things and is basically polite. Imagination and some interest in food promise unlimited variety.

Choosing What to Have

Party meals should be balanced in "weight" and color, and should make guests feel that you have taken special pains. Since the pivot of a meal is its main course, choose that first.

Meat, fish, or poultry? Assuming that you cook good dishes in all three categories, what else might influence the choice? What you feel like eating yourself, certainly, and what you feel like cooking at the particular time. (Only a hostess bored by food would care to cook the same meal for three parties in a row.) You also consider the season and the favorite foods, as far as you know, of the guests. Don't forget religious or health restrictions.

A safe rule is to avoid what one meat-and-potatoes host calls "queer food." While few foods, if cooked right, are not good eating, and it's fun to experiment with delicacies, parties are no place for wildly unusual dishes. To strike that line between novelty, which you want, and the bizarre, which you do not, serve popular foods cooked with as much originality as you, or your cookbooks, can muster, and save odd gastronomic delights—such as calves' brains and tripe—for people you *know* enjoy them.

Since French food is generally considered to be the best there is, a French repertoire will help, but beyond this, do not overdo foreign foods. You can expect guests to enjoy a well-known Spanish dish, but perhaps not an obscure one. Italian food has its charms, including garlic. But whiffs are better than clouds for parties here. For novelty, many a hostess will put on a Chinese banquet or a Hawaiian luau. Good idea—if guests can eat comfortably, which will not be the case if they are forced to grapple with chopsticks or to eat with their fingers.

As long as party food should be familiar, how do you avoid monotony? One way is by continually expanding the number of dishes you do well, watching and trying out recipes that sound good. Keeping records also helps. Just as you wouldn't duplicate a guest list exactly, you don't want to serve exactly the same menu twice to a particular group or couple, so you might jot down on your calendar the guest list, the main course, and dessert of each party.

Having decided on a main course, you must plan what goes with it. The rule of thumb is one vegetable, light and simply cooked, and a starchy or heavier vegetable of a different color from the first —such as corn or lima beans—or one that is cooked in a richer way: creamed onions, string beans in cheese sauce, or fried eggplant. Rice, potatoes, pasta, or pilaff can be the answer too.

Now think about the first course, if you are having one. The soup choices are endless. If the main course is meat, have a chicken, fish, or vegetable soup. If chicken is the main course, have a soup with a meat, fish, or vegetable base. Hot soup is always in order, but cold soups, simpler to serve with little or no help, are now appropriate all year round. Instead of soup, you might have easy-to-serve cold or hot fish dishes, shellfish, pâtés, artichokes with a sauce, stuffed tomatoes or stuffed eggs, aspics, melon with ham, antipasto, or *salade niçoise*. Almost anything begins a meal well, except a dessert, so please, no fruit cup. Though an American institution, it is not a proper opener for a meal.

A salad course is easy. Plain mixed green salad follows anything well. If you make a more elaborate salad just don't duplicate items from other courses. Always try for *green* salad, or add color with water cress or a few raw spinach leaves, beets, radishes, or tomatoes. Any sort of salad dressing is all right as long as it has enough bite in the seasoning and as long as you make your own. And as long as you don't pour it on until the last minute.

Desserts should simply be sweet and refreshing. Fruit in some form is perfect any time, and especially after a heavy main course; rich cream-butter-and-sugar desserts are better following lean meat or simply cooked chicken or fish. You can never go wrong passing a tray of hand-chosen fresh fruits with old-fashioned fruit knives and a good cheese.

Timing, too, influences the menu, if you agree that a good hostess can't spend much time in the kitchen after guests arrive. Luckily, almost everything except a roast or a fragile sauce can be cooked ahead and not suffer.

Finally, there's the serving. With a waitress to help, all courses could be the "watch carefully" type. Without help, they had better not be. If you're married to a deft carver you'll have lots of roasts. Or, wanting to skip carving, you'll choose dishes that don't need it or that taste just as good carved ahead and covered with gravy. When guests serve themselves you'll choose a menu that is easy for them to handle.

Sometimes, after you have mulled over a menu from all these angles, you are still undecided. Your usual specialties leave you uninspired, or the main course seems fine but you are puzzled about the rest. When this happens, take time for a reading session. Skim through cookbooks for an enticing, new-to-you soup or dessert. Perhaps you will find a recipe you always meant to try, or another that once seemed difficult, now seems easier. While no one should attempt a truly difficult recipe for the first time at a party, any good cookbook has dishes that you know will taste good, that you know you can do, without a rehearsal.

If you're still at a loss, think back to restaurant meals or to dishes you liked at other people's parties. Most hostesses are flattered to be asked for a recipe, but if you cannot borrow it, be of good cheer. Comb cookbooks at the library, and search newspapers and magazines. One day, there it is. And meanwhile you may have found a dozen other dishes that appeal.

If all else fails, make up a dream meal—one cooked by a famous chef and served by butlers. A fairy tale? Not necessarily. Perhaps the dream dinner is possible for *you* to do, or at least part of it—you can attempt the Roquefort mousse or the *sauce mousseline*, but not the oysters Rockefeller. No matter. You already have ideas that make the dinner seem interesting to you.

Making a Good Menu into a Good Meal

First, practice the art of "oncemanship," which is doing everything connected with the party only once. Make a master list and divide the work into categories—food, liquor, equipment, decorations. Attend to each category at once. If you need polish, think what else you might need from the housewares shop. Candles? Doilies? Table matches?

Before you start on silver, think of every piece you will need and do it all at once. Get out all plates and glasses at one time, all serving platters. Wash all that need it at one time.

When making out the grocery list, try to visualize the whole dinner. Have you parsley, extra cream, the right herbs, staples? It is frustrating to discover, elbow-deep in a recipe, that you are out of sugar, flour, or some seasoning that *makes* the dish.

Practice the art of oncemanship in scheduling your time, too. Divide the menu into cook-ahead and last-minute food, then reserve a few hours of uninterrupted kitchen time the day before the party and the afternoon of it. Do each dish all at once, without feeling rushed.

Have enough of everything. What is enough? It is really more than enough. You do not need an outsize meal—three vegetables, two desserts—but have an *ample* supply of what you do have. Very few women want more than "just a tiny bit" for second helpings, but there should be plenty for each man in the party.

Always try to present the dinner attractively. Use things that match or complement each other. They need not be expensive silver or china; in fact the more stove-to-table service equipment you have the better. Each year more items on the market are "presentable" at the dining table—enameled and crockery casseroles, ovenproof glass, metal platters and vegetable dishes. Perhaps not as glamorous as traditional serving things, they are well designed for today's parties, and professional-looking, the sort of thing restaurant chefs use for great creations.

When you serve a dish in transparent glass, wrap a napkin around it or buy pleated paper collars which, though not cheap, can be used many times.

Try to "party up the food," as one hostess puts it. Home cooking should not look fussed over but should appeal to the eye as well as the taste. Use parsley or water cress for garnish. Do put the paper ruffles back on the crown of lamb. Do sprinkle with chopped chives or dust with paprika or powdered sugar if the recipe suggests it. Laying fancy designs in the bottom of ring molds may be too much trouble, but when you unmold you can touch them up with little diamonds of pimiento, olive slices, or capers. Decorate desserts with a few fruit slices, candied flowers, or sprinkles.

What to Have to Drink

In the chapter on cocktail parties we campaigned for good brands of popular liquors in ample supply. This also applies to luncheon and dinner parties. The proper accompaniment to a good meal is wine. It adds to the party air, makes food taste better, and was proved to be an aid to digestion centuries ago. Water should be available, but only as a thirst quencher or for sipping. It should not be drunk in quantity during a meal. It isn't good for the digestion and it can drown subtle flavors. Washing down food with tea or coffee, American custom though it may be, is just as bad. Beer is right with certain foods, iced tea or coffee with summer luncheons. But, with those exceptions, serve wine—or nothing.

Good wines need not be expensive. Befriend a liquor dealer, give his suggestions a chance—and take advantage of his sales. Always go to the town's top dealer if you don't know much. Many small dealers don't either.

Many excellent imported wines and good American wines cost around two dollars a bottle. (If this is too expensive, skip wine.)

You do not need encyclopedic wine knowledge, just a few facts. Red wine goes with meat or game. There are two main red wine categories: Burgundy and Bordeaux (also called claret). Burgundy, rich in taste and bouquet, goes well with all red meats and with game. Genuine French Burgundies, from the famous Côte d'Or around the town of Beaune in Burgundy, are considered by experts the best you can get. Expensive in so-called "great years," good off-year Burgundies sell for modest prices.

Bordeaux, or claret, goes well with roasts, chops, pot roast, meat stews. Slightly lighter and fresher in taste than Burgundy, it suits any meat dish. Red wines of the Burgundy or Bordeaux type should never be chilled; their flavor and bouquet improve if the bottles are opened a few hours before the party and allowed to breathe, as they say, at room temperature. If you live in a hot climate, find a cool place. "Room temperature," to wine men, means 55 to 65 degrees.

Some poultry dishes call for red wine: *coq au vin* and other chicken dishes cooked in red wine, roast goose, domestic duckling, and turkey. (White wine for *cold* turkey, though.)

Most people feel that white wines go best with chicken or fish (though red is acceptable if you prefer it). Serve white wines chilled but not freezing cold. Most people prefer a *dry* (not sweet) white wine with a main course. Sweetish white wines are better with dessert.

Rosé, or pink, wines, whose delights are not yet fully appreciated on this side of the ocean, go especially well with roast pork, ham, highly seasoned fish, baby lamb. Usually not expensive, they really taste good with anything and make a perfect alternate to white wine at luncheon. Since rosés are served chilled, they can be the answer, too, when serving meat to people who like only cold drinks.

Champagne also goes well with anything. On a special occasion you could serve it right through dinner, or pass a bottle with dessert. Most people prefer dry champagne. "Brut" on the label means dry. Illogical as it may be, labels reading "Extra Dry," "Demi Sec," and "Sec," mean not so dry, sweetish, and sweet, in that order.

Sparkling Burgundy is usually not a rosy replica of champagne. Its bubbles are often artificial and its taste more grapy. It is popular, perhaps because, like champagne, it seems festive and looks pretty. But if champagne is really what you want, don't get sparkling Burgundy because you think it is cheaper. There are good New York State and California champagnes for the same price, and some equally fine French champagnes for four to five dollars a bottle. Many of the famous French champagne names, like Perrier-Jouët, Mumm's, Moët et Chandon, Lanson, Bollinger, have non-vintage varieties that are appropriately *brut* and less expensive than the same brands with a date on the label.

Bordeaux and Burgundy are by no means the only places with good vineyards. Loire and Rhone Valley wines are excellent. So are Italian Chianti, both red and white, and a whole series of Italian wines like Orvieto, Valpolicella, and Soave. There are famous German Rhine wines and Moselles, and Swiss, Portuguese, and Spanish wines that you will find palatable and cheap. American wines are getting better and better, too. Your dealer should know the ones you can serve with confidence.

Only an expert can make sense of vintages and labels. A "great year" may apply to this wine but not that. French labels often identify the *clos*, the actual plot of land where the grapes were grown: "Gevrey-Chambertin, Clos St. Jacques," or "Vosne Romanée, Clos des Réas." But for all amateurs know, the *clos* across the road may be better.

German wine labels tell all, if you know German . . . and wines. They state the town, the grower, the time of harvest, the additives if any, the vineyard slope, the castle on the hill. Everything. Our dealer presently has a Moselle with a label that reads, in part: Eitelsbacher Karthauser-hofsberger Burgberg, but the only way we know it is good is because he says so—and it costs $3.69 a bottle, on sale.

Let's just stick to "red," "white," and "rosé." Tell the wine dealer what you plan to eat, what you want to spend, and let him choose. Sample and learn under his guidance. And, unless you are having a wine expert to dinner, do not buy rare vintages, particularly if cocktails have been served—guests' taste buds won't be acute enough to tell a two-dollar from a six-dollar wine.

Port goes well with cheese. Genuine port comes from Portugal and is not cheap, but if you have cheese in place of dessert a glass is all anyone will take. Sweetish sherries also taste good with cheese, and literally any red wine teams delightfully with fruit, cheese, or nuts. Dry white wines are perfect with a salad bowl luncheon. Sweet German wines or French sauternes are right for dessert.

How many bottles should you have? It's hard to say exactly. Some guests drink several glasses during a meal, others only toy with one. Three people to a bottle is usually safe if one wine is served through most of dinner. If you have a second wine or champagne with dessert, you might cut back on the first. Allow one bottle of dessert wine for every six people.

Wineglasses. Connoisseurs like a special glass for each type of wine. The white wineglass is smaller than the red wineglass and bigger than the sherry glass. Rhine wineglasses have especially long stems and sometimes green bowls. Champagne glasses have long stems, often hollow, with balloon, basin, or V-shaped bowls. Since most of us have neither the budget nor the space for all of these, an all-purpose glass about the size of a red wineglass has come into fashion. The most popular model is tulip-shaped with a thin stem and, most important, a thin rim. Many department stores carry a nice version for about a dollar and a half.

Pouring wine. The person who pours the wine puts a little in his glass first to get out any pieces of cork that may be on top. Then he fills the other glasses, ending with his own. A wineglass is not filled full. If it is globular in shape a little less than half is right; a tulip shape is filled a little more than half full. These modest amounts encourage sipping, the correct way to drink wine.

Liqueurs

Rarely offered after lunch, they are added attractions after a dinner, though not really necessary. After coffee you can serve tall drinks or stop altogether. But liqueurs top off a good dinner and, rationalization though it may be, do seem to improve digestion.

There are literally dozens of liqueurs and cordials. Brandy, the gourmet's favorite, is not really a liqueur. "An ardent spirit distilled from wine," the dictionary says. "Brandies" are made by distilling the juice of the fruit itself to a high alcoholic content; "liqueurs" are the result of an infusion of fruit, or another flavoring, *in* alcohol.

Two types of grape brandy are considered superior. Cognac is made in the area of Cognac, France. (*Fine champagne* is a type of cognac especially smooth and palatable, made of combined wines from the French cognac districts, Grande and Petite Champagne.) The other first-quality grape brandy is armagnac, made in the foothills of the Pyrenees.

French brandy labels have distinguishing marks. Some are deceiving: the three stars often seen merely indicate the cheapest brandy in a firm's line and say nothing of its age. Other marks tell more, reliably: "V.S.O.P." (very superior old pale), "V.O." (very old), and "V.S.E.P." (very superior extra pale). Genuine Napoleon brandy was bottled before the Battle of Waterloo. There is none on the market today. A bottle of so-called Napoleon brandy might be modern brandy with a few drops of the old mixed in. Courvoisier, a first-rate cognac company, has trade-marked the subtitle, "The Brandy of Napoleon." This means cognac was Napoleon's favorite drink, not that you are getting something a hundred and fifty years old.

The famous names—Courvoisier, Rémy Martin, Monnet, Hine, Hennessey, Martell, etc.—produce great brandies, and good brandies at relatively moderate prices.

Always have brandy when you serve liqueurs, and then, since brandy is dry, offer at least one sweet choice. Crème de menthe, either white or green, is popular, and most refreshing when served over crushed ice. Other popular liqueurs are Cointreau and Grand Marnier, which have a base of oranges. Benedictine, a delicious liqueur invented by the Benedictine monks in France, starts with grapes, but dozens of herbs, spices, and seeds are added along with honey, cognac, and plain water. It is very sweet, but a nice compromise is to mix Benedictine half and half with brandy for a B and B.

Chartreuse, which has 130 different herbs, comes from a recipe of the Carthusian monks in Grenoble. A favorite of many, it comes in two colors: green, naturally, and yellow, the latter being a bit less expensive.

Those are some of the standard liqueurs served here, but there are many other choices. You might try an eau de vie, one of the brandies distilled from a fruit other than grapes. These retain the taste and aroma of the fruit but are as dry and strong as grape brandy. Among eaux de vie, we like Kirsch distilled from cherries, Mirabelle from plums, and, best of all, the raspberry eau de vie, Framboise. Eaux de vie are true brandies—that is, distilled fruit. So-called cherry, plum, or apricot "brandies," which are sweet and sticky, are really liqueurs—fruit syrups with alcohol added.

A few more liqueurs? Try Calvados, a mouth-watering apple brandy from Normandy. Try Strega, an Italian answer to Chartreuse. Try Tia Maria, a distillation of coffee from Jamaica. There are also German schnapps and Yugoslavian slivovitz, both clear, dry as the best French brandy.

Most liqueurs are expensive, because most good ones are imported, but you serve only a tablespoon or so, and a bottle lasts a long time. Granted that you want liqueurs at all, first pick a good brandy, then experiment with others. Incidentally, a bottle or two of liqueur makes a very special present for a man who says he doesn't want anything special for his birthday.

Gourmets take the serving of brandy very seriously. One we know puts a drop on his wrist first and sniffs it like perfume. While many people like to drink brandy in big balloon-shaped snifters or inhalers which they cup in the hands to warm the brandy and release its aroma, all brandies and liqueurs may be served in little glasses or "ponies" designed for this purpose.

Wines and liqueurs as recipe ingredients play a part in good eating. In many a recipe wine is what makes it; think of *filet de sole au vin blanc, boeuf bourgignon,* and *zabaglione,* to name but three. In other recipes, it adds only subtle flavor, but always add it. When a recipe reads "half a cup of dry white wine—optional," don't believe it. Though a gourmet might not agree, it has always seemed rank extravagance to cook with expensive table wine. Use instead inexpensive American table wines (but not wines labeled "cooking wine"). Get *dry* white wine, and a red wine with body. If you cook with wines often, there is saving in buying half gallons and storing them in the refrigerator.

For liqueurs there are no substitutes. A recipe that calls for a tablespoon of cognac had better have just that and not grocery store "cooking brandy." Flaming dishes also need the real thing. Fruit liqueurs, seldom used in the actual cooking of a dish, are added afterward or mixed into a sauce, and the success of the dish depends on the strength of the true liqueur. Fortunately a little goes a long way in a recipe.

Other After-Dinner Drinks

In place of liqueurs you might offer a stinger (brandy and crème de menthe shaken up with ice). If you have had champagne at dinner ask guests to take their glasses with them from the table and finish up the remainder in the living room. Whether or not you serve liqueurs, be prepared for tall drinks later on in the evening. Plan to refill the ice bucket and offer scotch, bourbon with soda or water, and ginger ale, tonic, and cola.

CHAPTER **17**

Easy Menus and Recipes

Here, suggested party menus, divided into the three main-course categories, meat, poultry, and fish, with an emphasis on dishes that taste and look professional and that don't need last-minute fussing over. Easy recipes for starred items are given. *Unless otherwise stated, amounts are enough for 10 people—with leftovers.* With calories as well as cuisine in mind we downgrade rice, potatoes, and floury gravy and upgrade fruit desserts. Each menu would be improved by a salad course, or you might pass up a first course and have salad instead. Salad can always be served, too, on a side plate *with* any of the main courses.

TWELVE PARTY MENUS WITH A MAIN COURSE OF MEAT

We have picked roast beef and roast lamb as the pivots. A whole cut of something always seems partyish and once you know your oven these are easy to cook, needing no watching or basting. Buy a pound of rib roast per person; a five-pound leg of lamb is plenty for ten people. Gourmets campaign for *rare* roast beef and *pink* lamb flavored with garlic. We agree.

Of course, many other meats could be substituted, as long as the meal stays balanced: with stews, stroganoffs, ham, or roast pork, have a lighter soup or dessert.

1.

Avocados Du Pont*
Roast Beef—Yorkshire Pudding, Chutney, String Beans with
  Slivered Almonds
Cherries Jubilee

With plenty of Yorkshire pudding, potatoes seem unnecessary, but might be added to the roasting pan. Indian chutney, or domestic chutney made from mangoes, is excellent as a roast beef condiment, and equally good with steak.

AVOCADOS DU PONT

3 cans jellied madrilène
5 ripe avocados
½ pint sour cream
4-ounce jar red caviar

Chill madrilène until thoroughly jelled. Just before dinner halve the avocados and lay on salad plates, supported by a lettuce leaf or two. Fill each half with the soup, top with a tablespoon of sour cream and then a teaspoon of caviar.

2.

Cold Bisque of Clams*
Roast Leg of Lamb—Roast Potatoes, Carrots, Mint Sauce
Mousse au Chocolat*

Cook the carrots in your favorite way or try this: slice them thin; boil them in salted water to cover, plus half a stick of butter and 2 tablespoons of sugar to every 4 cups of carrots (8 cups is ample for 10 or 12 people). Cook quickly over high heat until water boils away, letting carrots brown in the butter. Sprinkle with snipped parsley before serving. You can partially cook this dish the day before, putting the carrots in a casserole to brown over low heat during the first course.

Bottled mint sauce is fine but, to make something special of it, heat it with a couple of tablespoons of mint jelly until the jelly melts.

EASY MENUS AND RECIPES

COLD BISQUE OF CLAMS

3 cans condensed clam chowder
1½ tablespoons thyme
1 bottle clam juice
3 cans mushroom soup
1 cup heavy cream

Mix the undiluted clam chowder and thyme with the clam juice. Mix the mushroom soup, also undiluted, with the cream and stir both mixtures together over low heat until thoroughly blended. Strain to remove vegetables and chill in refrigerator. A day-before dish, it is equally good served hot.

MOUSSE AU CHOCOLAT

2 6-ounce bags semi-sweet chocolate bits
10 eggs, separated

Melt chocolate in top of double boiler, stirring well to melt bits completely. Beat egg yolks until lemon-colored. Beat egg whites until stiff and shiny. Pour melted chocolate into yolks. Mix well. Then fold in egg whites thoroughly with a wire sauce whisk. Pour into serving bowl (or individual cups) and chill 3 hours or overnight.

3.

Spinach Soup*
Roast Beef—Horse Radish Sauce,* Acorn Squash,* Brussels Sprouts
Deep-Dish Fruit Pie—Apple, Plum, or Peach—with Cream

SPINACH SOUP

Some spinach soups have a cream base; there's another in which chopped spinach is simply cooked in strong chicken stock. An easy cream one is made this way:

2 packages frozen chopped spinach, cooked
2 cans mushroom soup
Light cream
Salt, pepper, onion powder to taste

Combine ingredients and thin with a stock made from bouillon cubes (1 cube per cup of water). Purée in blender, thin with more stock if necessary. Good hot or cold, this can be made a day ahead.

HORSE RADISH SAUCE

1 cup heavy cream
Bottled horse radish, strained
Salt

A couple of hours before dinner, whip cream until stiff and stir in horse radish to taste—the hotter the better, we think. Add salt to taste and chill until serving. For a day-before version, mix the whipped cream half and half with softened cream cheese.

ACORN SQUASH

5 acorn squash
Salt and pepper
1 stick butter (¼ pound)
8 tablespoons brown sugar
4 tablespoons sherry
¼ cup cream

Wash squash, cut in half crosswise, and remove seeds. Sprinkle with salt and pepper and place, cut side down, in a baking pan. Bake in a 400° oven for 20 minutes. Mix remaining ingredients and spoon into squash halves. Return them to oven for 15 or 20 minutes. Don't forget teaspoons when you set the table.

4.

Creamed Crab Meat*
Roast Beef—Pickled Watermelon Rind, Twice-Baked Potatoes,
  Broccoli with Butter
Orange Ice with Cointreau*—Cookies

Since fresh crab meat is expensive, save this menu for a special event or have a cheaper main course. The crab-meat recipe makes a good lunch or dinner main course served with a colorful vegetable (carrots, beets, or peas) and rice. As a main course, two and a half pounds is necessary.

CREAMED CRAB MEAT

2 pounds fresh crab meat
1½ pints heavy cream
Bread crumbs
Sherry

Pick over crab meat for shells, trying not to break up big pieces. Line the bottom of a buttered baking dish (or individual ramekins) with a layer of crab meat, then cover with cream and sprinkle with a layer of bread crumbs. Repeat until all crab meat and cream have been used. Prepare ahead and refrigerate. Before serving, add ½ to ¾ cup of good sherry and sprinkle more crumbs over the top. Heat for 20 minutes or so in a 300° oven.

ORANGE ICE WITH COINTREAU

Serve orange ice in a bowl and pass a small decanter of cointreau (at room temperature) around the table. Chocolate cookies go especially well with this.

5.

Corn Soup*
Roast Lamb—Pickled Walnuts, Tomatoes Stuffed with Peas or Creamed Spinach, Scalloped Potatoes
Fraises Sarah Bernhardt*

Pickled walnuts are a favorite accompaniment to lamb in England although some people think it an acquired taste. Try to acquire it.

CORN SOUP

Use any cream of corn soup recipe, or make it this easy way. Take 3 cans of creamed corn. Rub through a coarse strainer—a bit of work but the result is all pulp, no kernels. Thin it to desired consistency with chicken stock, milk or cream or both, then salt, lots of pepper, and sugar to taste. Make ahead and reheat in a double boiler, or serve ice cold.

FRAISES SARAH BERNHARDT

While the genuine recipe consists of pineapple mousse surrounded by a sauce of strawberries and pineapple, with this relatively heavy menu the fruit alone seems plenty.

3 pints strawberries
1 large fresh pineapple (or 2 No. 2 cans pineapple cubes)
Sugar to taste
Curaçao or cointreau

Hull and wash strawberries. Cut pineapple into cubes, removing
any spiny bits and the core. (If using canned pineapple, drain it
well.) Combine fruits and sprinkle them with a little powdered
sugar. Pour over ½ cup or more of liqueur. Chill and stir once or
twice so that all fruit is washed by liqueur. Macaroons go well with
this.

6.

Pâté Maison*
Roast Beef—Mustard Pickles, Corn Custard,* Broccoli au Beurre*
Berries and Cream—Cookies

PÂTÉ MAISON

Perhaps you have invented your own *pâté maison*. If not, this is
excellent. Truffles are now more expensive than Beluga caviar, but
the one in this recipe can be left out. Serve each person a thick slice
of pâté with a couple of pieces of white toast, crusts removed.

1 small can truffles—this gives just one truffle
4 tablespoons brandy
1 pound liverwurst
1 envelope gelatin
½ can chicken broth, undiluted

Chop drained truffle fine and soak overnight in brandy. Next day
mash liverwurst, add gelatin which you have dissolved in the
heated broth, then brandy and truffle. Beat until smooth and chill
to harden. Beat again and put in a greased mold. Chill 3 or 4 hours
or overnight, unmold, and slice. You can skip the second beating,

but it makes the pâté lighter. An electric beater on low speed works well. If you skip the truffle, don't leave out the brandy, and lay a few slices of black olives on the pâté for the black accent.

CORN CUSTARD

4 eggs
2 cans creamed corn
3 tablespoons melted butter
2½ teaspoons sugar
3 cups warm milk
Salt and pepper
½ cup buttered bread crumbs

Beat eggs well. Mix all ingredients together except crumbs. Pour into greased casserole, sprinkle with crumbs, and bake in a 325° oven for 40 to 50 minutes. Mixed one day, refrigerated, and baked the next, this is still delicious; remove from refrigerator in time to let it warm up before baking.

BROCCOLI AU BEURRE

3 bunches fresh broccoli
Butter
Lemon juice

Strong as we are on frozen foods, this dish is best made from fresh broccoli. Wash and trim broccoli, cutting off the very ends of the stalks. Cut a few gashes in each stalk. Steam broccoli until tender but not soft. Place in casserole or heatproof serving dish and pour over one stick (¼ pound) melted butter to which you have added lemon juice to taste. Reheat slowly on top of stove before dinner.

7.

Cold Black Bean Soup*
Roast Beef—String Beans and Baby Limas Mixed with Butter, Mashed Potatoes
Lemon Mousse*

COLD BLACK BEAN SOUP

3 cans black bean soup, undiluted
3 cans condensed beef bouillon or equivalent amount
 of beef stock
½ teaspoon Worcestershire sauce
1½ cups sherry
1½ teaspoons powdered mustard
Sour cream

Heat all ingredients together except sour cream. Chill 3 or 4 hours before serving, or overnight. Ladle into soup plates and add a heaping teaspoon of sour cream to each.

LEMON MOUSSE

This is an easy version of an English cold soufflé. It serves 12 easily.

2 teaspoons grated lemon rind
1 cup lemon juice
2 envelopes unflavored gelatin
½ cup cold water
8 eggs, separated
1 teaspoon salt
2 cups sugar
2 cups heavy cream

Grate lemon rind, squeeze and strain lemon juice. Sprinkle gelatin over cold water to soften. Mix egg yolks with salt, lemon juice, 1 *cup* of the sugar, in the top of a double boiler. Cook over boiling water, stirring constantly, until slightly thickened. Remove from heat, stir in lemon rind and gelatin, and allow to cool.

Beat egg whites until stiff but not dry, then gradually add remaining cup of sugar, beating until the whites hold a peak. Use a big bowl for this as you will be adding everything else to it. Beat cream until stiff: pour over egg whites. Then add lemon mixture and fold all together with a sauce whisk. Pour into a big glass bowl and chill for 3 hours or more. For eye appeal, sprinkle surface with a little powdered sugar before serving, or put a trio of leaves or a single flower in the center.

8.

Boula Boula*
Crown of Lamb—Candied Carrots, Creamed Onions
Raspberries Gervais*

BOULA BOULA

This can be made with condensed pea soup but is infinitely better with fresh or frozen peas.

2 packages frozen peas
Sugar
2 large cans green turtle soup
Sherry
Salt and pepper
Whipped cream

Cook peas according to package directions, adding 1 teaspoon sugar. Pour peas and water in which they were cooked a little at a time into a blender. Blend thoroughly. Transfer to pan. Pour turtle soup into blender to purée turtle meat. Add to pan. Heat. Before serving add sherry to taste. Serve with a teaspoon of unflavored whipped cream on top, or, if you have the equipment, put hot soup into individual ovenproof bowls, add whipped cream and a dusting of paprika or grated black pepper, and pop under broiler until cream browns.

RASPBERRIES GERVAIS

Gervais is the French term for fresh cream cheese, which is hard to find here. You can achieve the same effect with the following:

4 pints raspberries
4 packages cream cheese
Heavy cream
Sugar

Wash and drain raspberries and place in serving bowl. Chill. Mash cheese and thin it with cream until the consistency is like thick whipped cream or whipped butter. Put it in a sauce bowl. Chill. Remove both berries and cream cheese during dinner so that they are not icy cold. Pass around a bowl or a sifter of sugar. While we prefer the rougher texture of granulated sugar with this, powdered sugar is just as good.

Note: A mock French *crème fraiche,* delicious with all fresh fruits, can be made by combining 2 parts whipping cream (beaten with a whisk until slightly thick) with one part sour cream. For 8 to 12 people use 1½ cups cream, 1 cup sour cream.

9.

Shrimp Baked in Wine*
Roast Lamb—Creamed Spinach, Shoestring Potatoes, from a can
Poundcake au Kirsch,* Whipped Cream

Another expensive dinner, because of the high price of fresh shrimp. If you like the sound of the recipe it can be served, with a green vegetable, as a main course for either lunch or dinner. In this case, have 3 pounds of shrimp for 10 people.

SHRIMP BAKED IN WINE

2 pounds fresh shrimp
1 stick butter (¼ pound)
1 clove garlic, minced
1 teaspoon dried tarragon
1 tablespoon chopped parsley
½ teaspoon each salt and pepper
½ cup bread crumbs
Dry white wine

Shell shrimp and cook for 4 minutes in boiling water to cover, with a slice of lemon, 1 teaspoon salt, and a bay leaf. We prefer shelling before cooking as the shrimp stay plumper that way. Blend the butter with the garlic, tarragon, parsley, seasonings, and bread crumbs. Place shrimp in greased baking dish and pour over wine to cover completely. Dot butter and crumb mixture over shrimps and run dish under the broiler for 5 minutes or so, until brown and bubbly.

POUNDCAKE AU KIRSCH

While this may seem *too* easy for a party dessert, just wait until you hear the compliments.

Make or buy a poundcake. Cut it into slices. Whip 1 cup of heavy cream. Pour kirsch into a pretty carafe and chill it. Arrange the poundcake attractively on a platter. Each guest takes a slice of cake, saturates it with kirsch, and adds a spoonful of whipped cream. The cream, not really necessary, just makes this dessert seem more elaborate.

10.

Fillet of Sole Normande*
Roast Beef—Harvard Beets, New Potatoes with Parsley Butter
Peach Cake*

FILLET OF SOLE NORMANDE

This is a good main course for a lunch or supper, served with plain string beans, peas, or beets, and boiled potato balls. It is a French specialty which can be cooked without supervision by a chef or anyone else. As a first course, allow 1 small fillet per person.

In a well-buttered baking dish lay fillets, sprinkle lightly with salt and pepper, and pour over dry white wine just to cover. Shake over some bread crumbs, add a few sprigs of parsley. Dot the fillets with lots of butter and bake in a 300° oven for 20 to 25 minutes. Now you have *sole au vin blanc*; it becomes *sole Normande* when you pour over 1½ cups heavy cream, during the last 5 minutes of baking. Return dish to oven, announce dinner. While guests come to table, remove parsley and run dish under broiler for 3 or 4 minutes, to get those professional-looking brown flecks on top. A cup of seedless grapes or sliced mushrooms can be added with the cream for an even more delicious dish.

PEACH CAKE

This is baking at its easiest, and can be done the day before. Since it is so good warm, turn off the oven after you take out the main course and let the cake warm slowly. Best with fresh peaches, well-drained frozen ones will do.

    1 cup sifted cake flour
    ¼ teaspoon salt
    1 teaspoon baking powder
    ½ cup granulated sugar
    ½ cup soft butter or shortening
    1 teaspoon grated lemon rind
    2 eggs, unbeaten
    4 or 5 sliced peaches
    ¼ cup granulated sugar
    ½ teaspoon cinnamon

Sift together flour, salt, and baking powder. Beat ½ *cup* sugar with the butter until creamy. Add lemon rind. Beat in eggs well, one at a time. Add flour mixture gradually, beating well after each addition. Spread half the batter in a greased pan. Lay on peach slices neatly. Spread with remaining batter and sprinkle the ¼ cup granulated sugar mixed with cinnamon on top. Bake in a 350° oven for about 45 or 50 minutes. Use either a square 8-inch pan or a round spring-form pan. This cake is good served with sweetened whipped cream or vanilla ice cream.

11.

Tomato Soup*
Roast Beef or Lamb—Purée of Peas, French Fried Potatoes
Blackberries Walterspiel*

TOMATO SOUP

All tomato soups are good openers. Try one made with canned tomato juice and stock, adding sugar, salt, and pepper to taste, and topped with whipped cream and fried croutons. Or add curry and cream to condensed tomato soup. Tomato juice is excellent added to vichyssoise or minestrone. Or try this:

3 cans condensed tomato soup
2 cans tomatoes put through a strainer or blended with
2 cups of the juice from canned tomatoes
1 cup cream
1 cup sherry
1 tablespoon or more dried tarragon

Mix all together and serve hot or cold. Serves 10 amply.

BLACKBERRIES WALTERSPIEL

This is a sort of German version of strawberries Romanoff. Blue-berries—the big hothouse variety—may be substituted for blackber-ries.

Croutons made from 6 slices of white bread
Kirsch or blackberry brandy
1½ quarts vanilla ice cream
2 pints blackberries, washed and drained

Toast croutons in oven; do not fry in butter. Put in a bowl and saturate with kirsch or blackberry brandy. Allow ice cream to soften slightly in the refrigerator. Just before serving, thoroughly mix ice cream, croutons, and berries together and transfer to a serving bowl.

12.

Crème Senegalese*
Roast Beef—Baked Potatoes with Sour Cream or Butter, Creamed
   Asparagus*
Apple Dumplings

CRÈME SENEGALESE

3 cans condensed cream of chicken soup
2 cups light cream
1 cup milk
2 or more tablespoons curry powder to taste
Coarsely ground black pepper to taste

Thoroughly mix soup, cream, and milk. Pour off a small amount and stir curry powder into it. (Repeat this if you add more curry, later.) Return curry mixture to soup and heat for 5 or 10 minutes, stirring constantly. Remove from stove and add salt and pepper to taste. Chill for 3 hours or overnight. If the soup should thicken, add more milk or chicken stock. Serve in consommé cups garnished with grated coconut, chopped white meat of chicken, or a thin slice of red apple with the skin left on.

CREAMED ASPARAGUS

While there is nothing better than asparagus cooked at the last minute and served with melted butter or hollandaise, this delicious recipe is easier for 10 people as it can be made ready ahead of time and heated up.

 2 big bunches of asparagus—about 50 spears
 3 cans condensed cream of asparagus soup
 Bread crumbs

Cut off tough ends of stalks and steam the asparagus or cook it in your usual way. Drain. Arrange neatly in a baking dish or casserole. Pour over the soup, undiluted, and top with buttered bread crumbs. At dinnertime heat for 40 minutes, uncovered, in a 325° oven, or for 30 minutes in a 350° oven. Serve from the casserole.

TWELVE PARTY MENUS WITH A MAIN COURSE OF POULTRY

Any of the first courses already listed which do not have a chicken base would go as well in these menus, as would the desserts, if colors and consistencies of the various dishes harmonize.

1.

 Hot Borsch with Sour Cream*
 Roast Squab Chickens Stuffed with Wild Rice—Wild Bramble
  Jelly, French Peas with Onions
 Baked Bananas*

This is a good winter menu; in summer a cold soup might be better, or omit soup and serve a crisp salad after the main course. While hot desserts, such as baked bananas, are good no matter what the season, a fruit and sherbet dessert or melon could be delicious too.

There is always something impressive about serving each person a whole bird. Squab chickens are generally more expensive than Rock Cornish hens and cheaper than real squabs (pigeons). Buy ten of whichever suits your taste and pocketbook. Stuff with partially cooked wild rice or a combination of wild and long-grain rice. You might use onion soup to moisten it, or add a small can of sliced mushrooms. Roast the birds at 350° for an hour or so, depending on their size. Baste frequently with butter or margarine mixed with the pan drippings. No need to make gravy.

Another delectable way to roast birds: leave them unstuffed, throw a pinch of salt, pepper, and orégano into each cavity. Rub the skins liberally with olive oil and lemon juice, then shake salt and pepper over and let stand an hour or more before roasting. Baste with Marsala wine—a cup or so—and turn oven high for the last few minutes to brown the birds well.

Wild bramble jelly is merely a strong, tart, English currant jelly that goes well with game. Domestic currant jelly is fine, though less strong. German *preisselbeeren* conserve is also excellent with game, guinea hen, squab chicken, or Cornish hen.

French peas and whole onions, from cans, partially drained, and heated up with butter, salt, and pepper, are easy. The milky look of the French version comes by mixing a little flour into a little milk and the juice of one can of peas. Cook until slightly thickened and pour over the drained peas and onions. A good dose of sugar always enhances the taste.

HOT BORSCH WITH SOUR CREAM

2 1-pound jars red cabbage
2 No. 2 cans undiluted beef consommé or 4 cups beef stock
2 1-pound, 4-ounce cans small whole beets
Black pepper
1 cup sour cream

In a blender purée 1 jar of cabbage with 1 can of consommé. Transfer to pot and purée remaining cabbage with consommé. Drain off juice of beets and add to pot. Slice 8 or 10 beets thin, cut into julienne strips, and add to soup. (Leftover beets can be eaten up next day.) Stir in black pepper (6 or 8 twists of the grinder).

Make a day ahead and decant into jars and refrigerate. Heat slowly and serve with a rounded teaspoon of sour cream in each cup. This recipe is equally good served cold.

BAKED BANANAS

Peel a dozen or more bananas and arrange pinwheel fashion in a large glass pie plate or shallow casserole, lavishly buttered. Mix a stick and a half of butter (melted) with 6 tablespoons brown sugar and ½ cup dry vermouth. Pour over bananas and bake in a 350° oven for 20 minutes or so, until the bananas are soft and the sauce bubbling. You might put the bananas in the oven as guests start the main course, and turn off the oven after 20 minutes, leaving the door open so that bananas will stay hot but not overcook.

2.

Salmon Mousse, Sauce Verte,* Sliced Cucumbers
Grilled Broilers—Succotash
Apple Pie and American Cheese

An any-season menu; in summer the broilers might be grilled over charcoal outdoors. In winter char the skin by putting broilers close to the flame.

Since the salmon mousse, sauce, and cucumbers is more of a first course than soup, one fairly heavy vegetable seems enough with the chicken. Use a standard cookbook recipe for salmon mousse or salmon loaf, using fresh or frozen fish if possible. If you use a ring mold fill the center with cucumbers; if not, pile them in a bowl edged with lettuce. Three big cucumbers are more than enough for 10 people. Slice them paper-thin, leaving the peel on one, for an attractive dark green accent, and soak in salted water in the refrigerator. Later, drain, and marinate in a light vinaigrette sauce to which you might add some dillweed for color and taste. Dark, thinly sliced, and buttered pumpernickel goes well with this dish. Try the mousse as a main course for lunch too.

SAUCE VERTE

While using grocery store mayonnaise is no crime, this sauce becomes superb made with homemade mayonnaise—pure olive oil and wine vinegar. To 1 cup mayonnaise add finely chopped chives, parsley, water cress, cooked spinach, 2 tablespoons of at least two of these. Add a drop of green vegetable coloring, if you think necessary. *Sauce verte* does not suffer if made a day ahead.

3.

Artichokes
Chicken and Oysters à la Crème*—Rice, Whole String Beans in
    Butter*
Crepes with Cranberry Sauce*

Wash, trim the tops, and cook artichokes according to any recipe. If served hot, have individual cups of hollandaise or melted butter. If served cold, strong vinaigrette sauce or homemade mayonnaise goes very well. For a lunch, you might have hot artichokes followed by cold chicken and a salad.

CHICKEN AND OYSTERS À LA CRÈME

This simple dish, needing little attention before serving, always seems to impress.

3 large broilers cut in serving pieces
3 teaspoons salt
1½ teaspoons pepper
1 stick butter (¼ pound)
1½ cups milk
1 teaspoon crumbled sage
3 dozen shucked oysters
1½ pints heavy cream
1½ teaspoons dried basil

Use only the meaty pieces of chicken, saving wings and backs for soup. Preheat oven to 375°. Sprinkle chicken with half the salt and pepper; sauté in the butter in a heavy skillet for 10 minutes or so, turning each piece once, to brown lightly. Place chicken in a shallow baking dish or casserole. Add milk, remaining salt and pepper, and sage. Cover dish, using foil if you have no lid. Bake 1 hour.

The above can be done ahead of time. The finale goes this way: Return casserole to 375° oven, heat to bubbling. Add well-drained oysters, cream, and basil, re-cover, and return to oven for 5 to 10 minutes, just to be sure the sauce is very hot. Oysters need little cooking; if overcooked they harden and shrivel.

WHOLE STRING BEANS IN BUTTER

Hardly a recipe, this is just a way to cook fresh string beans without the work of stringing or dicing. Snap the ends off 2 pounds of young string beans, wash, and drain. Half fill a big stew pot with water, add 1 teaspoon salt, and bring to a boil. Drop in beans a few at a time, always keeping the water boiling. Add 2 tablespoons sugar, and perhaps a pinch of baking soda to keep beans bright green. After boiling 10 minutes or so (beans should be crisp, not limp), drain and transfer to a top-of-the-stove casserole, add a stick of butter or margarine. Cover. Before serving reheat slowly over an asbestos mat.

Note: Leftover beans, peas, broccoli, etc., can be marinated in French dressing and served as salad with or without lettuce. To remove butter put vegetable into a colander and pour over boiling water. Marinate in refrigerator for an hour or more.

CREPES WITH CRANBERRY SAUCE

Crepes, always festive, are easier served to a smaller number than 10—you need two per person and making twenty takes time. They can be made the day before and stacked on a plate in the refrigerator. Once you learn the how-to of crepes they will serve parties in many ways: filled with creamed mushrooms, spinach, or sea food as a first course, filled with hash as a main dish, filled with jams for dessert. The indispensable utensil is an iron crepe pan, 6 inches in diameter, never used for any other cooking. A new pan must be "cured": fill it with vegetable oil and simmer for 2 or 3 hours. Pour out the oil and wipe with paper towels. Wipe it out after each use; keep it dust-free in a plastic bag. For 10 people, double this recipe:

⅔ cup sifted flour
1 tablespoon sugar
Pinch of salt
2 whole eggs and 2 egg yolks, well beaten
1¾ cups milk
2 tablespoons melted butter
1 tablespoon cognac

Sift dry ingredients together and add them to the eggs. Add milk and stir until smooth, then add melted butter and cognac. Let stand for 2 hours before cooking.

Now heat crepe pan over a medium flame and add a rounded teaspoon of butter. When it bubbles you are ready. Decant batter into a pitcher, and for each crepe pour in a good tablespoon or so— enough to cover surface of pan. Tip pan around until bottom is covered. Do not worry about any pinpoint air holes. Cook batter for a minute or so and test with a spatula to see if it's ready to turn easily. When you think that moment has come, turn and cook for another minute or so. (Sometimes the first couple of crepes will tear, probably because the heat of the pan is not yet right or there is too much butter. Don't worry. Eat the failures and proceed.) Halfway through you may need a little more butter. Pile up crepes on a platter and, when all are cooked, refrigerate.

Next day, butter a baking dish. Carefully lift a crepe from the pile and spread with a tablespoon or more of whole cranberry sauce. Roll up and put in the baking dish. When all crepes are rolled, sprinkle with sugar. As your main course leaves the oven, lower heat to 250° and put in the crepes. They will heat well during dinner. Serve from the baking dish. If you use another filling—lingonberries or jam—you might light the crepes with brandy at table. Warm a little brandy in a saucepan, pour over the crepes, and set aflame.

4.

Purée of Split Peas*
Roast Chicken with Wine Gravy*—Wild Rice and Long-Grain
    Rice, Half and Half, Tomatoes Filled with Creamed Spinach
Macédoine of Fruit*—Cookies

PURÉE OF SPLIT PEAS

You need a box of green split peas and a ham bone—the latter is essential. Follow directions for pea soup on the box. Save a few ham slivers to float on top of the soup. Since the purée should be fairly thin, add water as necessary. Serve with croutons fried in butter, if this appeals.

ROAST CHICKEN WITH WINE GRAVY

An easy dish, in which timing is somewhat elastic and taste memorable. Buy 2 5-pound roasting chickens. Rub cavities with a cut lemon, shake in salt and pepper, add some parsley sprigs and 1 teaspoon dried thyme to each bird. Rub outside with lots of butter or margarine and sprinkle with salt. Roast in a 350° oven for 1½ hours, or until legs move up and down easily. To carve easily, let sit 10 minutes or so out of the oven.

The gravy. In the afternoon put necks and giblets in a pan, with 1½ teaspoons salt, some parsley sprigs, 6 or 8 peppercorns, 2 small onions stuck with 2 cloves. Add a couple of carrots if you have them. Cover with water and dry white wine, half and half. Bring to a full boil and skim off the scum. Cover pan, reduce heat, and simmer gently for an hour or so. Strain. When the chickens are done, simply mix the pan juices into the heated wine gravy. You might reduce the gravy first by boiling it rapidly for a few minutes before adding pan juices, or thicken it with a little flour or with flour and butter kneaded together. If served as is, encourage guests to sop it up with French bread.

MACÉDOINE OF FRUIT

Well chilled, this is always a refreshing dessert. Use orange or grapefruit sections, seedless grapes, pineapple, fresh or canned, peaches or nectarines, pears, melon balls, whole berries, fresh or frozen. Add sugar to taste, or a mixture of honey and fruit juice, or some fruit liqueur, or a few pieces of crystallized ginger thinly sliced. Pile fruit in a glass bowl and chill well. Since a macédoine is juicy, you might serve it with cake or rich cookies—shortbread, macaroons, or brownies.

5.

Lobster Bisque with Sherry
Cold Poached Chicken in Jelly*—Mixed Vegetable Salad*
Fruit Pie à la Mode

A good menu for a summer outdoor lunch or supper, especially if fresh lobster is available. Or have another creamy soup—frozen clam or oyster bisque with cream added. If it's too hot for hot soup, serve a cold soup instead. Have hot bread or rolls with the main course, and heat the pie—as a pleasant contrast to the ice cream.

COLD POACHED CHICKEN IN JELLY

Buy 2 fowls or 3 broilers, cut in serving pieces. Prepare as you would for a chicken fricassee, simmering gently until tender in water (or white wine and water, half and half) with salt, peppercorns, a sliced onion, and a bay leaf. Simmer chicken until cooked through but still firm, let it cool in the broth, then skin and refrigerate. Strain broth and chill it and skim off fat. If the stock has jelled, melt it and pour half over the chicken arranged on a platter. Refrigerate again. The remaining stock must be made really stiff as it will be chopped. Mix 1 envelope unflavored gelatin in each 1½ cups hot stock. Jell in refrigerator. Just before dinner chop it coarsely and sprinkle it over the chicken. (Dampening the chopping board with a little cold water keeps the jelly in place.)

MIXED VEGETABLE SALAD

If possible, use mostly fresh vegetables. Cook or steam them as usual; then soak in refrigerator in a spicy French dressing for 2 or 3 hours. Try these together: string beans, baby limas, quartered peeled tomatoes, diced carrots, fresh peas or canned French peas, diced or sliced beets. For "crunch" add raw diced celery, green pepper, cucumbers, sliced or cubed, or sliced radishes. Thin circles of raw Spanish or Bermuda onion look well and are easily avoided by guests who do not care for them. Line a salad bowl with lettuce and mound the vegetables in the center.

If you'd like a creamy dressing with this, mix mayonnaise or sour cream half and half with French dressing. Remember when using beets that creamy dressings and other vegetables will turn pink.

6.

Madrilène (jellied in summer, hot in winter) with Lemon Slices
Chicken Paprika—Rice, Chopped Spinach
Profiteroles with Chocolate Sauce*

Chicken paprika, being thick and creamy, goes best with a simple soup and plain vegetable. Use a good Hungarian paprika in your recipe. Since sour cream can be tricky, this is the dish needing concentration just before dinner. Do everything else, dessert included, ahead, warming up rice and spinach over asbestos pads.

PROFITEROLES WITH CHOCOLATE SAUCE

Use 1 stick of cream puff mix. For each puff drop about ¾ teaspoon of batter on an ungreased baking sheet, leaving an inch of space between. Bake at 425° until golden brown—about 15 minutes. Cool, split, and fill each puff with 1 tablespoon of softened ice cream—vanilla, coffee, or chocolate. Put in freezer for an hour or more. Remove about 15 minutes before serving and pass with chocolate sauce (hot preferred).

7.

Avocados Filled with French Dressing
Oven-Fried Chicken Lois*—Tomatoes Filled with Wild Rice*
Gingerbread with Whipped Cream, Applesauce, or Both*

French dressing is a simple and tasty filling for ripe avocado halves. Other fillings are crab meat, grapefruit, or shrimp in Russian dressing. One hostess serves peeled or cubed avocados covered with Russian dressing on beds of lettuce. "Horribly rich," she admits, "but no one ever leaves a morsel." Since avocados must be prepared just before serving, they go well on this menu, which needs no other last-minute attention.

OVEN-FRIED CHICKEN LOIS

This recipe, perfect for a novice cook, is always applauded.

Lemon or lime juice
3 broiler-fryers cut in serving pieces
Flour
Salt and pepper
1 cup vegetable oil
3 cups chicken stock or broth made from chicken bouillon cubes

Sprinkle lemon or lime juice over chicken and roll in flour, seasoned with a teaspoon each of salt and pepper. Heat oil in a heavy skillet and brown chicken on both sides, turning with tongs to prevent breaking the flour crust. Transfer to a shallow baking dish or casserole. Pour in chicken stock and bake at 325° for 1½ hours. The dish needs no attention whatsoever; if guests are late, turn it off for a while. While 3 chickens allows plenty of meaty pieces for 10 people, use a few wings, too, as they crisp up deliciously. Save the others, plus necks, backs, and giblets, for the stock pot. The chicken livers may be added to the casserole for the last few minutes of cooking.

TOMATOES FILLED WITH WILD RICE

An easy, delicious way to serve two vegetables at once. Mix cooked wild rice with uncondensed mushroom soup or with sautéed sliced mushrooms and sour cream. Fill scooped-out and well-drained tomatoes with the mixture and bake for 30 minutes in the same oven as the chicken.

GINGERBREAD

Make gingerbread ahead from your favorite mix and serve it warm: after you remove the main course, turn oven off and put in the gingerbread. For 10, have whipped cream made from 1½ cups heavy cream. If you should use canned or bottled applesauce instead of cream, spice it with a few good shakes of cinnamon and nutmeg, to enrich color as well as taste.

8.

Onion Tart*
Broiled Chicken—Brussels Sprouts in Sour Cream,* Endive and
    Beet Salad on a Side Plate
Baked Pears

ONION TART

An easy and impressive first course. Make two tarts for 10 or 12 people. For *each* tart you will need:

Piecrust for a 1-crust 8-inch pie
2 cups sliced onions
Butter
Salt and pepper
Cayenne pepper
5 eggs, well beaten

Line the pie dish with the crust and chill while making the filling. Sauté onions in a frying pan with a tablespoon or more of butter until they are transparent but still firm. Shake salt, black pepper, and cayenne over them and spoon onto the piecrust. Pour over the beaten eggs and place in a 400° oven. After 5 minutes reduce heat to 225° and bake until custard is set and lightly browned on top—30 minutes or so.

Note: This makes an excellent lunch dish with a green salad and a fruit dessert.

BRUSSELS SPROUTS IN SOUR CREAM

3 pounds brussels sprouts
1 cup chopped onion
4 tablespoons butter
2 pints sour cream

Steam or boil sprouts until tender, cutting a crisscross gash in the bottom of each so that the tougher ends cook as quickly as the tops. Cook onion in butter until brown. Add sour cream and heat, stirring constantly. Mix in sprouts. Plenty for 12.

9.

Water Cress or Spinach Soup
Breast of Chicken with Grapes*—Puréed Baby Lima Beans,* Rice
Crème Brûlée

BREAST OF CHICKEN WITH GRAPES

12 chicken breasts, boned
1 stick sweet butter (¼ pound)
3 cups dry white wine
1 cup slivered, toasted almonds
1 pound seedless grapes

Shake salt and pepper over chicken breasts and sauté them in the butter in a heavy skillet until lightly browned. Place in a casserole. Pour wine in skillet to loosen any brown glaze, then pour over chicken. Cover and bake in a 400° oven for 15 minutes. Then add almonds and grapes and bake 15 minutes longer, or until chicken is tender.

PURÉED BABY LIMA BEANS

5 packages frozen baby limas
Butter
⅓ cup heavy cream
Parsley

Cook beans according to package directions. Then drain and purée in a blender or sieve, put in top of double boiler, add 4 tablespoons butter, salt to taste, beat in cream. Heat over boiling water. Serve dotted with more butter and chopped parsley. This can be done ahead of time. In the interim, cover the purée with cream to prevent a crust from forming.

10.

Gazpacho*
Chicken Tarragon*—Cauliflower Amandine,* Salad on a Side
    Plate
Ice Cream Pie*

This, a good summer menu, would be fine in any season.

GAZPACHO

An easy recipe for this famous soup. Make a day ahead and re-frigerate.

    3 cans tomatoes
    1 cup chopped onion
    2 cups chopped green peppers
    3 cups beef consommé
    2 garlic cloves, minced
    Juice of 3 lemons
    ½ cup olive oil
    1 tablespoon salt
    1 tablespoon paprika
    ½ teaspoon cracked black pepper

Chop the tomatoes or put them, with a little of their juice, into a blender, and blend for one second. Coarsely chop onions and peppers and put in a blender with a little of the consommé. Blend for one second. This makes crisp vegetables come out "chopped." Mix all the other ingredients with the tomatoes, onions, and peppers. Let stand at room temperature for an hour or so, stirring every so often, then chill (3 hours or overnight). You might garnish each cup with a sliced cucumber, and, if served in summer, add a cube of ice.

CHICKEN TARRAGON

    3 2½- to 3-pound broilers cut in serving pieces
    6 tablespoons olive or salad oil
    6 tablespoons butter
    2 cups dry white wine
    2 cups chicken consommé
    1 tablespoon salt
    ½ teaspoon pepper
    2 dozen sliced mushrooms
    3 teaspoons dried or 3 tablespoons fresh tarragon

In a big Dutch oven sauté chicken in olive oil and butter until brown. Add wine, consommé, salt, pepper. Cover and simmer 20 minutes. Add mushrooms and tarragon. You might do this much ahead, simmering for 10 minutes just before dinner.

CAULIFLOWER AMANDINE

Cook 2 heads cauliflower until soft but not mushy. Sauté 1 cup slivered almonds, 2 cloves garlic, minced, and 2 cups bread crumbs in ¼ pound melted butter until almonds are lightly browned. Pour over cauliflower.

ICE CREAM PIE

A fancy-looking dessert, this is easy to make ahead, easy to eat on laps at a buffet supper. Use any ice cream flavor that appeals; chocolate and coffee are traditional, peach or strawberry might be pleasant in summer. Decorate a chocolate or coffee pie with shaved chocolate, sprinkles, roasted slivered almonds, or shredded coconut. For a fruit ice cream pie, you might garnish the surface with coconut or chilled fresh fruit just before serving.

Allow one 9-inch pie for every 8 or 9 people. To make the crust for each pie: crush 20 single graham crackers until very fine (or break them in small pieces and pulverize them in the blender). Mix crumbs with ¼ cup sugar and ¼ cup melted butter, press onto the bottom and sides of a pie plate with the back of a spoon, and bake for 8 minutes in a 375° oven. For each pie use 1 quart of ice cream. Let it stand at room temperature until soft enough to spread. Fill pie shell and put in freezer compartment until firm. Remove about 15 minutes before serving.

11.

Salade Niçoise*
Chicken Albert*—Rice with Sautéed Mushrooms, Peas
Fruit Sherbet—Cookies

SALADE NIÇOISE

A great French salad which is an excellent opener for dinner or a good main course for lunch.
The basic ingredients:

Pitted black olives
Anchovy fillets
Tomatoes
Cooked string beans
Tuna fish

Popular additions:

Thin-sliced beets
Green peppers
Spanish onions
1 or 2 sliced potatoes or quartered hard-boiled eggs

Note: No lettuce. Serve chilled, mixed at the last minute with French dressing, in a big glass or pottery bowl to be passed hand to hand around the table.

CHICKEN ALBERT

Given to us by a bachelor who has little time for party preliminaries, this dish is almost too easy to include, but very good:
Have 3 broiler-fryers quartered. Sprinkle liberally with salt and pepper and put with 1 stick (¼ pound) butter into a casserole. Set the oven at 250° and cook for 1½ hours, basting two or three times. Shortly before serving, pour off some of the gravy, mix it with 1½ cups sour cream (or heavy cream), and return to casserole to heat through.

12.

Sliced Pimientos and Anchovies
Fricassee of Chicken—Chutney, Rice, String Beans with Almonds
Cold Zabaglione*

To serve the first course put a bed of lettuce on each salad plate. Lay on two or three slices of pimiento, and cover with a lattice of anchovy fillets. Pass cruet bottles of olive oil and vinegar around the table, along with bread sticks or hard rolls, and provide a knife as well as a fork.

COLD ZABAGLIONE

This recipe serves 8. You will have to make half as much again for 10 or 12, because the larger amount of ingredients won't go into an average double boiler. It can be made early in the day.

    6 egg yolks
    1½ cups granulated sugar
    4 teaspoons grated lemon peel
    5 tablespoons lemon juice
    1½ cups Marsala or dry sherry

In top of double boiler, beat egg yolks lightly. Add remaining ingredients. Cook over boiling water, beating every second. (A hand-model electric beater takes the work out of this.) When thick and fluffy, pour into individual sherbet glasses or big wine goblets and chill until serving time. The hostess who donated this recipe added, "Serve with lady fingers, if anything." A good idea with men present, since zabaglione is so light.

BUFFET SUPPER MENUS

These menus have two courses only. When people can sit at tables a first course might be added. All the main courses can be made the day before and are eatable with a fork alone.

1.

Chicken Curry*—Rice, Condiments, Water Cress Salad
Bowl of Mixed Fruits—Cookies

CHICKEN CURRY

This recipe, a classic strong curry, serves 12 amply and is easily doubled. It should be made the day before and left at room temperature to "ripen." On the day of the party there is plenty to do preparing condiments and dessert, anyway.

5- or 6-pound chicken cut in serving pieces
1 onion, sliced
1 carrot
1 bay leaf
1 tablespoon salt
⅔ cup olive oil
4 medium onions, chopped
6 stalks celery, chopped
3 apples, peeled and chopped
⅓ cup curry powder
1 level teaspoon ground ginger
1 teaspoon hot pepper sauce
1½ tablespoons Worcestershire sauce
Salt and pepper
3 tablespoons flour
1½ cups heavy cream
3 egg yolks, beaten well

Step 1: Put chicken in a stew pot, add water to cover, plus the sliced onion, carrot, bay leaf, and 1 tablespoon salt. Simmer gently until chicken is very tender, 1½ hours or more. Remove chicken and reserve broth.

Step 2: Heat olive oil in a top-of-the-stove casserole or Dutch oven, and cook chopped onions, celery, and apples until soft but not brown. Add curry powder and cook over low heat for 5 minutes. Add 4 cups strained stock, then the ginger, hot pepper sauce, and Worcestershire, salt and pepper to taste, and simmer 15 minutes more. Mix flour with water to make a medium paste and stir it in a little at a time and cook until the sauce is smooth. Turn off flame. Skin the chicken, discard bones, and cut meat into bite-size pieces. Then add it to the sauce.

Step 3: Now you have a rich, thick curry. Next day, reheat it slowly and a few minutes before serving mix cream and beaten egg yolks together and add them to the casserole. This thins out the curry to the right consistency. Serve with a big bowl of white rice.

Condiments are important both to the taste and to the party appearance of this dish. Alongside the curry and rice on the buffet table have the following: a big bowl of chutney, and smaller bowls of chopped peanuts, raisins (which you have plumped in boiling water), chopped parsley, shredded coconut, chopped candied ginger, and coarsely grated lemon rind. Bombay duck, a dried fish imported from India, is traditional, but crisp crumbled bacon is a good substitute, as is flaked dried codfish. All condiments except the chutney are to be sprinkled over the curry.

Orientals often serve poppadums, thin wafers which must be fried in fat, with curry. Some specialty shops have them, but good alternatives are rice wafers, or buttered and toasted English water biscuits, or pilot crackers.

Salad is not necessary, but if you care to have it, water cress with French dressing and a few orange sections goes well. Serve only beer, ale, or cola with curry, never wine.

2.

Brunswick Stew*—Rice, Corn Bread
Pecan Pie*

A Southern menu, this can be made anywhere in any season with frozen or canned vegetables. In summer you might have a lighter dessert—perhaps pineapple ice with crushed pineapple poured over, and a light cake.

BRUNSWICK STEW

While the original Brunswick stew was made with squirrels, chicken is the standard substitute. The easy recipe below should be refrigerated overnight if done the day before. Serves 16.

    6 tablespoons bacon grease
    6 good-sized onions, sliced
    2 5-pound chickens cut in serving pieces
    Salt and pepper
    4 cups canned tomatoes or fresh ones peeled and sliced
    4 cups corn kernels, fresh, frozen, or canned
    3 boxes frozen okra
    4 cups fresh or frozen baby lima beans
    1 teaspoon thyme
    2 tablespoons Worcestershire sauce
    Flour, optional
    1 cup sherry

Get out a stew kettle and a big casserole for top-of-the-stove cooking. Heat bacon grease in the casserole and sauté onions; then transfer them to the kettle. Sauté chicken lightly in casserole, using more grease if necessary. Put chicken in kettle, including necks and backs for a strong stock. Cover with boiling water, add salt and pepper, and simmer for 2 hours or so, until chicken falls from the bones. Remove chicken, skin it, and cut into good-sized pieces. Add strips from wings too. Put chicken in casserole, add the vegetables, thyme, and Worcestershire, and enough of the chicken stock to cover everything. If you have used fresh vegetables cook 25 minutes longer; with frozen vegetables 15 minutes is enough. For a thicker sauce mix in a little flour. Add sherry a few minutes before serving. Serve over rice in soup plates, especially if the supper will be eaten on laps. Toasted French bread is equally efficient as corn bread for sopping up the gravy.

PECAN PIE

For 16 people you will need two 8- or 9-inch pie plates. Since this is such a rich dessert the same amount easily serves 18. You'll need for *each* pie:

¾ cup dark brown sugar
Pinch of salt
3 well-beaten eggs
1 cup light corn syrup
1 teaspoon vanilla
1 cup pecan halves
Pastry for a 1-crust pie

Mix sugar and salt into the eggs. Add corn syrup, vanilla, and pecans. Line pie pan with pastry and pour in pecan mixture. Bake in a 425° oven for 15 minutes. Reduce heat to 325° and bake 35 to 45 minutes longer, until pie has set and crust is brown. It won't suffer if made the day before and left at room temperature. If using salted pecans, omit salt in the recipe. Serve pie as is or with a bowl of unsweetened whipped cream.

3.

Irish Stew*—Green Beans or Peas, Hot Buttered Rolls
Strawberry Tart*

IRISH STEW

Some people look down on Irish stew, wrongly; any gourmet will tell you that, made carefully, it is cooking at its best. This subtly flavored recipe, better made a day ahead, serves 6 amply; multiply ingredients for buffet suppers of 12 or 18.

3 tablespoons vegetable fat or salad oil
2 pounds boneless lamb, cut in 1½-inch cubes
⅓ cup chopped onions
2 tablespoons chopped green pepper
3 tablespoons chopped parsley
2 cloves garlic, minced
½ teaspoon leaf sage
Stock made from 4 cups boiling water and 2 bouillon cubes
4 large potatoes, peeled
½ teaspoon Worcestershire sauce
Salt and pepper

Heat fat in a top-of-the-stove casserole or Dutch oven. Sauté lamb gently, until it loses redness but is not brown. Add onions, green pepper, parsley, garlic, sage, and cook 2 or 3 minutes longer. Add the hot stock and simmer 1 hour.

Cut two of the potatoes into ½-inch slices and add to casserole with the two whole potatoes. Simmer 30 minutes longer, or until potatoes are tender. Remove whole potatoes, mash them, and return to casserole, mixing well. Add Worcestershire, and salt and pepper to taste.

Dumplings add something. You might use a standard dumpling recipe or a carton of ready-to-bake biscuits, and cover the pot for the last 15 minutes before serving. If stew is made a day ahead, don't make the dumplings until reheating at serving time.

STRAWBERRY TART

This recipe is usually praised both for taste and because it looks so professional. One tart will serve 8 or 10 people.

    2 packages frozen sliced strawberries
    1 8-ounce package cream cheese
    ⅓ cup butter
    1⅓ cups zwieback crumbs
    ¼ cup light cream
    4 tablespoons cornstarch
    1 pint fresh strawberries

Thaw frozen berries. Let cheese and butter soften at room temperature. Thoroughly mix crumbs and soft butter, then press with the back of a spoon on the sides and bottom of an 8-inch pie plate. Bake in a 350° oven for 8 minutes. Cool, then chill.

Beat cream and softened cheese together until fluffy. Strain frozen berries and cook the juice with cornstarch until thick and clear. Add sliced berries.

Remove pie crust from refrigerator and line with cream cheese mixture, then with strawberry mixture. Place the fresh whole strawberries, with points facing upward, over the surface.

To make this look even more professional, you might glaze the top: melt currant jelly and spoon it over the strawberries arranged on the tart. Return to refrigerator for a couple of hours before serving.

4.

Boeuf Bourgignon*—Green Salad, Garlic Bread
Hot Baked Fruits*

BOEUF BOURGIGNON

A good winter buffet supper dish, this serves 12 amply.

4 tablespoons bacon fat
4 pounds lean beef, cut in cubes
4 tablespoons sherry
24 small white onions
24 mushrooms, cut in quarters
3 teaspoons tomato paste
3 teaspoons meat glaze
6 tablespoons flour
2½ cups beef consommé
2½ cups red wine
Salt and pepper
2 bay leaves
½ teaspoon thyme
Chopped parsley

Heat bacon fat in a skillet and brown meat over high heat. Sprinkle sherry over and transfer meat to casserole. Lightly brown onions and mushrooms in skillet, then stir in tomato paste, meat glaze, and flour. Add consommé slowly and then ½ cup of the red wine, stirring constantly. When sauce comes to a boil, add salt and pepper to taste, and pour over the meat in the casserole. Add bay leaves and thyme, cover, and put in a 250° oven. Adding remaining wine every so often, cook for 3 or more hours, until meat cuts with a fork. Next day, reheat slowly and, before serving, sprinkle with fresh chopped parsley. Add more wine if you like a thinner sauce.

Mixed green salad goes well with this; so do string beans, carrots, or peas. A heavier accompaniment could be hominy grits with lots of butter, or spoon bread. Always have plenty of garlic bread for the gravy.

HOT BAKED FRUITS

For 12 people, use 3 1-pound, 14-ounce cans of fruit. You might have 1 can of pears and 2 cans of peach halves, or have 1 can each of pears, peaches, and apricots. Whole plums or prunes give good color contrast as well as flavor. In a low ovenproof dish or bowl arrange fruits neatly. Melt a stick (¼ pound) of butter, and mix it with enough brown sugar to have the consistency of thick soup. Pour over the fruits and dust with cinnamon. This can be done ahead of time. During the main course pour in ½ cup kirsch and cook in a 250° oven for 20 minutes. Serve with a pitcher of heavy cream and spicy cookies. Grated lemon rind, when you're feeling energetic, adds a good tang to this or any hot fruit dish.

5.

Steak and Kidney Pie*—Green Salad, Hot Breads
Fruit Shortcake

STEAK AND KIDNEY PIE

This recipe, ideal for brunch or lunch, too, serves 8. Have two pies for 10 to 16.

Piece of suet about the size of a golf ball
2 pounds round steak, cut in cubes
1 pound veal kidneys, thinly sliced
4 scallions, chopped
½ cup sherry
½ cup beef stock
Salt and pepper
1 teaspoon Worcestershire sauce
½ teaspoon marjoram
¼ teaspoon powdered cloves
Crust for a 1-crust pie

Melt suet in a stew pan and remove cracklings. Add steak, kidneys, scallions, and sauté until brown, stirring constantly. Add sherry and beef stock, salt, pepper, Worcestershire, marjoram, and cloves. Mix well, cover, and simmer for 1½ hours over low heat. Remove meat and thicken gravy with 2 tablespoons butter and 2 tablespoons flour mixed together. Grease a deep-dish pie bowl. Pour in meat and gravy and cover top with pie crust pricked in several places to let steam escape. If made the day before, refrigerate. On party day warm to room temperature. Bake in a 450° oven for 10 minutes, then reduce to 325° and bake 15 to 20 minutes longer, until crust is brown.

6.

Vitello Tonnato*—Mixed Cold Vegetables in French Dressing, Hot Rolls
Deep-Dish Blueberry Pie,* with Heavy Cream

VITELLO TONNATO

A superb Italian dish perfect for a hot-weather buffet luncheon or supper. The veal is thinly sliced before serving and cuts easily with a fork. Recipe serves 8 to 10 people.

Olive oil
3½-pound boned and rolled leg of veal
1 large onion, sliced
2 stalks celery, chopped
2 large garlic cloves, minced
2 carrots, chopped
1 can anchovy fillets
1 can tuna fish
1 cup dry white wine
4 or 5 sprigs parsley
2 bay leaves
¼ teaspoon thyme
½ teaspoon salt
½ teaspoon ground black pepper
Mayonnaise
Juice of 1 lemon
Capers

Heat enough olive oil to cover the bottom of your Dutch oven or stew kettle. Brown veal lightly on all sides. Add all remaining ingredients, except mayonnaise, lemon juice, and capers. Cover and cook gently on top of stove for 2 hours.

Remove meat and chill. Boil what remains in the kettle until reduced by one third, then purée in a blender or put through a sieve. Chill, then blend with 1 cup mayonnaise (preferably home-made) and the lemon juice.

To serve, slice cold veal as thin as possible; arrange neatly on a platter, sprinkle with capers. Serve the sauce in a sauceboat.

For the salad, any combination of mixed vegetables in French dressing may be used. You might add some cooked white rice or lentils for substance, or serve the sliced veal on cold white rice.

DEEP-DISH BLUEBERRY PIE

Wash 3 pints plump blueberries and put in a lightly buttered ovenproof glass dish. Sprinkle over about ¾ cup dark brown sugar —more if you like a very sweet dessert. Follow directions on the graham cracker box for graham cracker crust, using brown sugar. Press crust mixture gently on top of berries. Bake 30 minutes in a 350° oven, and serve warm with a pitcher of heavy cream. This recipe serves 10 amply.

7.

Veal Stew in Red Wine*—Noodles, Green Salad, Hot Rolls
Stewed Fresh Rhubarb and Strawberries*

VEAL STEW IN RED WINE

An easy version of a French ragout which serves 12 or 14.

    4 tablespoons butter
    1 pound lean bacon, cut in dice
    2 pounds small white onions, peeled
    5 pounds veal, cut in cubes
    Salt and pepper
    5 cups red wine
    Bouquet garni
    4 cloves garlic
    Flour (preferably potato flour)

In a Dutch oven melt the butter and sauté the bacon and onions. Remove when onions are lightly browned. Then add the veal, allow to brown, and sprinkle with salt and pepper. Add the wine, bouquet garni, and garlic. Return bacon to pot and simmer slowly for 1 hour. Return onions to pot and simmer 1 hour longer. To thicken, blend 2 tablespoons flour into a little red wine and add to the casserole. Simmer gently for 15 or 20 minutes. If made the day before, have 2 cans of whole onions in readiness to add 10 minutes before serving, in case the party runs late and the original onions become mushy.

STEWED FRESH RHUBARB AND STRAWBERRIES

2 pounds fresh rhubarb
2 cups granulated sugar
Baking soda
1 quart strawberries

Cut washed rhubarb into 1- or 2-inch pieces. Place in top of a big double boiler over boiling water. Cover and steam 30 minutes or so until tender. Do not stir. Mix sugar and ½ teaspoon baking soda into 1 cup hot water. When sugar is dissolved pour over the rhubarb and cook for 3 or 4 minutes more. While rhubarb is steaming, wash and hull strawberries and stew in 1 cup water until just tender, 4 or 5 minutes. When both fruits are done, mix together. If serving warm, transfer to an ovenproof dish and heat during main course in a slow oven. If serving cold, chill well in a pretty glass bowl. Sugar cookies, or plain cake, go well with this.

PARTY MENUS BUILT AROUND FISH

Even in communities where fresh fish is always available, it is less often served as a party main course than meat or poultry. Perhaps this is a mistake: from time to time guests might enjoy fish, it is often inexpensive, and many of the simplest fish recipes taste epicurean. Baked or poached fish can be prepared ahead of time and needs little or no attention during cooking. Since fish also broils quickly, it can cook while you light the candles and fill water glasses.

Whole fish—salmon, mackerel, or sea bass—will easily serve a small dinner party. Or you might have three or four smaller fish, or a single small one for each person. Inexpensive fish, such as cod, flounder, or halibut, can seem partyish with a good sauce. Shad and swordfish in season are sheer delicacies.

Most cookbooks contain excellent recipes for baking whole fish stuffed with, or laid on top of, vegetables. These, with boiled, baked, or scalloped potatoes, make a satisfying main course. Since it must be prepared ahead of time, cold poached fish served in jelly or with a sauce is a good summer choice.

The fish dishes listed as first courses in the meat and chicken menus above make good main courses. Below are a few more easy ones which usually bring praise. If a particular fish recipe is delicately flavored, gourmets speak out for simply cooked vegetables as accompaniment, and against highly seasoned salads. When ordering for a party, allow about ½ pound of fish per person.

Try scallops, preferably the small bay type, baked in butter and lemon juice for 10 minutes in a 375° oven. Pop under the broiler for 2 minutes at the end. Dry white wine, bread crumbs, and cream can be used instead of lemon juice.

Try smelts in season. Allow 3 to a person. Dip in cream, roll in flour or corn meal, and bake in a well-buttered dish for 5 to 10 minutes at 450°. Serve with tartar sauce.

Fresh shad roe is a perfect party dish. Allow one roe to a person, with a few extra. Parboil roes ahead of time and bake with butter and dry white wine for 25 minutes in a 350° oven. Or omit the wine and 10 minutes before serving sprinkle roes with slivered almonds. Serve with lemon quarters. A more elaborate dish is shad roes baked in a creamy white wine sauce with seedless grapes. To broil them, parboil ahead of time and while bringing out the rolls and vegetables put roes under the broiler flame for 10 minutes, basting with butter and turning once. Serve with crisp bacon and lemon.

Bluefish, salmon steaks, and trout are excellent this way: In an ovenproof dish make a bed of sliced onions, chopped celery, and parsley. Pour over lots of melted butter (inside, too, if the fish are split), to which you have added lemon juice and a good dash of Worcestershire sauce. Bake in a 350° oven for 25 minutes, or until fish flakes easily.

For a Friday or Sunday buffet supper you might have creamed finnan haddie. Bake it in milk according to any recipe, and use the pan juices as the basis of the cream sauce. Serve over toast with a green vegetable or with boiled potatoes or sliced hard-boiled eggs.

For a brunch or Sunday supper, kippered herrings may arouse jaded appetites. Butter the inside of each kipper, close, and roll in foil, sealing tightly to keep juice from escaping. Bake at 300° for 30 minutes. Serve with buttered rye or protein toast and lemon halves.

Instead of broiling lobster, try this Normandy coast method: Place split lobsters in roasting pans. Salt and pepper lightly. Dot liberally with butter. Bake at 325° for 25 minutes, or until tender. Ten minutes before serving, pour over lots of heavy cream mixed with dry sherry—two thirds cream to one third sherry. Put lobsters on big platters, pour over every drop of the pan juices, and serve with shoestring potatoes or French fries, and a lightly seasoned salad or plain green vegetable on a side plate.

When steamed clams are available they are fun for an outdoor party, cooked in kettles over the barbecue fire, or done inside and brought out. The day before the party buy 1 quart of clams per person, making sure shells are closed. To free clams of sand, submerge them in pots of cool water to each of which you have added 1 cup of corn meal. Refrigerate overnight; rinse well in cold water before cooking. For every 3 quarts of clams add ½ cup of water to the kettle. Cover and steam until shells open. Serve in soup bowls or deep plates with side dishes of melted butter. Strain the broth through cheesecloth and serve in consommé cups alongside. With oyster crackers, then salad, fruit, and cheese, you have a great meal.

Steamed mussels make a good first course, and served in quantity with salad, French bread, and white wine, they are an ideal main course for luncheons or Friday night parties, indoors or out. Use a recipe for mussels *marinière*, as is, or boil down the broth and mix it with heavy cream. This is Brittany's *moules à la crème*.

SALAD SUGGESTIONS

For good salads, lettuce deserves proper treatment. First, run cold water over the heads and put them in plastic bags in the vegetable section of the refrigerator. They will keep well for several days. Before serving, lettuce should be thoroughly washed and thoroughly dried. Some people shake it dry in a wire basket; others roll the leaves in dish towels. This method is the most satisfactory we have discovered: shake the leaves after washing. Lay them on a thick length of cheesecloth, cover with paper towels. Roll up the cloth and return to the vegetable compartment.

Try all varieties of lettuce. Romaine, chicory, escarole, and Bibb lettuce each have their special taste. Boston lettuce mixes well with any other green. Here are other suggestions:

Endive with minced beets in French dressing
Raw spinach leaves mixed with water cress and crumbled bacon
Raw spinach leaves mixed with a few spears of endive
Field salad served with French dressing alone, or with a few sliced beets

Try adding these to mixed green salads:

Marinated artichoke hearts
Canned hearts of palm, marinated
Croutons soaked in oil with a peeled clove of garlic
Spanish onion rings, sliced thin
Diced celery
Fresh tarragon, dill, or chives, coarsely chopped

Hard-cooked egg yolks put through a sieve and sprinkled over the surface of a mixed green salad makes Salad Mimosa. Canned Chinese Lichee nuts, carried by many delicacy shops, go well in any green salad with a sharp French dressing. More like fruit than nuts, they are pale pink, taste somewhat like grapes, only better.

Certain vegetables served without lettuce in a vinaigrette sauce make good first courses or are easily served, and eaten, from side plates with the main course. Try peeled sliced raw tomatoes or cooked asparagus, leeks or broccoli, chilled and marinated for a few hours. When marinating a vegetable to use in salad, use the marinade as dressing, adding more oil if necessary.

EASY COCKTAIL APPETIZERS

—Smithfield ham paste mixed with mayonnaise and cracked black pepper, spread on split beaten biscuit, or in celery stalks.
—Thinly sliced cucumber on white bread rounds spread with mayonnaise.

—Guacamole: Mashed avocado mixed with a little olive oil and salt, pepper, and chili powder to taste. To make an hour or so ahead without discoloration, leave the avocado pits in the mixture until serving. Pass in a bowl surrounded by corn chips.

—Shad roe. Parboil fresh or use canned shad roe. Chill it for several hours so it will cut easily. Wrap bite-size pieces in bacon, skewer with toothpicks, and broil or fry until bacon is crisp.

—Cheeses. For cocktail parties, strong cheese such as Stilton with port, Gorgonzola, or Roquefort is delicious and arouses thirst. Before a dinner, stick to smoky cheese spreads or blander cheese: Bel Paese, Gouda, Oka, Grappa, or Swiss. Guests should go to dinner with palates whetted, not exhausted.

—Vegetables, prettily pared and crisped in salted ice water, can be passed with seasoned salt or a sauce: cocktail sauce, Russian dressing, cheese spreads thinned with cream, sour cream with herbs, mayonnaise with mustard or curry.

—Roasted nuts. Re-roasting them, even if you've just opened the can, makes a big difference. Put nuts in a pan with some butter or olive oil and roast in a slow oven for 25 minutes or so, stirring occasionally. When nuts begin to brown pour into a paper bag to which you've added a teaspoon or more of salt or, better still, garlic salt, and shake well to absorb grease and spread salt evenly. Store in screw-top jars or cookie tins at room temperature.

—Cereals with seasonings. Mix several varieties of bite-size dry cereal with peanuts, almonds, or pecans, and pretzel sticks. Shake over lots of seasoned salt, garlic or onion powder, and crumbled marjoram. Dot with butter and bake in a slow oven for 30 or 40 minutes, stirring occasionally. Add more seasoning to taste during the cooking. This is equally good served hot or at room temperature and keeps well in covered jars.

—Cheese Taj Mahal. Get a good Wisconsin cheddar spread or club cheese. Let stand at room temperature until slightly soft. Mix in curry powder and chutney to taste, cutting up big pieces of chutney right in the bowl. This spread can be made days ahead. Cover and refrigerate. To serve, transfer to pretty bowls or china pots and surround with melba toast rounds.

—Tartar steak appetizers. Mix one pound lean, freshly-ground round steak with ½ cup chopped Bermuda onion, a whole egg, a little olive oil, salt and pepper to taste. Spread on ice-box rye bread slices and decorate with capers.

—Crab-meat canapés. To 1 can of crab meat, drained, broken up, and picked over for shells, add 2 heaping teaspoons mayonnaise, a few shakes of cayenne pepper, and a little lemon juice. Mix well and chill. Spread on rounds of white bread and decorate with parsley, pimiento, or leave plain.

—Breadless "sandwiches." With thin-sliced bologna, sliced American process cheese, and cream cheese thinned with milk or cream, make triple-decker "sandwiches." Use two slices of bologna and one of American cheese, or vice versa. Chill for 2 hours or so, then cut into rounds or diamond shapes with the smallest cutters you have. Skewer with toothpicks and chill until serving time.

EMERGENCY FOOD

While no one expects wonders from emergency meals, when guests come, or stay on, unexpectedly, there are good ways to feed them quickly and with little effort from a well-stocked kitchen.
Cocktail food:

> Nuts in tins or jars to be re-roasted and served hot
> Jars of Greek or Italian pickled peppers
> Canned pâté, anchovies, sardines, smoked oysters
> Olives, pickled mushrooms, or onions
> Assorted crackers or chips
> Canned crab meat, lobster, or minced clams
> Eggs, hard-boiled and stuffed

Soups: At a truly emergency meal, soup would not be expected before a main course, but doctored-up cans of cream soups, chowders, or minestrone, with rolls or a sandwich, could be the whole meal. Soups also serve well for short-order sauces and stocks.

For main courses, you might make containers of stew, beef stroganoff, or chicken pies. Store them in the freezer. Here are other ready-to-cook choices:

> Boxes of spaghetti or other pasta with canned sauces
> Canned whole ham or beef tongue
> Canned shad roe

Canned baked beans, easy to perk up with molasses, brown sugar,
bacon fat, and ketchup
Canned brown bread
Individual steaks or meat patties in the freezer which will defrost
quickly
Frozen Welsh rabbit to spike with beer and Worcestershire sauce
Canned and frozen vegetables, packaged potato mixes

Dessert isn't necessary for an emergency meal, but with a freezer
or freezer compartment you can always offer ice cream, or frozen pie
or cookies that bake during the main course. Canned fruits quickly
chilled or served hot with liqueur or spices are excellent. Sauces,
bottled or canned, go over cake, ice cream, or fruit. With 1 can of
pears, 1 can of chocolate sauce, and some vanilla ice cream you
have *poires Belle Hélène* in minutes.

Other choices:

Brandied peaches or marrons in syrup for ice cream
Canned *babas au rhum* to heat and serve with extra rum
Cake and cookie mixes
Canned applesauce for quick brown betty
Frozen strawberries for quick shortcake with a biscuit mix

Finally, staples. Eggs are perhaps the most versatile for emergency
cooking since they can be appetizer, main course, or the basis of
many desserts. If you are an omelet specialist you probably welcome impromptu parties. If not, read up on the hundreds of ways
of cooking shirred eggs or poached eggs with a sauce made from
condensed soup.

Like flour, potatoes, onions, and so on, the basic ingredients below keep well and can help you turn out expert eleventh-hour
dishes:

Consommé cubes   Ketchup
Meat glazes   Grated cheeses
Herbs most frequently used   Powdered or condensed milk
Mustards   for soups and sauces
Rice   Leftover wine
Bread crumbs   Condiments and conserves
Biscuit, bread, or potato mixes

18

Party Economies

Here, thoughts on economy—not how to give inexpensive parties, because every party raises the bills, and a party that seems cheap isn't a compliment to guests. But there are ways to prevent needless extravagance, waste, and skyrocketing grocery bills without losing the generous atmosphere a party should have.

Everyone's view of extravagance varies. Take these two couples, Host and Hostess A and Host and Hostess B. The A's live in a pretty but inexpensive apartment, have one baby who is taken care of by a nursemaid on weekdays since Mrs. A has a full-time job. They have no car, are economical about clothes and outside entertainment. But for parties Mr. A buys eight-dollar-a-bottle wines and usually orders a fifteen-pound smoked turkey. Of course they pay their friends a compliment by going all out, but isn't this being generous to a fault?

Hostess B impresses in the opposite way. She seems to get something out of nothing—or, to be logical, the most out of very little. Her extravagances might be home-roasted almonds or some good Bel Paese with cocktails. Her simple dinners become creations under her hand. She knows her herbs, makes a master's salad dressing, and has a feel for timing; food appears hot and never overcooked, at the moment you get really hungry. The delicacy shop in her life is the supermarket, reinforced by imaginative cooking.

While both hostesses give good parties, and neither is in deep at the bank, Hostess B gives *more* parties, perhaps because her economics make more sense.

Besides different views on extravagance, each person's economics can change. One week, when the future looks bright and secure, your party may have a few extra expenses. What's a few dollars when things go well? Another week, when you didn't get the raise or the furnace has broken down, you suddenly feel future-poor. A party may reflect that. You think twice about having expensive meat, buy beer instead or wine, or cancel the flowers. You may even decide to cancel the party. Not a bad idea, if it appears that purse strings really must be tightened. Spending seriously limited dollars on a party only adds worry, and the party gets off to a shaky start.

If the situation is less than desperate, accept the challenge of a limited budget and plan a party within it.

Economies in Food

Most potential savings on entertainment start in the kitchen. The choice of food is first but the kitchen itself may be a home savings bank. Lots of storage space and a big freezer mean that a hostess can buy and store things any time prices look good.

While you surely buy specials on everyday food as a matter of routine, watch for savings on party delicacies. Store managers, nervous for fear they won't move tiny potted shrimp, smoked oysters, imported French peas, often slash prices. Delicacies of this sort, not being perishable, can be saved for your next party—or the one after that.

One word of caution: we have all heard about shopper's syndrome, the inability to resist delicious-looking items seen in the store. When buying reduced delicacies, don't fall into this trap. Ask yourself if you would serve them with confidence at a party. Nothing is less economical than the unused bargain, and there's no kitchen big enough for eternal storage.

If you have a large freezer you can buy sides of beef or the cuts of meat you most often use for parties when they are priced low. In saving on meat, there is something in knowing just what is a bargain. Although no one seriously calls fillet of beef cheap, those staggering per-pound prices are for a cut that's all meat—no bones, no fat, no waste. Your butcher may have a special on the whole fillet, up to fifty cents a pound less than usual. You might get an eight- or ten-pound fillet for around fifteen dollars, have it cut in two and wrapped for freezing. The mathematical result is impressive: a main course for two dinners of eight, for about a dollar a serving. Economical? Well, you could have leg of lamb, ham, or roasting chickens for a lot less. But probably not a rib roast. The same mathematics goes for lamb chops. For a party they should be thick, which usually means too expensive. But when the butcher has a change of heart about the price of a whole rack of lamb, buy one, have it cut into chops. When a party day comes, you simply defrost.

Befriend your butcher, and watch his posters with parties in mind. Even a small freezer unit in the refrigerator might provide space for bargain meats. Some butchers also sell meat in bulk and keep it until needed in their big storage lockers.

Seasonal Economies

Buying things in season (and not when they're not) is more than economical. It's also a chance to be original in party menus. Instead of a soup, in summer you might start with *salade de tomates*—peeled sliced tomatoes chilled in a vinaigrette sauce—special because only vine-ripened tomatoes will do. Or boil up a few green or mild red peppers, marinate them, and serve them Italian style, under a lattice of anchovy fillets (bought on sale ages ago). When fresh shrimp is moderate use it as a first course baked in individual dishes. Five shrimp to a person is plenty. When oysters are in season buy a dozen to zip up frozen oyster soup, or if fresh crab meat is plentiful, mix a little into tomato or pea soup. These expensive-looking starters can be followed by a bargain main course without calling attention to pinched pennies. There are dozens of other seasonal choices: clams, fresh asparagus, melon, avocados.

At certain times of the year you can economize on main courses, too. There will be specials on ham, lamb, turkey.

If you live by the seaside or in lake country, fresh fish may also run cheap—you might serve baked smelts, stuffed sea bass, trout amandine, or bluefish in a special sauce. Once in a while you may see "fresh ducklings" advertised on your market window. A brace of these serves eight people nicely, and if you roast them with rosemary, oranges, or a can of cherries, you have a true party dish. There is always the old standby, chicken, never very expensive, and in certain seasons downright cheap. There are limitless chicken recipes that bury the economy under a delicious sauce.

Gourmets believe that the best dessert is fruit. It may be fruit and cake, cookies, ice cream, custard, tapioca, or fruit tarts or pies. But perfect fruit alone is not only partyish but cheap, bought in season: berries or grapes with cream or sour cream and sugar; hot fruit desserts made with peaches, pears, apricots, plums, or the underrated banana. Many a masterpiece can emerge from a couple of pounds of apples. Raw fruit combinations look, as well as taste, wonderful: mixed melon balls, or blueberries and strawberries, blackberries and raspberries, or whole nectarines mixed with black cherries on the stem.

Economical Ingredients

The first of these, margarine, has been coming up in the world and works just as well as butter for most *cooked* food. When you bake or baste, use margarine for a cut in cost which cuts nothing from flavor. Perhaps the only time *not* to use it is when a recipe calls for sweet butter, or when butter is to be served unadulterated, such as with lobster or steamed clams, or on hot biscuits.

Another staple, olive oil, becomes economical if mixed with a cheaper salad oil. Expensive imported olive oil flows freely in many French and Italian dishes, and on salads. But mixing pure olive oil half and half with domestic vegetable oil does not affect the taste of most recipes. The only exceptions are real mayonnaise—olive oil here makes all the difference—and a purist's French dressing, in which lettuce is bathed in oil with only dashes of vinegar, salt, and pepper. In an elaborate salad dressing, having paprika, garlic, mustard, or an overdose of cracked black pepper, a blend of oils won't be noticeable.

Among other economical ingredients are: bouillon cubes, instead of canned broth, for stock, and powdered instead of fresh milk—also economical calorically. When you need chopped tomatoes for a stew, tomato juice is a good substitute. If you often use recipes with wine, buy inexpensive half gallons of domestic red and white.

Using What You Have

When planning a party, search your closet to see if what's on hand might be worked into the dinner. Say you stocked up on canned soups during a sale and still have three cans each of clam chowder, split pea, and mushroom soup. Any of these could be the basis of a party first course. Perhaps it's summer and you still have black bean soup on the shelf. It's delicious iced; see the recipe in Chapter 17. Or you discover cans of creamed corn. Seems ridiculous to serve canned corn when fresh is in the market? Not if you add some eggs and milk for a corn custard that no one could tell came from the closet.

Back-of-the-cupboard surprises may come in very small packages. Half a jar of grated Parmesan can turn a routine salad dressing into an Italian masterpiece. Many another cheese, too dry to eat as is, can be grated into soups and sauces or sprinkled over vegetables. The remains of a can of shredded coconut can be floated on a curry soup, a custard sauce, or mixed into a fruit compote. An "old" bag of slivered almonds, freshly toasted, can do wonders for many a fish dish or green vegetable. Bake an unused layer of cake mix as the foundation for a fruit shortcake, or spread it with ice cream and, with a sauce, produce your own version of frozen cake, or baked Alaska.

All this may sound as if we recommend using leftovers on hand-picked dinner guests. Not at all. There is a great difference between clearing the closet of odds and ends and putting its hidden assets to use. You may stumble on something that becomes the specialty of the house. One October, a hostess put up gallons of apple butter, gave it away jars at a time, and served it at breakfast for months, but several jars remained as she was taking kitchen inventory before a party. The happy result was French crepes filled with apple butter. She happened to have the remains of a bottle of Calvados, and, as it was not enough to offer as an after-dinner liqueur, it went over the crepes. For repeats of her *crepes aux pommes* she uses ordinary brandy. Although invention, this was not experimentation on guests, since it didn't take an Escoffier to know that crepes and spiced apples would taste sensational together.

Using what you have might work this way: If you were having a party on Saturday and the Wednesday before had fried chicken for a family supper, you would use the necks, backs, giblets, and bones for a stock, and plan on breast of chicken or another party recipe that called for a good strong base. Or, if the refrigerator is full of eggs, that's no time to buy fruit or ice cream. Instead, have a mousse, soufflé, floating island, or meringue glacé.

Other Party Economies

Buying liquor and wine in quantity and food "on special" head the list, but other areas suggest economy also. Take laundry. Linen cloths and mats cost a lot to have laundered professionally, and cost valuable woman-hours if you do them yourself. Building a collection of lace mats, which won't need laundering each time, or spongeable plastic or wooden ones, saves time, and money in the long run.

You can also save on decorations. When the cost of fresh flowers seems prohibitive, there are long-lasting potted plants. If you are the type who can keep plants alive for months or years, having them is not only good party economy but makes the house look pleasant every day. If you are not blessed with a green thumb, buy greens— eucalyptus, ferns, lemon leaves, and such, which are not expensive and last in water for weeks on end.

Well-made fake flowers, expensive to buy, add up to savings over a long period of time but often look too static and grow musty more quickly than the time it takes to amortize their cost. Fake greens or trailing ivies can look attractive indefinitely (if dusted or sponged off) and can be long-term substitutes for fresh flowers. But *you* have to be sure. Buying fake greenery for long-term savings, then deciding it looks not quite right and buying fresh flowers for the party anyway is false economy.

A few more false economies. Economizing on *quantity* of food and liquor at a party is false. So is using a recipe that seems inexpensive but really isn't. Say you have a specialty-of-the-house soup, your own mixture of two cans of this, two of that, plus cream, herbs, lots of good sherry and croutons. Add up the cost of the main ingredients and you may be surprised. Main courses can fool you, too, especially casseroles and stews which call for stock, wine, special meat, or vegetables not in season. Before planning an elaborate casserole ask yourself if a leg of lamb, oven-cooked in a vermouth marinade, wouldn't be cheaper, and perhaps a little more partyish into the bargain? Or a crown roast of pork or a turkey.

One last point about party economies: when you or your husband get a raise, or Christmas brings a surprise check, it is normal to enjoy feeling flush. We should all splurge from time to time and a party is a good way to do it. But remember Parkinson's law, which seems especially apt here: "Expenditure rises to meet income." When planning parties through the years, during which we hope your income doubles and surprise checks pour in, remember that dollars spent on needlessly expensive dribs and drabs will be impossible to trace, making big changes in your life—a trip, a fur coat, a new rug—longer in coming.

Part Three

THE PARTY OF
A LIFETIME:
THE WEDDING

19

The Wedding
Preliminaries

Often in this book we have adjusted or altered party traditions to fit contemporary life. When we stand by old rules, it's because they still seem to work best or because good substitutes haven't come along.

We feel that wedding traditions should be embraced whenever possible. What you decide to spend and how you give the reception are variables, but they do not affect the religious ceremony or the main traditions. Sticking to custom is also easier: a wedding is a production, the event in a hostess' career that will make the most demands on her. No point complicating it with novelties.

The following survey of weddings and receptions goes by the *rules*, from the moment a girl comes whirling in to say she's engaged, until she goes off on the arm of her husband. Non-essential parties, such as showers and the bachelor dinner, are mentioned, as are wedding clothes and presents. All wedding details are covered.

THE ENGAGEMENT

Time was when a young man asked a girl's father for her hand in marriage and *then* proposed. Today the girl says "yes" first, and she is the one who tells her parents. It is still traditional for the young man to have a talk with the girl's father, no longer asking for his *permission*, perhaps, but hoping for the father's approval. The outline he gives of his prospects and plans, however modest and subject to change, starts things off right.

Next the parents of the young man get in touch with the parents of the bride-to-be. Usually the groom's mother telephones the bride's and asks when she and her husband may come to call. This is not as formal and stuffy as it sounds. While the polite reason for calling is to say nice things about their future daughter-in-law, there are also practical things to talk over: date and place of the wedding, the number to be invited, and so on.

This visit, especially when the parents know each other only slightly or not at all, can be agony for the young couple, both nervous for fear *their* parents may say something embarrassing or difficult. Though they probably will, the meeting is still important for the whole group, now closely linked for better or for worse, and especially important for the bride's mother. She not only has most of the work to do but wants to take everybody's wishes into account.

Announcing the Engagement

The official announcement is always given by the bride's parents at a party or in the newspapers, but before that both sets of parents tell relatives and close friends in person or in notes, and the bride and groom give their own friends the "secret" news.

The Engagement Party

This could be a cocktail party, a big luncheon or dinner, or just a simple meal including the groom and his parents, with perhaps a few relatives or close friends invited. Invitations to an engagement party need not tell the reason. During the party, for those who have not already guessed, the father of the girl calls for attention and makes the announcement.

An engagement party is not necessary because, as soon as the news is out, the groom's parents and others may offer to entertain bride and groom until they feel as exhausted as royalty on a state visit by the time they meet at the altar. But there are good reasons for having one. If the groom is a stranger to the community he can meet the bride's friends. Or the bride's father may feel that he must do something about business colleagues, yet does not want church and reception crowded with people who have never laid eyes on his daughter. Nor does he want business friends compelled to send presents, or even to feel that they must come to the wedding. (People-from-the-office often have a dull time at family affairs anyway.) A big engagement cocktail party is a good way around this. During the afternoon it comes out naturally that the bride plans a small wedding. This offends no one, and presents don't enter the picture since they are not expected at an engagement party—even though close friends may send them.

Announcing the Engagement in the Newspaper

The mother of the bride telephones the society or women's page editor and says when she would like the announcement to appear, giving at least a week's notice; women's pages often go to press before the rest of an edition. The editor may ask for a picture of the girl. This should be a 5 by 7 or 8 by 10 glossy head-and-shoulders shot, sent in an envelope with a typewritten announcement, to avoid the chance of the news being printed beside the wrong picture.

The copy should read:

"Mr. and Mrs. John Dean Whitman announce [or: have announced] the engagement of their daughter, Margaret Louise, to Mr. James Parker Hughes, Jr., son of Mr. and Mrs. Hughes of 100 Morningside Lane." [Or if the groom's parents live in another city: "of Baltimore, Maryland," leaving out the street address.]

Strictly speaking, that's enough. But people like a bit more detail, even if they have known the couple since infancy.

Something like this might be added:

"Miss Whitman graduated from the Merrywood School and received her B.A. degree from Barnard College. She is an assistant to the Curator of Drawings at the Fine Arts Museum.

"Mr. Hughes, a graduate of Theodore Roosevelt High School in Baltimore, and of Williams College, recently took his master's degree at Stanford, and is now with Jones, Morgan and Mayer, investment brokers, in this city. The wedding is planned for October."

The society editor, or pure enthusiasm, may inspire a more expanded announcement. Everyone is his own best judge of what else would be appropriate, but no one should let the typewriter run away, mentioning ancestors and relatives, unless they are so famous that it would seem unnatural to leave them out.

Two Visits to the Church

Around the time the engagement is announced the bride and her mother should call on their clergyman to make sure that he and the church are free at the time they would like the wedding, and to ask him to line up the organist and the sexton, who usually masterminds the procession and behind-the-scenes details. On this visit the bride and her mother should take a long look at the church. They may know it well, but it can look quite different when viewed as the setting for a wedding.

They should discuss decorations with the clergyman. He may have all the equipment necessary for flower standards, candles, or whatever they have in mind, but if not, a list must be made for the florist.

On the same visit the bride and her mother mention the rehearsal and fix a time when the clergyman, sexton, and organist can all be there.

The bride might also discuss the music. Since the organist will want to play anything she wishes, he must have time to look it up. If she has no idea what she would like he can make suggestions, and might run through these at the same meeting.

Wagner's Wedding March from *Lohengrin*, and Mendelssohn's from *A Midsummer Night's Dream* are most often played as the processional and recessional. While, to many of us, a wedding without them would be like a parade without Sousa, there is no real tradition about these selections. The bride and groom should have whatever music pleases them, as long as they choose something with a walking beat. Wedding attendants are usually nervous enough without the problem of keeping time to an obscure or difficult rhythm.

The second visit is the engaged couple's call on the clergyman.

Many dread this prenuptial tradition, since it seems so personal to discuss romance in a rectory office. But the clergyman must be convinced that the marriage is a good idea; it is his religious and legal duty. He will ask a few questions and sometimes give a little talk about his own views on marriage. Perhaps more to the point, he may also explain in detail the meaning behind each phase of the ceremony. Most of us know the vows so well that they may have lost their impact. A review may please and perhaps impress.

Who Pays for What?

Dowries and the deed to a rose-covered cottage may be things of the past, but the bride's parents still give the wedding and reception.

They give the kind of wedding they can afford—even if it's only fruit punch in the churchyard, and even if the groom's family would think nothing of spending ten thousand dollars on a wedding.

A complete list of the bride's parents' expenses includes:

Invitations and/or announcements
Church fees, organist, sexton, bell ringer
The bride's wedding costume and trousseau
All photographs (portrait of the bride and candid shots, if any, during the reception)
Transportation of the wedding party to and from the church
Flowers at church and reception, including bridesmaids' bouquets
Total cost of reception—food, drinks, music

The bridegroom or his parents pay for:

The wedding ring

The marriage license

The bride's bouquet, or a corsage for her to wear away from the reception

The clergyman's fee

Boutonnieres, gloves, and ties for the ushers, if any

Corsages for the mothers of bride and groom

The groom's expenses may not be as modest as they look. An engagement ring has been bought or, if the bride is given an old family one, perhaps reset. Then there is his parents' present to the bride, not obligatory, but who would fail to give one? It could be a jewel, a complete set of furniture, an expensive rug—any number of things, either practical or glamorous—that cost a great deal. The honeymoon tradition is a good one, even though a young couple might pass it up in favor of a down payment on something useful and lasting. So perhaps a check, earmarked for a trip, is the ideal way for the groom's parents to take part.

The groom, if he has ushers, will probably give each of them a souvenir of the wedding, and he may also give his bride a present on the wedding day, besides the ring. Also, since he is probably the poorer for courting her, he and his parents need not feel that the generosity is all on the other side.

GUEST LIST AND INVITATIONS

When the date is set and the church reserved, it is time to order invitations. The bride's parents have probably decided on the ideal number of guests. The groom's parents' list is generally about half that amount. It never works out perfectly. Both sets of parents may have friends in common; the bride and groom surely do. A groom's parents who live far away can expect few friends to come. Nevertheless, it's right to start with a round number and divide it evenly. Additions and subtractions come later. When you are calculating how many invitations to order, bear in mind that sending one to a friend who lives on the other side of the world is a nice way of saying. "We wish you could be with us."

The bride's mother asks the groom's to write a list including the groom's own friends. She and her daughter sit up nights working over their list; when both are complete she compares them for duplicate names and adds up the total. If the combined lists make too big a number, she asks the groom's mother to cut a few names and tries to cut an equal number from her own list. An easy way to work with a big list is to use a card index with names entered alphabetically on separate cards.

No matter what the total, it's wise to order extra invitations. It is virtually impossible to make up a complete list at the start, and sometimes the most obvious people are forgotten. For a list of two hundred and fifty or more, fifty extra invitations are not too many. Remember that invitations are sent as a politeness to those who already have the date on their calendars: the immediate families, the entire wedding party, and the clergyman and his wife.

Since invitations must be engraved, they should be ordered about two months ahead—engraving is not a fast process—and should be mailed three to four weeks before the wedding. Some jewelers keep supplies of the proper envelopes on hand so that addressing can be done while the invitations are being engraved.

The invitation reads:

Mr. and Mrs. John Dean Whitman
request the honour of your presence
at the marriage of their daughter
Margaret Louise
to
Mr. James Parker Hughes, Junior
Saturday, the fifth of October
at four o'clock
Saint Margaret's Church

In a big city where there is more than one Saint Margaret's, the address is engraved underneath. On a conventional invitation the word "Honour" is spelled in the English way.

Stick to traditional type faces. Plain script is the most traditional and formal. Up-and-down lettering, such as Antique or Shaded Roman, is popular and in good taste, but avoid a novel type face, even though the engraver has many examples to show you.

The invitation is always engraved on a double sheet of heavy white or ivory paper in black (if script) or in dark gray lettering. Choose the heaviest paper you can afford, with a dull, not a slick finish. (Glossy paper is used for invitations only in Europe.) Size varies. Some invitations are folded into the envelope, smaller ones go in unfolded. Size depends upon how much space is needed for the information. An outsize invitation is in poor taste.

Invitations are enclosed in two envelopes, an expensive tradition, but it is always done. The outer envelope is gummed like any other. The inner is not. It merely says, "Mr. and Mrs. Brown," or "Miss Wilson," or "Mr. Jones." Neither envelope is ever typewritten, and never say "Mr. and Mrs. Brown and family." If you are short of invitations and want to ask the Brown children, send one to all of them. The outer envelope would read: "The Misses Brown" and, underneath, "Master Peter Brown." The inner envelope reads: "Susan, Judy, and Peter." All grown members of a family should receive separate invitations. Since a return address is not usually put on the outer envelope, it is vital to write legibly and to check addresses.

The reception card, enclosed with the invitation, is a single piece of stiffer paper, exactly the same color as the invitation, with the same style of engraving. It reads:

Reception
immediately following the ceremony
703 Morningside Lane
R.s.v.p.

People often invite more people to the church than to the reception. On the face of it, this seems discriminatory: how does one decide between those asked to the service, the sacred part, and those asked to the social part? But in some circumstances asking more to the church makes sense. There may be many who are not close friends but who deserve some formal notice of the wedding. Send them an invitation to the church only because, though the formal place, it is also the more public; anyone may enter a church when its doors are open, invited or not. So the invitation to the church only is a mere announcement. And since people who receive it are not expected to send presents, there is no problem about "soliciting" one from those not invited for cake and champagne.

You might also send more church invitations than reception cards if your house, or wherever the reception will be, is so small that family members and the wedding party are all it will hold. If this *is* the case, ask no one else. News that a few outsiders have been invited will spread fast and may offend others.

Taking the opposite tack, often more people are asked to the reception than to the wedding. Anyone can understand a bride and groom wanting their marriage witnessed only by their nearest and dearest. Or the church may be tiny, or the ceremony may take place in a small living room, followed by a reception at a club or hotel or in a garden.

When the reception list is longer than the ceremony list the double-sheet invitation reads:

> *Mr. and Mrs. John Dean Whitman*
> *request the pleasure of your company*
> *at the wedding reception of their daughter*
> *Margaret Louise*
> *and*
> *Mr. James Parker Hughes, Junior*
> *Saturday, the fifth of October*
> *at five o'clock*
> *The Pine Meadow Club*
> *R.s.v.p.*

The small enclosure card, sent to those invited to the church, reads:

> *Ceremony at four-thirty o'clock*
> *Saint Margaret's Church*

Engraved enclosure cards are often skipped if the number invited to the church is small. Instead, the bride's mother invites people by telephone or letter, or encloses her visiting card with the reception invitation, writing in time and place of the ceremony by hand.

When the reception is being held in a church garden, or when the wedding is taking place some distance away, meaning that everyone who comes must automatically be asked to stay for the reception, both invitations can be run together like this:

Mr. and Mrs. John Dean Whitman
request the honour of your presence
at the marriage of their daughter
Margaret Louise
to
Mr. James Parker Hughes, Junior
Saturday, the fifth of October
Presbyterian Church
Greenville, Rhode Island
and afterwards at the reception
Greenville Country Club
R.s.v.p.
100 Morningside Lane

Note: The home address is engraved under the R.s.v.p.

Most stationers have samples of the conventional wordings for invitations when the bride's mother is a widow, has been divorced, or has married a second time. They also have the correct forms for the marriage of a young widow. (Older widows and divorced women have informal weddings and invitation is by letter or word of mouth, with perhaps engraved announcements sent afterward.)

Two politenesses that should never be forgotten: If the wedding or reception is held at a friend's house the invitation should read, under the line stating the hour, "at the house of Mr. and Mrs. William Goodhue," with their address underneath. But since the Goodhues do not want to receive the replies or wedding presents, the bride's home address is added under the R.s.v.p.

Second: If a club to which the bride's parents do not belong is used, the name of the member arranging for it is engraved in the right-hand corner opposite the R.s.v.p.: "Through the courtesy of Mr. and Mrs. Alexander Blackwell." To omit this detail makes a false claim and is rude to the Blackwells, unless the club throws open its door regularly to make up the deficit, and you don't need the backing of a member.

Informal Wedding Invitations

If the wedding is to be small, or there is no time for engraved invitations, the mother of the bride writes notes to everyone. This is the most flattering invitation of all, because it is so personal:

Dear Caroline,
Margaret is being married to John Parker Hughes, Jr., at Saint Margaret's at noon on Saturday, October fifth. We do hope you and George will be there and will join us here afterward for a small breakfast.

Love,
Kate

Or to a friend of the bridegroom:

Dear Mrs. Smith,
As you may know, our daughter Anne and Frank Palmer are being married on Saturday, October fifth, at Central Methodist Church. The wedding will take place at four-thirty. We hope that you and Mr. Smith will be there and will join us here afterward for a glass of champagne.

Sincerely,
Dorothy Williams

A bride-to-be who has no parents, or a woman marrying for the second time, writes the same sort of letter:

Dear Mrs. Livingston,
John Hughes and I are to be married in the Lady Chapel of Saint Patrick's on Saturday, October fifth, at eleven o'clock. We hope that you and Mr. Livingston will come, and go afterward to a small reception that my cousins, Mr. and Mrs. Bruce Wendell, are giving for us at 6 Orchard Drive.

Sincerely,
Margaret Whitman

Replies to Wedding Invitations

Invitations to the church do not have R.s.v.p. and require no reply. The form for accepting the invitation to the reception is:

Mr. and Mrs. Winston James
accept with pleasure
the kind invitation of
Mr. and Mrs. James Dean Whitman
for Saturday, the fifth of October

There is no need to add anything else.
    A regret reads:

Miss Lucy James
regrets that she is unable to accept
the kind invitation of
Mr. and Mrs. James Dean Whitman
for Saturday, the fifth of October

An excuse is not necessary, but always answer the invitation; the bride's parents need to know how many to expect.

When an invitation is written by hand, reply just as you would to any other first-person invitation, with a short note saying "Yes" enthusiastically, or "No" with a polite excuse.

What Hour Should the Wedding Be?

In the Northeast the traditional Protestant or Jewish wedding is held in the afternoon at four, four-thirty, or five. Roman Catholic weddings are usually held in the forenoon at ten or eleven or, if there is to be a high nuptial mass, at noon. In the South and West many Protestant weddings are held in the evening at eight or nine o'clock, to avoid the heat of the day. Catholics may sometimes be married in the evening by special permission.

While there is nothing against marrying at an unusual hour, if the Church approves, a big wedding will probably work better if you conform to local custom. A small informal wedding followed by breakfast might take place at nine in the morning if the couple were catching a noon plane.

Protestant and Catholic weddings are usually not held on Sundays or during Lent. Jewish weddings are not held on the Sabbath (sundown Friday through sundown Saturday), or on specific holy days or in holy periods during the year.

Wedding Announcements

Announcements are sent in place of invitations under circumstances such as these:

—If the bride and groom have a small wedding to which only a few friends are invited by handwritten letter, the announcement informs everyone else.

—If the marriage is sudden, with no time to arrange a traditional wedding, an announcement is usually sent, both to those who have been at the wedding and to those not invited. Usually the engraver will make a special effort to produce the announcement quickly.

—If there has been illness or death in one of the families and a small wedding takes the place of a big one, announcements go out to everyone who might otherwise have been invited.

The traditional announcement is always engraved on a double sheet and reads:

Mr. and Mrs. William Evans Goodwin
have the honour to announce
the marriage of their daughter
Eve Caldwell
to
Mr. Paul Rogers Wainwright
on Friday, the sixteenth of June
One thousand nine hundred and sixty-four
Trinity Church
San Francisco, California

"Mr. and Mrs. Goodwin have the honour of announcing" is equally correct, as is "Mr. and Mrs. Goodwin announce," though this seems flat compared to the other wordings. The name of the church may or may not be included, but the city always is. Announcements should be mailed on the day of the wedding or as soon after as possible.

While no one need acknowledge a wedding announcement, and no present is expected, a letter of good wishes or a present will be happily received. This is a matter of inclination only because the announcement is exactly that—a way to inform that a marriage has taken place—nothing more.

Often a card is enclosed with the announcement giving the couple's new address and the date they will be settled in their house or apartment. Here are three versions of such a card:

(1)

Mr. and Mrs. Maxwell Wilson, Junior

After the tenth of August   *16 Cypress Avenue*
Newton, Vermont

(2)

At home
after the tenth of August
16 Cypress Avenue, Newton, Vermont

(3)

After the tenth of August
16 Cypress Avenue   Newton, Vermont

The date given is not necessarily the very day the newlyweds arrive back from the honeymoon. It might be a week or so afterward, to give them time to themselves before the telephone starts ringing.

When There Is a Change of Plans

A *broken engagement* always involves temporary unhappiness and tension, but it is wiser than getting married when in doubt. Since nerves may be raw it is nice that there are routine ways of coping.

When the engagement has been announced, but invitations to the wedding have not been mailed, a notice is given to the newspaper: "The engagement of Miss Phyllis Webster, daughter of Mr. and Mrs. Harold P. Webster, and Mr. Paul Mason Cooper, has been terminated [or: broken] by mutual consent." Close friends and relatives are usually told by word of mouth, and tactfully keep questions and opinions to themselves. The time for talking it over may or may not come later, but the matter should never be brought up by outsiders.

Recalling invitations. If invitations are out and the wedding must be postponed for some reason, every person on the list must be notified. This can be done by telephone, letter, or telegram. But the simplest, time permitting, is for the bride's family to have a card printed (not engraved, because it takes so long) saying:

Mr. and Mrs. Ernest Clark Andrews
regret that
owing to the death of Mrs. Andrews' mother
the invitations to
the wedding of their daughter
Priscilla
to
Mr. Peter Walker
must be recalled

OR:

Owing to the illness of their daughter
Mr. and Mrs. Ernest Clark Andrews
are obliged to recall their invitations
for Tuesday, the sixteenth of May

When a wedding is definitely called off, not just postponed, after invitations are out, the announcement reads:

Mr. and Mrs. James Williamson
announce that the marriage of their daughter
Elizabeth Morgan
to
Mr. Stephen Van Dyke
will not take place

If there is no time for a printed or typewritten announcement —when there is sudden illness or the bride and groom call it quits at the eleventh hour—the mother of the bride telephones or telegraphs everyone. The telegram might read: "Invitations to the wedding of Elizabeth Andrews and Stephen Van Dyke have been recalled" or: "This is to inform you that the marriage of Elizabeth Andrews and Stephen Van Dyke has been postponed [or: will not take place]." Since telephoning is a mammoth job, the mother of the bride might divide the list among a few close relatives or friends. They say that they are "calling for Mrs. Andrews to say that the wedding, which was to have taken place this Saturday, has been canceled." Those called only reply, "Thank you for letting me know," out of tact, and to keep each call short.

If a wedding is canceled, every present must be returned, and the bride gives back her engagement ring and any other presents to the groom.

ON WITH THE WEDDING

Now that those dreary details are out of the way, let's return to the sunny side of the street.

To keep track of replies to invitations you need a system. When an acceptance comes, "A" goes beside the name on the list, "R" next to those who regret. Or, if you use a card index, remove the cards of those who regret.

Presents and Thank-You Notes

Wedding presents begin to arrive. Before a single package is opened the bride should have a wedding-present book. She enters the donor's name, the present, when it was sent, and where from (important if she decides to return it). When the thank-you note is written she checks off the entry.

A bride should try to keep up with thank-you notes. Writing five notes a day is not overwhelming, but if she skips three days and is faced with fifteen she feels swamped. People are usually tolerant of engaged girls, understanding they are busy and want time to enjoy being engaged. But tolerance changes to admiration with prompt thanks for presents.

Perhaps the reason so many brides fall behind in their letters (and in some cases *never* write) is because they feel that each letter should be a gem. No one expects that. All the sender wants to know is: "Did Elizabeth get my present?" A thank-you letter need say no more than:

Dear Mrs. King,

The beautiful salad plates arrived today. I adore them, and we need them! We both appreciate your thought of us more than I can say, and will think of you gratefully every time we use the plates.

We are so pleased that you and Mr. King will be at the wedding.

Affectionately,

Elizabeth Andrews

Clocked on a stopwatch and written fast but legibly, that letter took three and a half minutes, including the envelope. Any short enthusiastic letter is more than adequate, especially if sent immediately. The bride should mention what the present was, not just say, ". . . your lovely present," because the sender wants to be sure the bride knows what he or she picked out.

A boon to the bride is a table set aside for desk work with the invitation list and addresses (helpful for addressing thank-you notes), the present book, writing paper, pen and ink, and a roll of stamps. Nothing else. If the desk is in the same room as the wedding presents, so much the better.

If a present comes without a card, the bride immediately calls the store (or writes, if it is out of town), describes it, gives the order number if there is one, and asks the salesman to track down the sender.

Before the wedding, presents are always addressed to the bride alone, unless they are something intended solely for the groom, such as cuff links or some equipment for his favorite sport. A present sent after the wedding is addressed to both bride and groom.

What to send as a wedding present. Here tradition is changing, for the better. The old custom was to send something lasting for the household: silver, china, linen. Nowadays people send anything they think the couple would like or need: practical equipment from a cookbook to a dishwasher. Personal things—underwear, bath towels, and bed linen—in the past given only by the bride's parents or close relatives, may be sent by anyone. But it is a good idea to check on whether the bride wants them before monograms are sewn on.

A check or a gift certificate from a good store is sure to make a hit. Wedding presents *are* money, merely translated into goods, and if you don't know what to send, let the bride do the translating herself. It may spare her returns and exchanges.

Returning presents. No one wants a young couple to keep something that they do not like or will never need. The bride should not worry about offending friends who don't see their vase or ashtray when they come to inspect the house. If they are offended, they are unreasonable.

As prices and taxes rise, older people more and more often send something of their own as a wedding present: a set of plates or a useful piece of silver too expensive to buy at today's prices. This can be wonderful. But since the bride can only keep a "pass-on" present or sell it, the giver should choose carefully, not just discard unwanted things.

A bride is wise not to make hasty decisions about returning duplicates or things that seem at the time, unusable. Pairs—of lamps, decanters, casseroles—are often more useful than a single one. Extra breakables such as plates, glasses, platters, pitchers, and vases might be kept against the time when others have been swept away in pieces. Many a wife of ten years regrets having returned something which seemed too elaborate at first but which would have fitted beautifully into her present life.

20

Planning the Wedding Reception, the Ceremony, Wedding Parties, Wedding Clothes

The mother of the bride starts making reception plans even before the engagement is officially announced, if possible. Once the date is cleared with the clergyman, she moves quickly.

If the reception will be at a club or hotel, she reserves the ballroom or suite, and the rooms which the bride and groom will use for changing into their traveling clothes. She gives the manager a general idea of the size of the reception; it doesn't have to be definite, just something to help him line up an approximate number of waiters or waitresses.

Refreshments are discussed. The bride's mother might choose punch, alcoholic or otherwise, or one punch of each persuasion. Champagne, the traditional wedding drink, might be the only drink, or there can also be whisky and soda, coffee, milk, or soft drinks for teetotalers and children.

At an afternoon wedding the food can be simply wedding cake, or before it is cut trays of sandwiches could be passed. Since afternoon receptions are like cocktail parties (without cocktails), any cocktail party food suits.

If the wedding is in the early morning a true breakfast might be served: eggs with sausages or bacon, creamed chipped beef on toast, followed by wedding cake and coffee. This is the only "wedding breakfast" that is a breakfast; a wedding at eleven or twelve is followed by lunch. If there will be tables for all guests, this might consist of hot consommé or clam broth, a chicken or fish dish, and ice cream and wedding cake. Champagne would be served throughout, and coffee passed with the dessert.

At a lunch where guests will serve themselves and eat on their feet, soup would be skipped, and the main course would be eatable with a fork—hot creamed chicken, sea food Newburg, or cold salmon mayonnaise. The dessert might be ice cream in individual molds, or mixed fresh fruit, and wedding cake—or cake only.

At an evening wedding the "breakfast" could be a full supper, or merely drinks with sandwiches and cake, as at an afternoon reception.

If the reception is going to be at home, and big, the hostess loses no time getting in touch with a good caterer. She asks him to the house and discusses every detail. Furniture and kitchen arrangements are of special concern, and a floor plan must be outlined: location of the receiving line, refreshments, coats, wedding presents, and so on.

A hostess' list of things to ask the caterer might read:

> Receiving line in hall or living room?
> Buffet table in dining room or in living room cleared of furniture?
> Champagne where? Passed by waiters from kitchen?
> Music where?
> Coats in master bedroom and guest room or in cellar playroom?
> Room to display wedding presents?
> Parking? Will caterer round up men to park cars, or do we?
> Ask 3rd Precinct to send policeman to control traffic?
> When will caterers start setting up?
> How many rooms should storage company clear?
> How many cases of champagne?
> Will he supply it or should we buy it?
> Ice? How will he keep champagne cold?

Big question: how many people does caterer think we have room
  for?
Ask him to send estimate of total cost.

The caterer will have reassuring answers to these and other
questions. He may say that the whole thing will be impossible
without a tent set up in the garden. If this happens, the bride's
mother may reconsider the size of the reception (and the father
try to talk his daughter into eloping). If a marquee is within
the budget, the caterer will advise where to set it up. Many cater-
ing firms have their own marquees in different sizes, or can recommend awning companies that rent them.

Music

Just as in church, you must have music at the reception; try
going to one that doesn't have it! You might have a piano player
or accordionist, or even a small dance orchestra. There's no problem about dancing in a hotel or club, but at a house reception
a room must be cleared. The caterer can arrange for a mover to
store rug and furniture for a day or two.

Flowers

Flowers are an expensive necessity for both church and reception.
Give the florist your ideas and ask him to look over the church and
the reception room, make suggestions, and submit an estimate.

In the church the minimum would be a vase of flowers at either
side of the altar. At a wedding where money is no object, the
chancel might be banked with flowers, and bouquets might be
tied to the end of each pew, beneath tall candles wound with
vines. But there is a line between extravagance and vulgarity even
if the bride's father has signed a blank check for decorations.
The happy medium might be a couple of high flower standards or sprays of blossom in the chancel, and white flowers on
the altar. (In winter, holly or hemlock, or a chancel lined with
unadorned Christmas trees, could be lovely.) The end of every

fourth or fifth pew on the center aisle might be tied with flowers or greens. Or sprays could be alternated, zigzag, every three or four rows, if the aisle is narrow. At a wedding where there will be many family members, a single bouquet on either side of the aisle separates the family pews from the non-reserved section behind.

Flowers in the church are usually white, though at a midwinter wedding the vivid reds of poinsettias, camellias, or Jerusalem cherry bushes might look warmer and give an attractive medieval effect.

Flowers for the reception. In some rooms a single arrangement on the buffet table would be enough. While other rooms would profit by much more decoration, creating a bower seems wrong for a party lasting so short a time. Movable arrangements which can be sent later to a hospital are better. Wide wall expanses can be decorated with inexpensive greens. The key place for a beautiful display is where the bride and groom receive. It is like the centerpiece of the reception. Any color scheme that goes in the room and does not clash with bridesmaids' dresses or bouquets is fine. The bride herself is *the* white flower anyway.

WEDDING CLOTHES

The Wedding Dress

The bride's dress at a big wedding should be a version of the traditional dress every girl dreams about, white or off-white (depending on what is most becoming to her skin), with sleeves, long or short, and usually a train. The neckline may be high or low, but never as revealing as an evening dress. The material may be lace, tulle, faille, velvet, organdy, or—most traditional—satin, according to the season and what becomes the bride. At a summer garden wedding satin would look as out of place as piqué in December. In any season, if the bride has a low budget, satin is not the best choice since cheap satin has a too shiny look.

The dress might be trimmed with family lace, pearl embroidery, or buttons and bows. But the bride, the object of all eyes, should stand out, rather than be submerged in detail. Clean graceful lines and a good fit are what counts, especially since she is more often seen from a distance—in church, in the reception line, dancing—where intricate dress details blur or vanish. The bride should also consider how a dress looks from the back as she will be studied most closely standing at the altar.

No bride should assume that her figure will change miraculously on the wedding day. If she is short, she should not be swallowed up in a tent of satin and tulle. Nor should she have a long train—its weight will pitch her forward. If a girl has a generous bust, it is even more important to choose a "little" wedding dress, with a narrow skirt and short train, or a train of lace or tulle; transparent materials give an airy look.

Most American girls have slim waists, a belt line that goes in where it should below a flat midriff. If this is not a bride's strong point, she can play it down with a not too full skirt, so that it will not spread to an extreme width at the floor.

Waist cinchers do a lot for anyone, but a bride should practice wearing one before the wedding, to avoid possible discomfort, or even old-fashioned swooning, on the big day.

Since many girls have less than beautiful upper arms, it's nice that sleeves are traditional. With a short-sleeved dress, long white kid gloves are the answer. The third finger of the left glove is cut at the seam, and the bride slips her finger out for the ring.

The veil or headdress can be anything that suits the bride and goes with the dress. Usually only the very young bride wears a face veil. This, of plain tulle, is thrown back after the clergyman pronounces the blessing. Sometimes it is not attached to the headdress but merely tucked under or held with a couple of hairpins to the bride's hair. As she turns from the altar, the maid of honor gently pulls it away.

A short girl should choose a fingertip veil topped by a wreath, or a long plain tulle veil attached to a diadem of pearls or stiffened lace. A tall girl should choose something flat, such as a snug lace cap or a veil laid on like a scarf. Every bride should stand at a distance before the fitting-room mirror. No one can tell from a sitting position whether she looks pinheaded or topheavy.

Shoes match the dress and have closed toes. A bride, who should walk as though trained for the stage or royal life, will find that perfectly fitting shoes with reasonable heels are her greatest hidden asset.

Managing a wedding dress. No bride wants to drag her dress around the store or house to see how it moves; yet she wants to look comfortable in it. Perhaps she also lies awake nights wondering whether it will get crushed on the way to the church. Let's erase these worries. First, she should never buy a dress that seems really uncomfortable or unmanageable. It won't look right, and neither will she. Second, a dress rarely crushes on a short ride to the church, if it is handled right. The maid of honor, or a saleswoman from the bridal shop, can help the bride into the car and arrange dress and veil around her. If the car has a jump seat the bride might settle for it, letting the skirt spill over the back. Her father gets into the car first and sits on the side farthest from the door the bride will use. When they arrive at the church he steps out on his side, comes around, and helps her down.

The thing *not* to sit on is the veil. More crushable than most dresses, it may also be pulled askew. As the bride gets into the car, she, or someone else, holds the veil up in loose folds which are laid beside her. As she steps out it unfolds naturally.

When the bride enters the church, someone arranges dress and veil in "starting position" and she is all set to go.

Photographing the Dress

A bride who is wearing a traditional wedding dress may want a portrait photograph taken. During the sitting she has a chance to move in the dress and to practice with train and veil.

If possible, the sitting should be a week or so before the wedding—earlier if the picture will be sent to newspapers. If the bridal shop is set up for photography, have the picture taken there to avoid wear and tear on the dress (and the bride's nerves), by carting it to and from a studio.

A bouquet will have to be ordered for the picture unless the photographer has a fake one. Or sometimes he arranges with the florist for a cut-rate replica of the bouquet if he feels he will get a big order for the posed pictures and is to take candid shots during the wedding too.

The Bride's Dress for Smaller Weddings

This could be exactly the same as for a big wedding, minus a long train if the ceremony is in a small chapel or at home. Instead of a veil, she might wear a cap or a simple coif.

At a garden wedding, organdy or piqué and a picture hat with streamers could be the most charming thing imaginable. Or, in place of the hat, a wreath of flowers. Any bride's wedding clothes, being a *costume*, do not have to follow current fashions to the letter. To press the point, all that's necessary is something simple, becoming, covered, and white. The dress might be day length at a tiny wedding, and *should* be if the ceremony is performed by a magistrate or other official who is not a clergyman. It could be a day-length white or pastel dress, in a dressy fabric, or a pale or neutral wool traveling suit.

A woman being married for the second time never wears all white; any color but black is suitable.

Since fashions change so fast, few brides today have big trousseaux of outfit upon outfit meant to last for years. The going-away costume with new accessories and a few new things for the honeymoon are enough.

The Bridesmaids' Dresses

Once bridesmaids always wore long dresses, but now day-length dresses are also in favor, perhaps because they are more wearable afterward. Nevertheless, if a bride wants long dresses, so be it. Nothing looks prettier coming down the aisle, and there is no problem about uneven hemlines. Choice of color and material is the bride's. For a variety of complexions and figures, clear colors and fabrics with body—taffeta, ribbed silk, velveteen—usually look better.

The maid of honor's dress may match the others or be the same cut in a different color, or a different shade of the same color. She can also carry a bouquet in a different color from the rest.

All bridesmaids wear headdresses—real hats or coifs or, better still, flowers, which are adaptable to most hair-dos and universally becoming. Flower headdresses are paid for, along with the bouquets, by the bride's family.

The shoes bridesmaids wear should all be alike; feet will be seen whether dresses are short or long. The bride picks out an inexpensive white pump, leaves a color sample for dyeing with the shop, and each bridesmaid goes to be fitted. She pays for her own shoes, too.

Jewelry

The bride need wear no jewelry at all, except her engagement ring, but might wear a string of pearls or diamonds (if she is lucky enough to have one in the family). Her earrings could be small pearls or diamonds. Colored jewelry should not be worn. The bride wears her engagement ring on her right hand during the ceremony, returns it to the left afterward.

Bridesmaids usually wear pearls. Their necklaces or earrings should be as much alike as possible.

Clothes for Mothers and Women Guests

Mothers. Shoppers often turn down dresses with the remark, "No, it's too mother-of-the-bride." A good warning, since gray lace or blue moiré, unless cut by a master, can be the opposite of chic. Mothers of brides and grooms *should* look chic, up to date, and as young as they can.

The mother of the bride decides what length dress she will wear and tells the mother of the groom. Full length is standard, but day-length cocktail dresses or suits are also in fashion. The mother of the bride picks her color and tells the groom's mother, or gives her a sample, so that their dresses don't clash in the receiving line.

Here are some costumes that would win votes for a Best Dressed Mothers contest:

At a fall wedding the groom's mother wore a short dress and jacket of pale beige-on-beige brocade, with a rather straight skirt, straight loose buttonless jacket, brown velvet beret, and brown silk shoes and bag.

At a winter wedding one mother chose dull silk satin in navy blue with a high neckline in front, lower at the back, three-quarter sleeves, and a short flared skirt. Her shoes and bag matched the blue and her hat was a bright red velvet turban.

For a city spring wedding one mother wore floor-length Mediterranean blue corded silk with a boat neckline, elbow-length sleeves, and tulip-shaped skirt. Her hat: the never-out-of-style pillbox, this time of flowers in many blues.

At a country wedding in summer, pale linens, cottons, or silk shantungs would be good for short dresses or suits. Long dresses might be chiffon (if it is deftly cut to have a shape), or embroidered linen, cotton, or plain silk in a popular weave. Or, in very hot weather, something sleeveless would do, worn with a matching jacket in the church.

Women guests wear their best cocktail-time clothes—preferably not black, certainly not daringly cut—to an afternoon wedding. For a noon wedding, dressy suits or tailored silk dresses are appropriate. In the evening the little dinner dress or suit serves for any wedding except the most formal. To this, women would probably wear true evening dresses—covered at church by a jacket or coat—and veils or coifs which could be removed at the reception.

The Clothes of the Men

All male principals at a wedding, including the fathers, wear the same thing, as nearly as possible—and look the better, as men always do, for being "in uniform."

At a formal daytime wedding men wear morning coats (or cutaways, as they are often called), pale gray waistcoats, and gray and black striped trousers, similar but not necessarily identical. Sometimes instead of the tailed morning coat the men wear pepper-and-salt Oxford jackets, cut like the jacket of a business suit, with the gray vest and striped trousers.

They all wear black calfskin shoes, black socks, white stiff-collared shirts, and four-in-hand neckties, striped gray and black. With the trend toward simplicity, stand-up wing collars and striped gray ascots are rarely seen. While hats don't really count, since they are not seen in church, a silk hat or gray topper goes with the cutaway, a black homburg or bowler with the Oxford jacket. White boutonnieres and gray gloves (worn by ushers in church, but not by the groom and best man) complete the costume.

Men in the wedding party usually have to rent their outfits. The groom suggests a renting agency and several days before the wedding each usher goes in to be fitted to coat, vest, and trousers, and pays the rental fee. The groom often buys ushers' neckties and gloves, not so much as a gift as to be certain all are alike.

The groom's boutonniere is often different from those of the ushers, to follow the nice tradition that he is really wearing a spray from the bride's bouquet—even though he isn't. Ushers usually have white carnations or pompon chrysanthemums, and the groom might have a few lilies of the valley or a small gardenia.

At a less formal daytime wedding the men in the party might wear navy-blue suits, stiff-collared white shirts, and blue and white striped or dotted ties. With this outfit go white boutonnieres but no gloves. In summer, white flannels with navy-blue blazers or all white suits are appropriate, as are gray flannels and white linen jackets. Again, no gloves. With a white jacket, the boutonniere might be a bachelor's button.

Although this phenomenon is seen all over the country on a Saturday afternoon, evening clothes, such as white summer dinner jackets with black bow tie, should never appear at a daytime wedding.

At a formal evening wedding men wear white tie and tails, with a stiff-bosomed shirt, stand-up wing collar, white piqué waistcoat, and patent-leather shoes—not opera pumps. White gloves and white boutonnieres are worn.

At a less formal evening wedding the groom and his ushers would wear dinner jackets, with black bow ties, patent-leather shoes, white boutonnieres, no gloves.

Men guests in the daytime are always right in a dark blue or gray suit with a white shirt and quiet necktie. At evening weddings they usually copy the degree of dressiness decided on by the women. A man whose wife was wearing a long dress to a formal evening wedding might wear white tie and tails. If she was wearing a dinner dress or theater suit he would wear his dinner jacket.

P.S. *for the groom:* If he wears new shoes which have light soles, they should be blackened; otherwise, when he kneels at the altar everyone smiles. An unremoved price tag has the same effect.

PARTIES BEFORE THE WEDDING

During the weeks before the wedding many people want to give parties for the bride and groom. Though kind of them, it's what often causes tubercular-looking brides and shaky-handed grooms at the ceremony. When someone offers a party, the sensible bride picks a time no later than a week before the wedding, saying that she and the groom are just too busy nearer the date. Until a week before, parties are fun. They need not always be big cocktail crushes or buffets. The couple might prefer dinner with four or five others, or going with you to a play or concert. Get two pairs of tickets so that the fiancés can hold hands and not even pay attention if they don't want to. Asking an engaged couple for tea or a cocktail alone gives them a chance to see you (and vice versa), but to get away early.

Showers

Bridal showers are like rain showers in this respect: one or two are all right, but more are a bore.

A shower seems unnecessary for a girl whose family is able to give her everything she needs, since its main purpose is to provide practical things. A shower's secondary purpose—the chance for the girls to meet for a good talk about the wedding—is pleasant, but perhaps everyone could have as much fun at a lunch without presents.

Judging by the mass of invitations and wrappings in stationery stores, the bridal shower has become part of pre-wedding custom. But no bride should allow more than two showers to be given for her (and one is better). They are too expensive for her friends, and no doubt she would prefer one good wedding present to several insignificant shower gifts.

While a shower is supposed to be a surprise, the hostess should get the bride to hint what she would like. On invitations the hostess writes "Kitchen shower" or "Linen shower" or whatever kind it will be. Perhaps a top price might be stipulated: "Kitchen utensils under $5.00." Or it could be a no-expense shower: "Bring your easiest good recipes," with dividends to the groom who doesn't want to start married life on a diet of hamburgers and canned spaghetti. A how-to shower is helpful too; each guest brings, typed on a card, some housekeeping advice she has learned the hard way: "How to uncurdle hollandaise," "How to remove candle grease from a table top or tablecloth," "Peeling onions without tears."

At an afternoon shower, tea, coffee, or soft drinks might be served, or sherry or Dubonnet with appropriate sandwiches or cookies. At an after-dinner shower, the hostess might have coffee, hot chocolate, and a cake. At an all-girl party it does not seem right to serve hard liquor. Showers are best held in the afternoon or at lunchtime, because many of the women will have dates or, if married, will not want to leave their husbands at night. Never invite men to a shower. They may come to be good sports, but will wince at cries of "Oh, what a darling casserole!" and "I always wanted a blanket cover like that." And women will find that they inhibit this normal shower conversation.

Bride's Luncheon

A lunch given by bride for bridesmaids used to be one of the standard pre-wedding parties but is scarcely necessary. Enough happens without it. At the lunch, the bride usually gave presents to bridesmaids and they a joint present to her. These could be given at a shower or another pre-wedding party. Or the bride could have bridesmaids' presents at the reception, and the bridesmaids could send their present to her house with a card signed by each.

Both presents should be something lasting. The bride might be given a silver frame for her wedding picture, a compact engraved with her new initials, or something for the house that she wants—a special piece of furniture, an addition to a china collection, a clock. The bride usually picks some small piece of jewelry for her attendants—a pin or charm, or a picture frame engraved with initials and the date. Other original and useful choices might be a small cut crystal vase, a porcelain bird, ashtray, or cup, suitable for any shelf or table.

The Bachelor Dinner

This is the one party where women are not involved, but just for the record, here's what takes place.

Traditionally, the bridegroom gives the dinner for his ushers and any other close friends he wants. Often his father and the father of the bride are included. He usually takes a private dining room somewhere; there are cocktails followed by dinner, then, we are told, speeches which last well into the night.

Since such a party is bound to be expensive, the groom's father may foot the bill, or the ushers may pay for it, dividing the cost. In this case the best man or an usher pays for everything and later sends the fair share of the bill to each of the others.

During the evening the bridegroom usually gives ushers their presents. He might choose silver paperweights, stamp boxes, or beer mugs engraved with the date and monogram, or gold tie clips or key chains. His presents could also be something much less expensive: leather wallets, table-model cigarette lighters, or leather calendars or pocket engagement books, marked with initials. While all ushers' presents should be alike, the best man might be given something a bit more lavish.

The ushers usually give a present to the bridegroom. The silver cigarette box engraved with facsimile signatures is standard. The groom might also like a cocktail shaker or water pitcher, some new luggage, sports equipment, or a briefcase fit for a Prime Minister. Since the present is usually expensive and the groom might as well have something that he wants, the best man might consult him and buy the present; later each of the ushers would pay his share.

At some point during dinner the groom toasts the bride. This tradition may include breaking his glass, on the theory that it should never be put to less important or less sentimental use. If he does break it everyone else follows suit, and therefore the head-waiter should be warned beforehand to provide cheap glasses, replacements, and be prepared to clear the debris.

Bachelor dinners, sometimes given on the eve of the wedding, are more often held a few days earlier with the last night devoted to a dinner or supper for the entire wedding party.

The Wedding-Eve Dinner

Not part of long-time tradition, the wedding-eve dinner has probably come in because the rehearsal is often held on the afternoon before the wedding, and going on to a party seems natural—and fun. It should start early and end early.

The party is usually given by the parents of bride or groom, and includes everyone taking part in the ceremony, their wives and husbands, and, if there's room, relatives or godparents of the couple. There are speeches and toasts, attendants' gifts may be presented. Usually the wedding party is seated together, and the bride and groom always sit beside each other. Beyond these details, the party runs like any other. It could be formal with everyone in evening dress, or the simplest buffet supper. There is champagne or some other wine for toasting. After coffee the bride and groom should leave and everyone else follows soon after.

The Wedding Rehearsal

Every wedding, whether in church, house, hotel, or garden, which has music and a procession should be rehearsed. Having settled on a time with the clergyman, the bride's mother sends typed notices to the wedding party. These might give information about wedding-day timing too.

The notice to bridesmaids might read:

Rehearsal at five o'clock, Friday, May 4th, Saint Margaret's Church, Jefferson Road:

We will go direct from the rehearsal to the bridal dinner at the Country Club.

Saturday, May 5th:

Please be at our house in your bridesmaid's dress no later than 3:15. You will be given your bouquet and headdress when you arrive.

Bridesmaids will be driven to the church at 3:45 sharp.

OR:

Saturday, May 5th:

A car will call for you between 3:15 and 3:30. Please be dressed and waiting. You will be driven to the side door of the church. Please go into the vestry room, where you will be given your bouquet.

The same information about the rehearsal is given to the ushers. The rest of the notice might read:

Saturday, May 5th:

Please be at Saint Margaret's no later than three o'clock. You will be given your boutonniere when you arrive.

Following the ceremony, please go to the reception in your own car, or in one of the cars for the bridesmaids which will be waiting outside the church.

Every member of the wedding party should rehearse—especially children. Unrehearsed flower girls and pages have been known to sit down in mid-aisle or at the altar, to forget to throw petals, or to call to their mothers or leave the procession to visit them.

Everyone should be prompt. It takes time to get organized. The procession in Catholic, Protestant, and Jewish weddings varies, and the clergyman will first assemble everyone to go over the marching order. Then all take their places and the organist strikes up the processional. The superstition that a bride should not take part in her rehearsal has a point in its favor. She and her mother can stand aside and watch the procession objectively, to see if it is too slow or too closely spaced, and to decide whether the organ is too loud or soft. The wife of an usher or someone else stands in for the bride.

The sexton usually stays at the entrance to the nave to pace the procession, and to start ushers and bridesmaids off on the right foot.

When the practice processional has ended, attendants simply stand where they are told while the clergyman goes over the ceremony with the bride, groom, maid of honor, and best man. The bride, if using a stand-in, takes a place nearby.

Then there's a practice recessional, and, just to be sure, the clergyman may go through the whole thing again. If ribbons and a white carpet will be used, he also shows the appointed ushers how to cope with them.

Everyone is in high spirits at a wedding rehearsal, but since it is practice for a religious ceremony, good church deportment—low voices, quiet footsteps—is in order.

THE WEDDING DAY

Now the great day has arrived and the word for everyone is *promptness*. Time should be allowed for emergencies that don't arise. In bad weather, guests as well as the wedding party should leave for the church earlier than otherwise.

All principals should be dressed half an hour before their first cue. Bouquets, corsages, and boutonnieres should be on hand before anyone has time to begin worrying about them, and, hopefully, the florist will have had the church to himself several hours before the service.

Lunch or Supper on the Wedding Day

One party on the day of the wedding, the reception, is technically enough. But when the ceremony is in afternoon or evening, attendants and out-of-town guests might appreciate something more. Since the bride's mother has enough on her hands, this is a good opportunity for the groom's family to take over. If they, too, are from out of town, other friends and relatives of the bride might entertain. Following an afternoon wedding, the parents of the bride, simultaneously let down and wound up, may find having something to do a blessing.

The Best Man on the Wedding Day

So far he may have done nothing but enjoy himself at the parties, or come to the rehearsal and bridal dinner. But on the wedding day he whips into action.

First he sees to the bridegroom's clothes, taking his traveling things to wherever the reception is to be held and hanging them up in the room assigned. He then collects both bride's and groom's suitcases and checks them into the hotel where they will be staying or at the station or airport, making sure the stubs get into the groom's wallet. If the couple want to take their bags with them from the reception, he has them put near the entrance, then into the car at the right time.

As temporary travel agent he also makes sure that the groom has necessary tickets, driving license, or passports in his wallet.

With all this out of the way, the bride, her parents, or the groom's parents may consult him about other details. The groom is, and should be, considered unequal to tasks of any importance on this day. The best man substitutes, and also serves, as the wedding hour nears, as gentleman's gentleman, helping the groom to dress and trying to ease the tension.

Before escorting the groom to the church he makes sure he has the envelope with the clergyman's fee *and* the ring, his supreme responsibility. When the moment comes for him to present the ring, he may fumble or forget which pocket it is in, but he must *have* it. Good insurance is to keep the ring in its box, in a deep pocket of his trousers. When the ceremony begins, he carries the box in his hand, opening it only when the clergyman signals for it.

Duties of the Maid of Honor

Bridesmaids' duties are not taxing; they must be on time for all events, look and act their best. They may also help the bride to dress or to change afterward. The maid of honor plays a more important role at the altar. She holds the bride's bouquet, helps with the veil and train. She is indispensable to a bride in full wedding regalia, if only because it's comic for the bride's father to hold a bouquet and struggle with a long train.

The Ceremony

The last few minutes before something so serious and emotional are bound to be tense for everyone closely involved. The bride and groom, especially, wish to heaven it would begin. Although it *is* hard to wait doing nothing, infinitely worse is a nervous scramble at the last moment, or a breathless arrival because the veil wasn't secure or the tie wouldn't tie right.

Groom and best man should be in the church no later than fifteen minutes before the ceremony. Ideally, the bride drives up at the exact hour, or one minute after, to give leeway to late-comers. If there is a room at the back of the church where the bride can hide out with her bridesmaids, she might come early and wait there nervously, just as well as at home.

In the meantime, ushers have arrived at the church about an hour before the ceremony, pinned on their boutonnieres, and decided upon a division of labor. Several ushers will be assigned to the center aisle and one each to the side aisles, if any. A brother or brother-in-law of bride or groom, or some other relative, is a good choice for the center aisle, as he may recognize family and special friends who should be given seats near the front.

The bride's family sits on the left, the groom's on the right. If the groom comes from another town and has only his parents with him, some of the bride's relatives might sit in the front pews on his side. This looks better than one side packed and a lonely couple sitting on the other. Parents have the aisle seats in the first pew on each side.

As guests arrive, the ushers go forward to meet them at the door into the nave. A woman guest is always escorted by an usher, who offers his arm and asks whether she is a friend of the bride or the groom. If she has arrived with her husband, he follows behind her and the usher. When a whole family arrives together it speeds things up if the usher offers his arm to the oldest woman in the group; her husband or one of the other men escorts any other woman. Young girls don't need to be escorted by an usher.

Husbands and wives often arrive at the church separately if the wedding is on a weekday. They might plan to meet outside, or the one who arrives first is seated alone and watches out for the other to come in. They usually get together with little trouble.

Making a seating plan in church for all the guests, or even just families, is complicated and often inefficient. Some people fail to come, and it slows things down for ushers to look up names on a list. A bride's mother who has definite ideas about where certain people should sit might mail each of them a card with a pew number on it. Ushers are told to reserve certain pews and guests with cards hand them to an usher on arrival.

The bride's mother is the last to come in. After she takes her place no one else is seated. If a white carpet and ribbons are in the plan, ushers, usually the two who will lead the procession, draw these down the aisle. As soon as they have returned to the rear of the church the wedding march begins. Most churches have a buzzer or light at the organ console, which the sexton flashes on from the rear of the church to signal that the moment has come.

When the wedding march begins, the groom and best man walk in from the side and stand on the right of the altar steps. The clergyman takes his place at the same time. All the guests stand.

After the Ceremony Is Over

When the minister has given the blessing the organist strikes up the recessional. The maid of honor returns the bride's bouquet, turns the train, and picks up her own bouquet.

It is unattractive for the bride and groom to fall into a Hollywood embrace before so many people *and* before the altar of a church. A brief kiss is fine, and the bride may also pause on her way down the aisle to kiss her parents and her in-laws. These are matters of impulse, not a formal part of the proceedings.

When the recessional is over, the ushers go right back to escort family members out of the church. The ribbons are then removed and everyone leaves.

Manners in Church

Even though it is gay, and the most social event in church, guests should remember where they are, no matter how excited they feel. A word to the usher who escorts them, a smile or quiet hello to people sitting near is all right; to wave, crane your neck, or to keep up a whispered chat is not. Neither is turning completely away from the altar during the procession, even though it's tempting.

Guests who belong to a religion different from the bride and groom need not follow unfamiliar ritual. A Protestant, for instance, does not genuflect or cross himself during a Roman Catholic mass. But everyone should conform to the religious atmosphere by bowing or kneeling during prayers and paying attention to what is going on at the altar.

During the ceremony, ritual controls the manners of the bride and groom. Bridesmaids and ushers should stand at attention and follow the service. Going up the aisle, they should walk well and look happy, instead of as if headed for a frightening precipice.

Taking flash pictures is not correct in church. The photographer might go to the balcony and take a time exposure of the couple as they stand at the altar. He can also take flash pictures from the outside as the couple enter and leave.

During the recessional the bride and groom, though understandably ecstatic, and relieved that the service is over, should not race up the aisle but stick to the tempo set by the organist. At the rehearsal a fast-paced but not hustling beat can be chosen.

The Wedding Reception

The bride and groom, having left the church first, arrive at the reception ahead of everyone else, to be followed shortly by parents, bridesmaids and ushers, and then the guests. If the wedding reception is being held in the parish house or church garden, or if the ceremony takes place in the bride's house, guests should mill around for a few minutes before going into the reception area, to give the bride and groom time to catch their breath, and perhaps to toast each other alone.

When the wedding is in a club or hotel the person in charge greets the couple as they arrive, offers them a glass of champagne and the chance to freshen up.

After parents and bridesmaids appear the music starts and the receiving line forms, following this pattern: Nearest the door stands the bride's mother, unless there is an announcer, in which case he comes first. Next to the bride's mother comes the mother of the groom, and then the bridal couple. The bride always stands on the groom's right no matter which side of the room the receiving line comes from. If the guests come from the left, for instance, the bride stands next to her new mother-in-law. If they come from the right, the groom stands between his mother and the bride. Next comes the maid of honor, then the bridesmaids.

Usually the fathers do not stand in the receiving line, though they may if they wish, next to their wives. Often they can be more helpful standing near the end of the line to guide guests to the champagne and to make introductions. Or they just circulate around the room.

Ushers and flower girls do not stand in line, except for the official pictures. It would make too much handshaking, and children would fidget.

If there is no announcer, guests introduce themselves to the mothers and make some quick comment about the beautiful wedding or how pretty the bride looks. Then to the bride, "You look beautiful," and to the groom, "Congratulations!" is enough, with a quick compliment to the bridesmaids, about their bouquets, dresses or whatever. Sometimes there is a sort of bucket-brigade introduction: as a guest moves along the line each member of the wedding gives the name of the next person in it. Guests introduce themselves as they shake hands even though it seems a wasted effort—who could remember all those names? But not to say, "I'm Polly Jackson," or "I'm Phil Wright," makes "receiving" ridiculous, and the smiles and handshakes meaningless.

If there is dancing the bride and groom have the first dance alone. Then the father of the bride cuts in, and the groom invites the bride's mother to dance. After that there is no special dancing order. The groom should dance with both mothers and with all the bridesmaids. All the men in the wedding party take a turn with the bride. After the dance of the bridegroom, bride, and bride's father, guests drift onto the dance floor at will.

The Bride's Table

Sometimes everyone has a seat at table for luncheon or supper. Sometimes only the bridal party is seated. This always has a gold-fish-bowl atmosphere if the reception is held in one big room, with guests standing and staring at the seated in-group. It is better if there is an alcove or separate room off the main one for the wedding party's table, leaving the big room for standing guests.

The seating at the bride's table is in this order: Bride and groom sit next to each other at the head, or in the center if it is a long banquet table set on only one side. The wedding cake goes directly in front of them. The bride is on the right of the groom. On her right, the best man. The matron or maid of honor is on the groom's left, then ushers and bridesmaids alternate around. If the parents are seated, the groom's father sits at the bride's mother's right, and the groom's mother at the right of the bride's father. The clergyman included at a bridal table (and it is nice if he is) sits at the left of the bride's mother, and his wife left of the bride's father.

The toasts begin with the groom's to the bride or with the best man's to the bridal couple. Everyone rises and joins in. The bride may toast the groom if she feels like it, but it is no slight if she is shy and does not. Both fathers usually make toasts, and the groom pleases if he toasts his mother and mother-in-law. If there are telegrams, the best man might read them to the whole company.

At a stand-up reception it is better to skip all toasts except the best man's to the couple and the groom's to the bride, since it's awkward to call a standing crowd to order more than once. The bride, groom, and best man go to the cake table, which is placed in some central spot. The best man calls for silence, then makes his toast. The groom follows.

After the toasts the bride cuts the cake, dividing the first slice with the groom. Then a waiter slices the rest. The bride's cake is usually a white or pound cake in two or more tiers, with white icing and perhaps a white wedding bell or bouquet (but preferably not a toy bride and groom) on top. If the cake is big enough everyone at the reception might be offered a slice. An expensive but nice addition is a pile of small boxes of fruitcake on a table near the door for souvenirs. Unmarried guests are supposed to put these under their pillows and, it is said, are fated to marry whomever they dream about. A more reliable and romantic reason for souvenir cake is that the bride and groom can save some to eat on wedding anniversaries. Fruitcake keeps indefinitely and can be refreshed twenty years later with splashes of brandy.

Leaving the Reception

As at all other parties, the time suddenly seems right for people to go. While guests may leave a reception any time after going down the receiving line, it is nice if they stay until after the bride and groom have left—a good reason for the couple not to linger. All wedding attendants wait to see them off. When the couple decide to leave, the bridesmaids gather and the bride throws her bouquet. When there is only a maid or matron of honor, unmarried women guests also try to catch the bouquet, but when there are several unmarried women in the wedding party no one else joins in.

The bride with her bridesmaids, or alone with her maid of honor or mother, if she prefers, goes to change into traveling clothes. So does the groom. When both are ready they either return to the reception to say good-by or guests wait near the entrance to cheer them as they run out. Parents usually say private good-bys upstairs.

As they rush to the car, the couple are showered with rice or rose petals. Many clubs and hotels forbid rice, with reason. It is a slippery hazard on bare floors and difficult to sweep up. Petals are better, too, because they are easy to see and shake off. Let's spare the bridal couple the embarrassment of rice showering from pockets and hat-brims as they check in at the hotel or airport.

Manners at a Wedding Reception

Since the hostess will be in the receiving line at first, and not able to make introductions, guests don't wait for them. The reception hall, even if a hotel ballroom, is on this occasion the "home" of the bride and her parents, and being under their roof is sufficient introduction for everyone to talk to everyone. Good guests make a point of speaking to strangers and people who have no companions.

After the receiving line breaks up the hostess moves about and tries to speak to as many guests as she can. She makes sure that the groom's parents, especially if they are from another city, have company at all times.

The bride always looks overjoyed at a big reception, but the groom, who may find it tedious and exhausting, must try never to show it. All eyes are on him, and he should act as if he preferred nothing better than talking to old aunts, dancing with bridesmaids, and being slapped on the back by fifty men in as many minutes. As head of a new family, his performance makes a great impression on everyone; he should keep smiling, even if his cheeks hurt.

One bride and groom did something at their reception which isn't tradition but ought to be for the boost it gave. Before going to change, they went around the room together, speaking to everyone at every table. All two hundred guests left convinced that the couple were especially delighted to see them.

This wonderful pair also took time on their honeymoon to write each member of the wedding party, thanking them for their friendship and moral support on the wedding day. (Somehow, everyone remembers this couple's anniversary every year.)

After the wedding it is nice if guests write a short note to the mother of the bride. Granted, it is only a gesture, but here is a hostess who has worked beyond capacity, and suddenly all is over. If her party was especially pleasant, her daughter beautiful, her choice of flowers original, she would love to hear it, for it was the party she wanted to be her best.

General Index

Address, form for boys and girls, 96
After-dinner drinks, 195–96. *See also* Liqueurs
Afternoon coffee party, 106–7
Age groups, in guest list, 13
Announcements, wedding, 263–64
Appearance. *See* Dress, for parties
Artificial flowers: as centerpiece, 47; outdoor parties, 85
Artificial fruit, as centerpiece, 47
Ashtrays: cocktail party, 33; dinner, with no maid, 52; outdoor party, 79; small seated dinner, 48–49
At home cards, 264

Babies, 14; parties for, 97
Bachelor dinner, 281–82
Bal de tête, 73
Ball, -dance, difference, 67
Bar equipment gadgets, 172–73
Bartender: cocktail party, 30, 34; uniform, 184
Behavior, formal dinner, 116–17. *See also* Manners
Best-ness, 4
Black-tie: dinner, hostess dress for, 156–57. *See* Evening dress
Boat picnics, 86–87
Brandy, 193–94. *See* Liqueurs
Breakfast, wedding, 270
Bridal showers, 279–80
Bride's luncheon, 280–81
Buffet lunch, outdoor party, 78
Buffet suppers: check list, 62–63; hostess' dress, 156; invitations, 15, 20; man's dress, 161; outdoor party, 78; perpetual mo-

tion, 56–59; "seated," 59–62, multipurpose, 59, serving, 61–62, setting up for, 59–61; serving, 58–59; table setting, 57–58; types, 56
Butter plates, formal dinner, 114

Candles: formal dinner, 115; lunch party, 55; seated buffet supper, 61; small seated dinner, 47
Caterer, 113–14; cost, 122; formal dinner, 113–14; operational method, 183; team, 183; waiters' uniforms, 184; wedding reception, 270–71
Centerpieces: food, 84; formal dinner, 115–16; outdoor parties, 84; small seated dinner, 46–47
Champagne, 191–92; at a dance, 70–71; formal dinner, 114. *See also* Wedding reception
Check list: cocktail party, 38–39; coffee party, 108; tea party, 102
Children, at parties, 14
Children's parties: decorations, 97; family affairs, 95–97; going and coming, 97; invitations, 95–96; manners, 96
Christmas, 90, 93, 94; Eve supper, 94; "syndrome," 95. *See* Family affairs
Cleaning. *See under* House
Clothes. *See* Dress, for parties
"Clutcher," 25–26
Cocktail party, 30–41; ashtrays, 33; bar, 34–35; beverages; 34; bowls, 32; check list, 38–39; cleaning,

37–38; doilies, 32; engagement, 252–53; flowers, 38; food, 35–37, 39; glasses, 31–32; guests, number of, 175; help for, 30–31, 182; ice, 31; introductions, 126; invitations, 15, 17–19; kinds, 30; liquor, 33–34; man's dress, 161; martini, 34; pets, 40; R.s.v.p., 19; serving equipment, 32; small, 40–41; telephoning invitations, 19; when to give, 30; written replies to invitations, 24

Coffee parties, 106–8; afternoon, 106–7; check list, 108; evening, 107; morning, 106

Coffee service, 133; small seated dinner, 50; large seated dinner, 54

Compotes, 48

Conversations, 132. *See also* Language

Cook, hiring, 55

Costume parties, 73

Crumbing the table, 50, 51, 119

Dance, 64–77; -ball, difference, 67; behavior at, 75–76; decorations, 71–73; dinners before, 68; ending, 76–77; food, 69–71; guest list, 64; host, 75; hostess, 75, dress, 156–57; invitations, 65–67; liquor, 69–71; music, 68–69, 74–75; place, 65; seated buffet supper, 59; subscription, 76; time schedule, 73–75

Decorations: children's parties, 97; dance, 71–73; desserts, 190; formal dinner, 116; outdoor party, 81–82; wedding, 254, ceremony, 271–72, reception, 272

Delicacies, purchasing, 243

Dessert service: formal dinner, 114; seated large dinner, 53

Dinner(s): announcing, 129; bachelor, 281–82; before a dance, 68; formal, 109–22, hostess dress, 156–57 (*see* Formal dinner); guests, number of, 175; help for, 182; introductions, 126; invitations, 16, 20–22; seated dinner (12–18), 53–55; small seated dinner, 42–52, hostess dress for,

156; separating after, 133–34; wedding-eve, 282

Doilies, cocktail party, 32

Dress, for parties, 5; accessories, 157–59; appropriateness, 153; caring for, 159–60; economical, 157–58; fashionable, 152–53; figure and fit, 155; hostess, 155–57; man's-woman's complementary, 162; for men, 153–54, 160–62; openmindedness, 153–54; outdoor party, 78–79; tastefully, 154; uncertainty about, 155–56; women, for dinner at home, 162; your age, 154

Drinking manners, 145–46, 158

Drinks: after-dinner, 195–96; choosing, 190–93; liqueurs, 193–95. *See* Liquor; Wine

Dull people, seating, 130

Easter, 90, 93. *See* Family affairs

Eating. *See* Table manners

Economy: in décor, 247–48; false, 247–48; party, 242–48

Ending a party, 136–37

Engagement: announcing, 252, 253–54; broken, 264–65; party, 252–53; ring, 276, returning, 266

Entertaining. *See* House

Entertainment, family parties, 93

Equipment: formal dinner, 112–14; picnic, 87–88; tea party, 99

"Etiquette," 6–7

Evening coffee party, 107

Evening dress: buffet supper, 56, 59; women's, 155–56. *See also* Black-tie

Family: affairs (*see* Family affairs); father as host, 139–40; inviting to party, 13–14

Family affairs, 90–97; after dinner, 92–94; children's parties, 95–97; entertainment, 93; guest list, 90; making most of, 94–95; place cards, 91; planning meal, 91–92; serving, 92; spirit of, 93; timing meal, 91–92; traditions, 94–95

Finger bowls, 46; formal dinner, 114, 119

Flatware: buffet supper, 57; small seated dinner, 45–46

Flowers: cocktail party, 38; church wedding, 271–72; men in wedding party, 278; wedding reception, 272

Food: bridal shower, 280; buffet supper, 56–57, 226–35; centerpieces, 84; choosing, 186–90; cocktail party, 35–37, 39, 40–41; dance, 69–71; desserts, 188, decorating, 190; dinner, 52, 197–210, 210–25, 235–37; familiarity, 186–87; formal dinner, 112, 120–22; holiday parties, 91; kinds, eating, 142–45; outdoor party, 80–81; "party up," 190; picnics, 85–87; second helpings, formal dinner, 118–19; small cocktail party, 40–41; small seated dinner, 50; tea party, 100–2; wedding breakfast, 270; wedding reception, 269–70

Formal dinner, 109–22; behavior, 116–17; caterer, 113–14; dessert service, 114; equipment, 112–14; food, 112, 120–22; guest list, 110; help, 112–14; hostess, 113; invitations, 110–12; late arrivals, 116; menu cards, 117; menus, 120–22; place cards, 115; receiving line, 116; serving, 118–20; table setting, 114–16; wines, 114–15

Formal parties, wording used, 22

Gate crashers, 138

Glasses, cocktail party, 31–32

Guest list: big party, 12; dance, 64; family parties, 90; formal dinner, 110; pointers, 12–14; record-keeping, 87; repetition, 10; small party, 10–11; special events, 23; wedding, 256–57

Guest(s): after dinner, 148; arrival, hosts and, 126; behavior, 141 ff; choosing, 4; drinking manners, 145–46; of honor, seating, 129–30; -hostess, thanking, 149; imitation, 151; language, 150–51; late-stayers, 136–37; leaving, 135–36, 148–49; "nucleus," 10; politeness, 147–48; punctuality, 141; smoking manners, 146; table manners, 142–45; uninvited, 138

Help, 176–85; cocktail party, 30–31; directing, 177–81; engaging, 9; formal dinner, 112–14; holiday parties, 91; lists for, 178–80, 182; men, uniform, 184–85; pay for, 183, 185; problems, 185; for seated dinner (12–18), 53; several, 182–83; small cocktail party, 40; speaking to, 181–82; troublesome, 185; uniforms, 178, 184–85; women, uniforms, 184. See also Caterer

Holiday parties: food, 91; help, 91. See Family affairs

Host: behavior, 125 ff; conversation, 134–35; at a dance, 75; formal dinner, 116–17; imitation, 151; party spirit, 4; role, 138–40; uninvited guests, 138

Hostess: behavior, 125 ff; conversation, 134–35; creating correct atmosphere, 7–8; at a dance, 75; dress, 155–57; ending a party, 136–37; formal dinner, 113, 117; -guest, thanking, 149; imitation, 151; party spirit, 4; poise, 137–38; refusal of help, 132; rules for, 7–8; thanking, 149

House: cleaning, 164–69; furniture arrangement, 173–74; household gadgets, 171–73; kitchen, 170–71; lighting, 169; neatness, 163–64; party capacity, 175; ready for entertaining, 168–69; single girl's apartment, 174

Husbands-wives: conversation, 147; dress, matching, 162; separating, 128

Imitation, virtues of, 151

Informal parties, 22

Introductions, 116, 126–28; etiquette of, 127; hostess behavior after, 128–29

Invitations: accepting/regretting, 24–25, 27; big party, lists, 12; buffet supper, 15, 20; children's parties, 95–96; cocktail party, 15, 17; dance, 65–67; dinner parties, 16, 20–22; formal dinner, 110–12; giving, 15; list, making, 12–14; menaces, 25–27; outdoor party, 78–79; people you dislike, 12; recalling, 28; reminders, 23; repaying, 28–29; replying to, 24–25; small party lists, 10–12; special events, 23; telephoning, 15, 19; visiting cards, use of, 16–18; wedding, 256–60, informal, 261, recalling, 265–66, replies to, 262; when to send, 9–10; written, 15, 16–19

Kitchen, 170–71

Language, 150–51
Late arrival, 26–27, 141; at formal dinner, 116
Lateness, 26–27
Lighting, outdoor party, 81–82
Liqueurs, 193–95; cost, 195; glasses, 195; serving, 54
Liquor: cocktail party, 33–34, 41; at a dance, 69–71; outdoor party, 79
Lunch: bride's, 280–81; buffet, outdoors, 78; dress for, 153; hostess dress, 156; leaving, 148; man's-woman's dress, 162; parties, 55; on wedding day, 284; wedding, 270; wine with, 192

Maids. See Help
Manners: children's parties, 96; church wedding, 288; drinking, 145–46, 158; formal dinner, 116–17; as morals, 6–7; and party spirit, 7; smoking, 146, 158; table, 142–45; wedding reception, 292
Men: party clothes, 160–62; wedding clothes, 277–79. See also Host
Menu. See Food
Menu cards, formal dinner, 117

Morning coffee party, 106
Music: dance, 68–69, 74–75; wedding, 254–55; wedding reception, 271

Newcomers, as guests of honor, 129–30
New Year's Day open house, 94
Nicolson, Harold, 6
Novelty, at parties, 4–6
Nut dishes, 115

Obligations, fulfilling or not, 12
Open house, 138; New Year's Day, 94
Outdoor parties: at home, 78–85; cleaning up, 79–80; clothing, 78–79; cooking and serving, 80; decorations, 81–82; food, 80–81; furniture, 79; invitations, 78–79; lighting, 81–82; liquor, 79; man's dress, 161–62; picnics, 85–89; table settings, 83–85; types, 78

Parties: atmosphere, 4–8; best-ness, 4; economies, 242–48, in food, 243–44, ingredients, 245–46, seasonal, 244–45; leaving, 148–49; manners, 6–7; novelty, 4–6; "oncemanship," 189; spirit, 3–8, in family affairs, 93; types, 9
Pets, 14, 40
Photographs: flash, at church wedding, 288; wedding dress, 274
Picnics, 85–89; equipment, 87–88; food, 85–87; kinds, 85–87
Place cards, 131; family affairs, 91; formal dinner, 115
Place mats, 44–45
Place plates, 118
Poise, 137–38
Post, Emily, 7
Presents: bride-bridesmaids, 280–81; groom-ushers, 281; wedding, 267–68, returning, 266

Receiving line: formal dinner, 116; wedding reception, 289
Reception, wedding, 269, 288–92

Repaying invitations, 28–29
R.s.v.p.: cocktail invitation, 19; dinner invitation, 20, 22; position of, 22; wedding invitation, 260

Seasonal economies, 244–45
Seated dinners: ideal size, 42; serving, 53–54; small, 42–52
Seating arrangements, 129–31
Second helpings, 145
Serving: buffet supper, 58–59; formal dinner, 118–20; instructions for inexperienced help, 179–81; order of, at table, 53; outdoor party, 80; seated buffet supper, 61–62; small seated dinner, 49–52; tea, 103–5
Shopper's syndrome, 243
Showers, bridal, 279–80
Silver, polishing, 37, 166–67
Single girl: apartment, 174; as hostess, 139–40
Small seated dinner: centerpiece, 46–47; food, 50; outdoor party, 78; place mats, 44–45; serving, 49–52; table setting, 42–49; types to eliminate, 11
Smoking manners, 146, 158
Special events: guest lists, 23; invitations to, 23; picnics, 85
Subscription dances, 76
Substitutes, for party list, 14
Supper: on wedding day, 284; buffet (see Buffet suppers)

Tablecloths: buffet supper, seated, 61; small seated dinner, 43–44
Table manners, 142–45
Table settings: buffet supper, 57–58; formal dinner, 114–16; lunch party, 55; outdoor party, 83–85; small seated dinner, 42–49
Take-you-in card, 117
Taste, in dress, 154
Tea parties, 98–105; arranging, 99–100; check list, 102; dress, 153, 156; equipment, 99; food, 100–102, 105; guests, number of, 175; serving tea, 103–5; spring and summer, 105

Telephones: guest, 147–48; hostess, 132–33
Thanksgiving, 90, 94. See Family affairs
Thank-you note: to hostess, 149; to mother of the bride, 292; for wedding presents, 266–67
Toasts, 119–20; formal dinner, 119; groom to bride, at bachelor dinner, 281–82; wedding-eve dinner, 282; at wedding reception, 290
Traditions, family affairs, 94–95

Uninvited guests, 27

Victoria, Queen of England, 112
Visiting cards: crossing out engraved name, 25; as invitations, 16–18

Waitresses, uniform, 184
Wedding: announcements, 263–64; attendants, 225; bachelor dinner, 281–82; best man, 285, 286, 290; bridal showers, 279–80; bride, 286, dress, 272–75, luncheon, 280–81, mother at ceremony, 287, parents' expenses, 255, 276; bridesmaids, 289, 290, 291, dresses, 275–76; cake, 290–91; Catholic, 262–63, 283; ceremony, 286–87, planning, 254; change of plans, 264–66; clothes, 272–79, men, 277–79, mothers, 276–77, women guests, 277; day, 284–92; dinner, 119; engagement, 252–56; -eve dinner, 282; flowers for men in party, 278; groom, 285, 286, clothes, 277–79, parents' expenses, 256; guest list, 256–63; hour for, 262–63; invitations, 256–63, informal, 261, recalling, 265–66; replies to, 262; jewelry, 276; Jewish, 262–63, 283; lunch, 270; maid of honor, 285–86, 287, 290, 291; manners in church, 288; mothers' clothes, 276–77; music, 254–55; parties before, 279–82; preliminaries,

251–68; -present book, 266; presents, 259, 266, 267–68, returning, 266; Protestant, 262–63, 283; reception, 269–72, 288–92, bride's table, 290–91, cards, 258, 259–60, leaving, 291, receiving line, 292; rehearsal, 253, 282–84; thank-you notes, 266–67, 292; ushers, 286–87, 289, 290; veil or headdress, 273–74; who pays for what?, 255–56

White lies, 26

Wine: amount needed, 192–93; champagne, 191; in cooking, 195; cost, 190; domestic, 191, 192; formal dinner, 114–15; French, 191, 192; German, 192; glasses, 193; guest and, 145; Italian, 192; pouring, 193; red, 190–91; rosé, 191; serving, 54, 145–46; sipping, 193; with special foods, 192; temperature, 191; white, 191

Wives. *See* Husbands-wives

Menu and Recipe Index

Acorn squash, 200
Appetizers:
  avocados Du Pont, 198
  breadless "sandwiches," 240
  cereals with seasonings, 239
  cheese, 239
  cheese Taj Mahal, 239
  cocktail, 238–40
  crab meat:
    canapés, 240
    creamed, 201
  creamed crab meat, 201
  guacamole, 239
  onion tart, 220
  pâté maison, 202–3
  roasted nuts, 239
  shad roe, 239
  shrimp baked in wine, 206
  tartar steak, 239–40
  vegetables, 239
Asparagus, creamed, 210
Avocados Du Pont, 198

Bananas, baked, 212
Beef:
  boeuf bourguignon, 231
  party menus, 198, 199, 200, 202,
    203, 207, 208, 209
Bisque of clams, cold, 199
Black bean soup, cold, 204
Blackberries Walterspiel, 209
Blueberry pie, deep-dish, 234
Bluefish, 236
Boeuf bourguignon, 231
Borsch with sour cream, hot, 211–
  12

Boula boula, 205
Broccoli au beurre, 203
Brunswick stew, 228
Brussels sprouts in sour cream, 220
Buffet supper menus, 226–35

Cakes:
  gingerbread, 219
  peach, 208
  poundcake au kirsch, 207
Carrots, 199
Cauliflower amandine, 223
Cereals with seasonings, 239
Cheeses:
  as appetizers, 239
  Taj Mahal, 239
Chicken:
  Albert, 224
  breast of, with grapes, 221
  Brunswick stew, 228
  cold poached, in jelly, 217
  curry, 226–27
  oven-fried, Lois, 219
  and oysters à la crème, 213–14
  roast, with wine gravy, 216
  tarragon, 222–23
Cinnamon toast, 101
Clams:
  bisque of, cold, 199
  steamed, 237
Cocktail appetizers, 238–40
Cold poached chicken in jelly, 217
Corn:
  custard, 203
  soup, 201

Crab meat:
  canapés, 240
  creamed, 201
Creamed crab meat, 201
Crème fraiche, 206
Crème Senegalese, 209–10
Crepes with cranberry sauce, 214–
  15
Curry, chicken, 226–27

Desserts:
  baked bananas, 212
  blackberries Walterspiel, 209
  blueberry pie, deep-dish, 234
  crepes with cranberry sauce, 214–
    15
  fraises Sarah Bernhardt, 202
  fruit, 245
    hot baked, 232
    macédoine of, 216
  gingerbread, 219
  hot baked fruits, 232
  ice cream pie, 223
  lemon mousse, 204
  macédoine of fruit, 216
  menus, 188
  mousse au chocolat, 199
  orange ice with cointreau, 201
  peach cake, 208
  pecan pie, 228–29
  poundcake au kirsch, 207
  profiteroles with chocolate sauce,
    218
  raspberries gervais, 205–6
  stewed fresh rhubarb and straw-
    berries, 235
  strawberry tart, 230
  zabaglione, cold, 225
Dinner menus:
  fish, 235–37
  meat, 197–210
  poultry, 210–25

Emergency food, 240–41

Fillet of sole Normande, 207
Finnan haddie, creamed, 236
Fish and sea food:
  amount per person, 236
  bluefish, 236
  clams:
    bisque of, cold, 199

  stewed, 237
crab meat:
  canapés, 240
  creamed, 201
dinner party menus, 235–37
fillet of sole Normande, 207
finnan haddie, creamed, 236
kippered herring, 237
lobster, 237
mussels, steamed, 237
party menus, 235–37
salmon steaks, 236
scallops, 236
shad roe, 236
  appetizer, 239
shrimp, baked in wine, 206
smelts, 236
trout, 236
Fowl. See Poultry and fowl
Fraises Sarah Bernhardt, 202
Fruit:
  bananas, baked, 212
  blackberries Walterspiel, 209
  blueberry pie, deep-dish, 234
  crème fraiche, 206
  desserts 245
  fraises Sarah Bernhardt, 202
  hot baked, 232
  macédoine of, 216
  raspberries gervais, 205–6
  rhubarb and strawberries, stewed
    fresh, 235
  strawberry tart, 230

Gazpacho, 222
Gingerbread with whipped cream,
    applesauce or both, 219
Guacamole, 239

Horse radish sauce, 200

Ice cream pie, 223
Iced tea, 105
Irish stew, 229–30

Kippered herring, 237

Lamb:
  Irish stew, 229–30
  party menus, 198, 201, 205, 206,
    208
Lemon mousse, 204

Lima beans, baby, puréed, 221
Lobster, 237

Macédoine of fruit, 216
Marmalade toast, 101
Meat:
  beef:
    boeuf bourgignon, 231
    party menus, 198, 199, 200,
      202, 203, 207, 208, 209
    dinner party menus, 197–210
  lamb, Irish stew, 229–30
  party menus, 197–210
  steak:
    and kidney pie, 232–33
    tartar, appetizers, 239–40
  veal:
    stew in red wine, 234–35
    vitello tonnato, 233–34
Menus:
  bridal shower, 280
  buffet supper, 56–57, 226–35
  choosing, 186–90
  cocktail party, 35–37, 39, 40–41
  dance, 69–71
  desserts, 188, 190
  dinner, 50, 52
    with fish, 235–37
    with meat, 197–210
    with poultry, 210–25
  first course, 187
  formal dinner, 112, 120–22
  holiday parties, 91
  keeping records, 187
  outdoor party, 80–81
  picnics, 85–87
  salad course, 187–88
  tea party, 100–102
  timing, 188
  wedding breakfast, 270
  wedding reception, 269–70
Mixed vegetable salad, 217
Moules à la crème, 237
Mousse:
  au chocolat, 199
  lemon, 204
Mussels, steamed, 237

Nuts, roasted, 239

Onion tart, 220
Orange ice with cointreau, 201

Pâté maison, 202–3
Peach cake, 208
Pecan pie, 228–29
Pies:
  blueberry—deep-dish, 234
  ice cream, 223
  pecan, 228–29
  steak and kidney, 232–33
Poultry and fowl:
  chicken:
    Albert, 224
    breast of, with grapes, 221
    Brunswick stew, 228
    cold poached, in jelly, 217
    curry, 226–27
    oven-fried, Lois, 219
    and oysters à la crème, 213–14
    roast, with wine gravy, 216
    tarragon, 222–23
  dinner party menus, 210–25
Poundcake au kirsch, 207
Profiteroles with chocolate sauce, 218
Purée of split peas, 215

Raspberries gervais, 205–6
Rhubarb and strawberries, stewed fresh, 235
Roast chicken with wine gravy, 216

Salade niçoise, 224
Salads, 237–38
  on menus, 187–88
  mixed vegetable, 217
  niçoise, 224
  suggestions, 237–38
Salmon steaks, 236
"Sandwiches," breadless, 240
Sauces:
  crème fraiche, 206
  horse radish, 200
  verte, 212–13
Scallops, 236
Sea food. *See* Fish and sea food
Shad roe, 236
  appetizer, 239
Shrimp baked in wine, 206
Smelts, 236
Sole. *See* Fillet of sole
Soups:
  bisque of clams, cold, 199
  black bean, cold, 204

borsch with sour cream, hot, 211–12
boula boula, 205
corn, 201
crème Senegalese, 209–10
gazpacho, 222
purée of split peas, 215
spinach, 199–200
tomato, 208–9
Spinach soup, 199–200
Squash, acorn, 200
Strawberries:
 and rhubarb, stewed fresh, 235
 tart, 230
 (*see* Fraises Sarah Bernhardt)
Steak and kidney pie, 232–33
Stew:
 Brunswick, 228
 Irish, 228–29
 veal, in red wine, 234–35
String beans, whole, in butter, 214
Supper menus, buffet, 226–35

Tartar steak appetizers, 239–40
Tomato(es):
 filled with wild rice, 219
 soup, 208–9
Trout, 236

Veal:
 stew in red wine, 234–35
 vitello tonnato, 233–34
Vegetables:
 as appetizers, 239
 asparagus, creamed, 210
 broccoli au beurre, 203
 brussels sprouts in sour cream, 220
 carrots, 199
 cauliflower amandine, 223
 corn:
  custard, 203
  soup, 201
 lima beans, baby, puréed, 221
 mixed salad, 217
 onion tart, 220
 spinach, soup, 199–200
 split peas, purée of, 215
 squash, acorn, 200
 string beans, whole, in butter, 214
 tomato(es):
  filled with wild rice, 219
  soup, 208–9
Vitello tonnato, 233–34

Zabaglione, cold, 225